The Church's New Front Door

The Church's New Front Door

Technology as a Means for Christian Engagement in the Twenty-First Century

DANIEL TOPF

WIPF & STOCK · Eugene, Oregon

THE CHURCH'S NEW FRONT DOOR
Technology as a Means for Christian Engagement in the Twenty-First Century

Copyright © 2024 Daniel Topf. All rights reserved. Except for brief quotations in critical publications or reviews, no part of this book may be reproduced in any manner without prior written permission from the publisher. Write: Permissions, Wipf and Stock Publishers, 199 W. 8th Ave., Suite 3, Eugene, OR 97401.

Wipf & Stock
An Imprint of Wipf and Stock Publishers
199 W. 8th Ave., Suite 3
Eugene, OR 97401

www.wipfandstock.com

PAPERBACK ISBN: 979-8-3852-2095-3
HARDCOVER ISBN: 979-8-3852-2096-0
EBOOK ISBN: 979-8-3852-2097-7

08/12/24

Scriptures taken from the Holy Bible, New International Version®, NIV®. Copyright © 1973, 1978, 1984, 2011 by Biblica, Inc.™ Used by permission of Zondervan. All rights reserved worldwide.

Source for Table 3: Companies Market Cap. Used by permission.

To Jeff Hittenberger,
the inspiring educator who first told me
about the Fourth Industrial Revolution

Contents

List of Tables | ix

Acknowledgments | xi

Abbreviations | xiii

Introduction | 1

1 Mobility | 16

2 Work | 34

3 Education | 54

4 Entertainment | 72

5 Healthcare | 88

6 Security | 106

7 Productivity | 124

8 Energy | 144

9 Space | 161

Conclusion | 176

Bibliography | 183

General Index | 217

Scripture Index | 221

List of Tables

Table 1. Comparison between the Neolithic and the Industrial Revolution | 7

Table 2. Characteristics of the First, Second, Third, and Fourth Industrial Revolutions | 9

Table 3. The Ten Largest Car Companies by Market Capitalization in 2021 | 18

Table 4. The Five Levels of Autonomous Driving | 23

Table 5. The Changing World of Work | 40

Table 6. Largest US Companies and Their Employee Numbers | 48

Table 7. Becoming Future-Ready: The Top Five Soft Skills and Hard Skills | 57

Table 8. The Top Ten Bestselling Video Games of All Time | 73

Table 9. Data Sizes from Byte to Quettabyte | 129

Table 10. The Largest Exporters of Crude Oil in 2022 | 157

Table 11. Distances in Our Solar System | 164

Acknowledgments

WRITING THIS BOOK HAS been a breathtaking experience, simply because the disruptive technologies of the Fourth Industrial Revolution touch on so many fascinating topics. Throughout this journey, I have received a lot of encouragement and helpful feedback from various people, for which I am profoundly grateful. In particular, I would like to thank Jeff Hittenberger and Oskar Gruenwald, who encouraged me regarding this project early on. I also received valuable insights and support from Randy and Amy Murray, John and Amie White, Daniel Allegri, and Nelson Jennings.

This is my first volume designed for a broader audience. I appreciate that Wipf & Stock agreed to publish it and all the help I received from hard-working individuals like George Callihan, Michael Thomson, Matt Wimer, and Elisabeth Rickard. Special thanks go to my wife, Annali, who remained such a joyful presence in my life, even when I disappeared for hours and hours at times in order to author this book.

Above all, I want to praise our God and Father in heaven, who sustained me during the entire process and allowed me to produce this volume—*soli Deo gloria*.

Abbreviations

3D	three dimensional
5G	fifth generation of cellular technology
AACS	American Association of Christian Schools
ACC	adaptive cruise control
ACCS	Association of Classical Christian Schools
ACSI	Association of Christian Schools International
ADHD	attention deficit hyperactivity disorder
AEI	American Enterprise Institute
AGI	artificial general intelligence
AI	artificial intelligence
AIED	Artificial Intelligence in Education
AIMM	Artificial Intelligence of Maneuver and Mobility
AK-47	Avtomat Kalashnikova 1947
AR	augmented reality
ARK	Active Research Knowledge
ARPA	Advanced Research Projects Agency
ARPANET	Advanced Research Projects Agency Network
ATA	American Trucking Associations
ATM	automated teller machine
AV	autonomous vehicles
BAT	Basic Attention Token

BYD	Build Your Dreams
CDC	Centers for Disease Control and Prevention
CES	Consumer Electronics Show
ChatGPT	Chat Generative Pre-trained Transformer
CIO	chief information officer
CKE	Carl Karcher Enterprises
CNBC	Consumer News and Business Channel
CNCA	Carbon Neutral Cities Alliance
COP	Conference of the Parties
COVID	coronavirus disease
CRC	Chemical Rubber Company
CRISPR	clustered regularly interspaced short palindromic repeats
CT	computed tomography
DANS	Dubai Air Navigation Services
DARPA	Defense Advanced Research Project Agency
DNA	deoxyribonucleic acid
DVD	digital versatile disc
DW	*Deutsche Welle*
EIA	Energy Information Administration
EMS	Evangelical Missiological Society
ERA	Engineering Research Associates
eVOTL	electric vertical take-off and landing
FAA	Federal Aviation Administration
FAANG	Facebook, Amazon, Apple, Netflix, and Google
FLOPS	floating operations per second
FPS	first person shooter
GB	gigabyte
GDP	gross domestic product
GPS	global positioning system
HIV	human immunodeficiency virus

HP	Hewlett-Packard
HTC	High Tech Computer Corporation
HTS	*Hervormde Teologiese Studies*
IBM	International Business Machines
ICE	internal combustion engine
IED	Institute of Entrepreneurship Development
IEEE	Institute of Electrical and Electronics Engineers
IIHS	Insurance Institute for Highway Safety
IIoT	industrial internet of things
IMARC	International Market Research and Consulting Group
IMF	International Monetary Fund
IoE	internet of everything
IoT	internet of things
IoV	internet of vehicles
ITER	International Thermonuclear Experimental Reactor
JET	Joint European Torus
KSTAR	Korea Superconducting Tokamak Advanced Research
LAWS	lethal autonomous weapons systems
LiDAR	light detection and ranging
MIT	Massachusetts Institute of Technology
MOBA	multiplayer online battle arena
MOOC	massive open online course
MRI	magnetic resonance imaging
NASA	National Aeronautics and Space Administration
NEI	Nuclear Energy Institute
NHTSA	National Highway Traffic Safety Association
NIF	National Ignition Facility
NLP	Natural Language Processing
NPR	National Public Radio
NSA	National Security Agency

OECD	Organization for Economic Cooperation and Development
PHMSA	Pipeline and Hazardous Materials Safety Administration
RNA	ribonucleic acid
RSSRail	Reliability, Safety and Security of Railway Systems
RTA	Road and Transport Authority
SAE	Society of Automotive Engineers
SCM	Student Christian Movement
SIL	Summer Institute of Linguistics
STEM	science, technology, engineering, and mathematics
SWB	solar, wind, and batteries
TAE	Tri Alpha Energy
TED	Technology, Entertainment, Design
TTO	Tactical Technology Officer
TX-0	Transistorized Experimental computer zero
UBI	universal basic income
UI/UX	user experience/user interface
USDA	US Department of Agriculture
VHS	video home system
VPN	virtual private network
VR	virtual reality
WEF	World Economic Forum
WFP	World Food Programme
WHO	World Health Organization
WION	World Is One News
XR	extended reality
YWAM	Youth With A Mission

Introduction

BEGINNING IN 1971, POLITICIANS, entrepreneurs, and celebrities have conducted an annual meeting in Davos, Switzerland, to discuss the future trajectory of the world economy and other global issues. This exclusive and influential gathering was initiated by Klaus Schwab, a professor of business policy, who became the founder and executive chairman of the World Economic Forum (WEF).[1] During the 2015 annual meeting in Davos, Schwab highlighted the significance of an epochal development sometimes described as the Fourth Industrial Revolution. This term goes back to the year 2011 when the German federal government began to promote the concept of Industry 4.0 as the next milestone in the future of manufacturing.[2] However, it was Schwab who popularized the term and made it known to a wider audience, particularly through his landmark book *The Fourth Industrial Revolution*, which he published in 2016.

As Schwab emphasizes, the Fourth Industrial Revolution is not only changing the technological and economic realities of our time—"it changes *us*."[3] This is because, in the Fourth Industrial Revolution, a significant number of innovative technologies converge, creating a new environment that is about to radically transform the way people live and work—and, through advances in gene editing, may even change the very fabric of human beings.[4] These powerful technological innovations that, taken togeth-

---

1. Pigman, *World Economic Forum*, 1–11.
2. De Propris and Bailey, *Industry 4.0*, 7–8.
3. World Economic Forum, "What Is the Fourth Industrial Revolution?" Emphasis in the spoken original.
4. For a definition of technology, a good starting point is an essay by Stephen J. Kline in which he defines four major categories: (1) manufactured articles, that is to say, hardware, or artifacts; (2) manufacturing hardware (or manufacturing equipment), which, more broadly speaking, is "a sociotechnical system of manufacture"; (3) knowledge, technique, methodology, or know-how; and (4) "sociotechnical systems of use,"

er, will shape the age of the Fourth Industrial Revolution include artificial intelligence (AI), advanced robotics, blockchain technologies, quantum computing, biotechnology, genomics, virtual reality (VR), nanotechnology, autonomous vehicles, 3D printing, the internet of things (IoT), space technologies, materials science, geoengineering, and energy storage.[5]

This is quite an impressive list of technologies, each with its own challenges and opportunities. As the futurist and bestselling author Bernard Marr recognizes, "Many of these technologies by themselves would have a massive impact on business and society, but collectively the change will be beyond what many of us can imagine today."[6] In this volume, I introduce some of these technologies, explaining what the current state of development is and how these innovations may impact humanity in the future. This is then followed by an evaluation from a theological point of view. My goal is to make the discussion about these topics accessible to everyday people, to those of us who are not part of the elites meeting in Davos every year. It is not my intention to commend the WEF or anything it stands for. On the contrary, I believe there is much worthy of criticism in those circles.[7] However, the ideas coming out of Davos are influential, and I therefore think it is important to engage with them.

In particular, writing from the perspective as a follower of Jesus, I want Christians to be aware of these developments, considering the Fourth Industrial Revolution not only has far-reaching political, economic, and social consequences, but important ethical and spiritual implications as well. As former Secretary of State Henry Kissinger and his coauthors rightly acknowledge in their publication on the impact of AI, "while the number of individuals capable of creating AI is growing, the ranks of those contemplating this technology's implications for humanity—social, legal, philosophical, spiritual, moral—remain dangerously thin."[8] I believe this gap creates an opportunity for the church to participate in the *missio Dei* in new ways, by increasingly addressing a variety of current issues, particularly when it comes to the promises and perils associated with technology.

---

which is "a system of combinations of hardware, people (and usually other elements) to accomplish tasks that humans cannot perform unaided by such systems—to extend human capacities." Kline, "What Is Technology?," 215–17.

5. Schwab and Davis, *Shaping the Fourth Industrial Revolution*, 7, 238.
6. Marr, *Tech Trends in Practice*, 283.
7. For a recent critique of the WEF, see Roth, *You Will Own Nothing*, 69–74.
8. Kissinger et al., *Age of AI*, 27.

To be missional, the church needs to be relevant, and in order to be relevant in the twenty-first century, believers need to engage with the topic of technology in knowledgeable and applicable ways.[9] A considerable number of Christian authors has already addressed issues related to technology, especially with regards to phenomena like the smartphone and social media, as well as AI and transhumanism.[10] Regarding the former, books like *12 Ways Your Phone Is Changing You* (by Tony Reinke) and *The 40-Day Social Media Fast* (by Wendy Speake) point to the limitations of technology, and why it is important for Christians to develop countercultural habits in some of these areas that are so profoundly shaping our daily lives nowadays.

Devices like the smartphone and applications like search engines make use of what is known as narrow AI, which is designed to solve very specific and limited tasks.[11] By contrast, some futurists envision the advent of artificial general intelligence (AGI), which means machines could become so advanced one day that they would far surpass humans in every aspect, a development also known as superintelligence, strong AI, or technological singularity.[12] In order to compete within such an environment, some believe humans will have to augment their capabilities, which is a worldview or movement called transhumanism. Some of the important authors in this area include the futurist Ray Kurzweil, who wrote *The Singularity Is Near*, and the Israeli historian and public intellectual Yuval Noah Harari, the author of *Homo Deus*.

Christians have responded to these challenges with books like Jacob Shatzer's *Transhumanism and the Image of God* and *2084: Artificial Intelligence and the Future of Humanity* by John C. Lennox, who, with his title, points to the dystopian totalitarianism described in George Orwell's classic *1984*. I agree with these authors that many aspects of AGI and transhumanism are deeply concerning, especially when examined from a biblical and theological perspective. However, some of the discussions about these

---

9. I began to explore this principle in the essay Topf, "Global Crisis of Unemployment," 9. For recognizing the importance of the Fourth Industrial Revolution in missions, see Moon, "Missions from Korea 2017," 124.

10. For instance, Detweiler, *iGods*; Gay, *Modern Technology*; Reinke, *Competing Spectacles*.

11. Broussard, *Artificial Unintelligence*, 10–11, 32.

12. Bostrom, *Superintelligence*, 3–4, 22, 26.

topics are quite speculative at this point, specifically when it comes to AGI, which may still be hundreds of years away (or may never be achieved).[13]

In the present volume, I limit myself to engaging with concrete technologies, especially those that are likely to be relevant in the next ten to twenty years or so. This book is also unique in that it introduces not just one particular technology or phenomenon, but rather a sample of current trends within the framework of the Fourth Industrial Revolution.[14] By doing so, my aim is to address a variety of questions in order to spark a conversation about these important topics within the body of Christ. A bit of history might be helpful to understand these groundbreaking developments. After all, if there is a fourth revolution, there must also have been a first, second, and third revolution. In the following, I therefore begin with a brief overview that places the Fourth Industrial Revolution in its historical context.[15]

A BRIEF HISTORY OF TECHNOLOGY

Human beings have taken advantage of various technologies for centuries and, at a more basic level, have always used tools.[16] The earliest human communities made stone tools like cutting blades, axes, celts, and chisels.[17] Equipped with such tools, humans gained an advantage in terms of

---

13. Writing in 2005, Kurzweil set the date for the Singularity as 2045, and I think it is extremely unlikely this prediction will come true. Kurzweil, *Singularity*, 136. For a variety of time lines regarding the arrival of AGI, see Tegmark, *Life 3.0*, 40–42. For a critique of Kurzweil's predictions, see Crouch, "Alchemists' Dream," 48–50.

14. Jason Thacker also addresses various societal developments in his book, but his focus is on AI, not on the Fourth Industrial Revolution. Thacker, *Age of AI*. Lodewyk Sutton specifically mentions the Fourth Industrial Revolution in his article's title, but he writes mostly about the dangers of narcissism in an age dominated by social media. Sutton, "Appropriation of Psalm 82."

15. Schwab, "Fourth Industrial Revolution"; IED Team, "Brief History." For a more detailed description, see chapter 2 ("Revolutions We Had") and chapter 3 ("Revolution Has Started") in Donovan, *Profit and Prejudice*, 19–74.

16. Together with the development of language, toolmaking has often been considered a unique feature of the cognitive abilities humans have. However, the abilities of various animals to make use of tools in their quest for survival are also noteworthy; see, for instance, Shumaker et al., *Animal Tool Behavior*; Sanz et al., *Tool Use in Animals*. Nonetheless, there are important differences between animals and humans in this respect: "Only humans, however, could not survive without tools, and only humans have in turn been shaped by the tools they use." Headrick, *Technology*, 1.

17. Pruitt, "6 Major Breakthroughs." In the biblical account, the early chapters of Genesis highlight how humans engaged in agriculture, made musical instruments,

food preparation, whether it was through hunting animals or clearing areas of land for their agricultural endeavors. After the Stone Age, which is commonly divided into the Paleolithic Period, the Mesolithic Period, and the Neolithic Period, came the Bronze Age and the Iron Age that enabled humans to create tools that were sharper and more durable, making them more effective. Subsequent civilizations invented increasingly sophisticated tools, including paper, printing, gunpowder, and the compass (the four great inventions of ancient China), while also achieving engineering marvels like the building of roads, canals, bridges, and aqueducts.[18]

Further improvements came about in the Middle Ages, which produced inventions such as the spinning wheel, mechanical clocks, windmills using a horizontal axis and large sails, spectacles, and tools used for nautical navigation, like the astrolabe.[19] And while centers of advanced learning had existed long before in various parts of the world, the first modern universities were founded in European cities like Bologna (in AD 1088), Paris (AD 1150), Oxford (AD 1167), and Cambridge (AD 1209).[20] This emphasis on comprehensive and systematic study contributed to the cultivation of knowledge, an emphasis on science, and the empirical method that laid the foundations for the (First) Industrial Revolution.

The technological, social, and intellectual developments of the Middle Ages, the Renaissance, and the Protestant Reformation set the stage for the Industrial Revolution that, beginning with England, would transform entire countries from the eighteenth century onwards. The significance of these events can hardly be overestimated. As Peter N. Stearns

---

used iron and bronze to make tools, and began to build cities (Gen 4:2, 20–22; 6:14–16; 10:10–12; 11:3–4). Dyer, *From the Garden to the City*, 78–80; Reinke, *God, Technology, and the Christian Life*, 80–88.

18. Fan et al., "Four Great Inventions," 161–300. For the advances of the ancient Greeks and Romans in building bridges and aqueducts (as well as other technologies), see various chapters in Oleson, *Oxford Handbook of Engineering and Technology*.

19. See chapter 6 (on technology) in Cipolla, *Before the Industrial Revolution*, 137–59.

20. Significant ancient centers of learning include Buddhist monasteries in Nalanda and Taxila, India; Plato's Academy in Athens, Greece (around 380 BC); China's imperial academy in Beijing (from the third century AD); the Library of Alexandria in Egypt; and the University of al-Qarawiyyin in Fes, Morocco (founded in AD 859). Palfreyman and Temple, *Universities and Colleges*, 3–6. Nonetheless, the following assessment by Hastings Rashdall (1858–1924) still carries weight: "The Universities and the immediate products of their activity may be said to constitute the great achievement of the Middle Ages in the intellectual sphere. Their organisation and their traditions . . . affected the progress and intellectual development of Europe more powerfully, or (perhaps it should be said) more exclusively, than any schools in all likelihood will ever do again." Rashdall, *Universities of Europe*, 5.

affirms in *The Industrial Revolution in World History*, "The industrial revolution was the most important single development in human history over the past three centuries."[21] One reason why the Industrial Revolution was such a crucial event is because it is a historical occurrence that "continues to shape the contemporary world" in profound ways.[22]

Over time, the Industrial Revolution caused a transformation of all of society. In this regard the Industrial Revolution is comparable in its impact only to the Neolithic Revolution, which began around 10,000 BC.[23] Before the Neolithic Revolution, humans lived together in nomadic bands and survived through hunting animals and gathering edible plants. The economic surplus was essentially zero, and thus population growth was extremely low as well. But once people began to concentrate on farming, they were able to settle down and generate a modest surplus.[24] Population growth was still slow, however, interrupted by times of stagnation and sometimes even decline (as was the case during the Black Death pandemic in the fourteenth century).[25]

These dynamics of limited output changed with the advent of the Industrial Revolution.[26] In a radical shift and departure from prior lifestyles, people began to live primarily in urban (rather than in rural) settlements, and while previously almost everybody had to work as a farmer, now a number of professions developed as more and more people concentrated on manufacturing non-edible goods. Some of these goods, such as tractors and fertilizers, could be used to increase agricultural output. Consequently, the economic surplus of industrializing societies increased noticeably and, for the first time in human history, there was substantial population growth (Table 1).[27]

21. Stearns, *Industrial Revolution*, 1.

22. Stearns, *Industrial Revolution*, 1, 319.

23. Stearns, *Industrial Revolution*, 7.

24. Mazoyer and Roudart, *History of World Agriculture*, 65, 119, 311; Barker, *Agricultural Revolution*; Boyle, *Human Geography*, 71–77.

25. The Black Death dramatically affected Europe, but also parts of China and India, as well as various Middle Eastern countries and Egypt. Within a few years, the European continent "lost twenty-five million of its seventy-five million inhabitants," a staggering percentage of truly apocalyptic proportions. Kelly, *Great Mortality*, 11–12.

26. The population explosion that took place due to economic growth in the context of the Industrial Revolution has been highlighted by a variety of authors, such as Maddison, *World Economy*, 29–45; Myers, *Walking with the Poor*, 23–24; Harari, *Sapiens*, 247, 305, 351.

27. I obtained the idea for this table by reading Stearns, *Industrial Revolution*, 7. See Susskind, *World without Work*, 13–14.

Table 1. Comparison between the Neolithic and the Industrial Revolution

	Primitive Societies	*Neolithic Revolution*	*Industrial Revolution*
Basic work	hunting/gathering	farming	manufacturing
Living arrangements	nomadic bands	rural communities	life in cities
Economic surplus	virtually zero	above sustenance	wealth accumulation
Population growth	minimal	slow	substantial

The Industrial Revolution was a historic event of gigantic proportions. At the heart of the first phase of this historical development was the improvement of the steam engine by James Watt (1736–1819), which radically expanded the range of transportation and production capabilities.[28] The reason the First Industrial Revolution and those that followed it were so impactful was because these technological innovations had far-reaching economic, social, and political implications.[29] For example, as new kinds of jobs were offered in factories, farmers started to leave the countryside, which led to increasing levels of urbanization, the formation of a new working class, and later to the distinction between blue-collar and white-collar workers.[30] Significant changes also occurred in areas like leisure and free time, consumption patterns, and family dynamics.[31]

However, it is important to highlight these kinds of changes did not happen overnight.[32] In fact, for the majority of the population, life in the

---

28. The invention of the steam engine goes back to a French refugee in Holland in the late 1600s, and Thomas Newcomen improved the steam engine around 1700 in England—but it was James Watt who perfected it to the point that it could be "applied to industrial use." Stearns, *Industrial Revolution*, 26. However, the first design for a steam engine was probably created by Heron of Alexandria, who lived in the first century AD. Rosen, *Most Powerful Idea in the World*, 4–8.

29. Hahn, *Technology in the Industrial Revolution*, 20.

30. Stearns, *Industrial Revolution*, 160–61.

31. For example, children from poor families had to work in the early factories, often under problematic conditions, something that began to change after the introduction of child protection laws. Once children did not work anymore, they increasingly became a cost factor, rather than a potential source of income. Due to longer schooling years for children, "New concepts such as adolescence came into play in acknowledgement of the in-limbo stages of development between literal childhood and a life of work." Stearns, *Industrial Revolution*, 78.

32. For this reason, some observers are reluctant to use the term "revolution" to describe these events. Historians studying the developments in England have shown that "measurable changes were in many ways surprisingly slow," taking "several decades." Stearns, *Industrial Revolution*, 3. Stearns acknowledges both sides of this debate when he evaluates the Industrial Revolution as follows: "Overnight revolution, clearly

United Kingdom at the end of the eighteenth century had not changed all that much. Some of the developments related to industrialization only gained momentum toward the end of the nineteenth century. For instance, "By 1850 there were still as many craft workers as factory workers and as many rural people as urban. Industrialization had changed the work lives as well as the prospects and outlook of the nonfactory majority, but it had not yet revolutionized them."[33]

Considering these time frames, some historians and economists prefer to not only speak of the Industrial Revolution, but to describe this early phase as the First Industrial Revolution, which laid the foundation for further changes down the road.[34] While the First Industrial Revolution was mostly powered by the steam engine, the Second Industrial Revolution was characterized by the advent of electricity. Electricity not only became the foundation for modern tools of communication, such as the telegraph and the telephone, but also revolutionized the daily lives of people, particularly through the invention of the light bulb by Thomas Edison (1847–1931) in 1879.[35]

More changes came about in the twentieth century, often at a rapid pace, bringing about a new era. The Third Industrial Revolution brought innovations like automation, digitization, and electronics, thereby paving the way for the computer age. Some of these developments had already begun in the first few decades of the century. Hewlett-Packard (HP), for instance, was founded in Palo Alto, California, in 1939, thereby becoming one of the first tech companies located in Silicon Valley.[36] However, many of the most crucial events took place after World War II, notably

---

not, but massive transformation, almost certainly yes." Stearns, *Industrial Revolution*, 4.

33. Stearns, *Industrial Revolution*, 10.

34. Not everybody agrees with this kind of differentiation. Stearns, for example, is aware of the discussion about dividing the Industrial Revolution into four distinct phases, but argues: "To speak of a second industrial revolution in the West may be misleading, for it downplays the unique significance of the initial conversion from an agricultural to an industrial economy that had already occurred." Stearns, *Industrial Revolution*, 153. Those following a classification by Joseph Schumpeter would argue that there have been already five waves of industrialization: (1) the first, powered by the steam engine, in the 1780s and 1790s; (2) iron in the 1840s and 1850s; (3) steel and electricity in the 1890s and 1900s; (4) electromechanical and chemical technologies in the 1950s and 1960s; and (5) the present era based on information and communication technology. Atkinson, "Shaping Structural Change," 104–5.

35. Morris, *Edison*, 631; Freeberg, *Age of Edison*.

36. Malone, *Bill and Dave*, 1, 71, 77.

Intel's first commercially produced microprocessor (in 1971) and the invention of the World Wide Web in 1989.[37]

As in the previous examples, the transitions between the eras are fluid. In some sense, the invention of the internet at the end of the twentieth century already points beyond the Third Industrial Revolution. However, in the 1990s, the internet was just beginning to influence the socioeconomic realities of nations, particularly in the United States. Many of the most influential developments, such as the presentation of the first iPhone in 2007 by Steve Jobs (1955–2011), only took place later, in the twenty-first century (Table 2).[38]

Table 2. Characteristics of the First, Second, Third, and Fourth Industrial Revolutions

	First Industrial Revolution	Second Industrial Revolution	Third Industrial Revolution	Fourth Industrial Revolution
Chronology	18th century	19th century	20th century	21st century
Energy source	coal	oil/gas	nuclear	sustainable
Powered by	steam engine	electricity	computers	data
Key applications/industries	mechanization, factories, textile industry	railroads, internal combustion engine, chemical industry	automation, digitization, electronics, aviation	cyber-physical systems, internet of things, AI, robotics

More importantly, in its early years the internet was primarily a tool for facilitating communication between humans. In the Fourth Industrial Revolution, however, the internet will increasingly be used for communication between smart devices, which is why experts speak of the internet of things (IoT). The IoT goes beyond standard devices like laptops or smartphones that are connected to the internet, encompassing things like wireless inventory trackers and smart home devices like connected appliances, light switches, and thermostats.[39] In the year 2018, there were still more humans than IoT devices on Earth (7.5 billion versus seven billion).

37. Cressler, *Silicon Earth*, 6.

38. Merchant, *One Device*, 3, 72, 88. In focusing on a few main players, I am choosing a conventional approach here in telling the story of the various phases of industrialization. For a critique of this approach, see Tim Unwin, who is concerned that "the Fourth Industrial Revolution is in large part a conspiracy to shape the world ever more closely in the imagination of a small, rich, male and powerful élite." Unwin, "Five Problems," §31.

39. Thomas, "30 Internet-of-Things Examples."

However, just one year later, in 2019, the number of active IoT devices reached 26.7 billion, a number that will continue to grow exponentially in the coming years and decades.[40]

This is just one example of how sophisticated machines are increasingly dominating the economic and technological landscape of our time, which is why the classification of a Fourth Industrial Revolution seems warranted. Historically, the United Kingdom and the United States have played a crucial role in bringing about these radical changes that began in the late eighteenth century. Shortly after this period, other countries (like Germany, France, and Russia) went through their own process of industrialization. Other important players in this regard include Japan, Israel, Brazil, Mexico, Turkey, South Korea, China, and India.[41]

Not every country will see the need to go through every aspect of industrialization; for instance, the driving factor of the First Industrial Revolution—the steam engine—does not play a vital role in today's economy anymore. However, every society will have to face the threats and opportunities associated with the Fourth Industrial Revolution. As the South African scholar Tshilidzi Marwala emphasizes, "In many ways, we may have seen the last three industrial revolutions pass us by, but we cannot afford to be passive observers of this one."[42] As Christians, I believe we are facing a similar challenge and have to ask ourselves: How are we to respond to the technology-driven changes the Fourth Industrial Revolution is bringing about?

EVALUATING TECHNOLOGY FROM A CHRISTIAN PERSPECTIVE

Christianity seems to have an ambivalent relationship with science and technology. On one hand, it has been argued it is no coincidence that the scientific revolution took place in Europe, within the confines of Christendom—rather than, for instance, in ancient China, or in the Islamic world.[43] (This phenomenon is even more astounding considering that,

---

40. Maayan, "IoT Rundown for 2020."

41. These are some of the countries highlighted in the global perspective on the Industrial Revolution given by Stearns, *Industrial Revolution*, 204, 207.

42. Marwala, *Closing the Gap*, 223.

43. Some of the books that emphasize the positive role of Christianity, particularly for the development of the West, include Stark, *Victory of Reason*; Hannam, *God's Philosophers*; Holland, *Dominion*.

for hundreds of years, these two civilizations were ahead of the West). The theistic beliefs rooted in Christianity gave Europeans the confidence that the universe had been created in an orderly fashion by a God who was holy and accessible at the same time. In addition, the Protestant work ethic paved the way for capitalism, thereby contributing an important socioeconomic component to the Industrial Revolution.[44]

On the other hand, Christianity is sometimes considered a hindrance to scientific progress as well. An often-cited example is the conflict between the Italian astronomer Galileo Galilei (1564–1642) and the Roman Catholic Church, which—apparently on biblical grounds—was not willing to embrace the idea that the Earth orbits the sun, rather than the other way around. Following the Copernican view, the heliocentric model Galileo was proposing based on observations conducted with the telescope that he had invented threatened to revolutionize the way people looked at their place in the universe. Eventually, Galileo was summoned by the Inquisition in Rome, put under house arrest, and pressured to formally recant the very discoveries that today are commonly accepted. However, the story is more complex than it may at first appear. Some scholars have argued the conflict between Galileo and the pope was not so much a conflict between faith and science, but rather a confrontation between two strong-willed individuals.[45]

Nonetheless, it is still fair to say the church in this particular instance attempted to block the publication of newly discovered scientific insights.[46] This is as unfortunate as it is unnecessary, considering all truth is God's truth—a highly significant principle that has been more recently

---

44. This idea was propagated by the German sociologist Max Weber (1864–1920) in his most influential work, *Protestant Ethic and the Spirit of Capitalism*. Nowadays, scholars are increasingly questioning Weber's theses, but many still recognize religion can be a principal factor in explaining how the Industrial Revolution unfolded. Stearns, for instance, highlights how religious minorities in England saw entrepreneurship as a way to find social recognition in a society which usually marginalized them. Stearns, *Industrial Revolution*, 53, 122. Considering the emphasis Protestantism placed on literacy for the masses, so that people would be able to read the Bible for themselves, it might be "better to talk about the Protestant *word* ethic," as the historian Niall Ferguson suggests (emphasis original). Ferguson, *Civilization*, 264.

45. The conflict between science and Christianity (or lack thereof) as symbolized in the interactions between Galileo and the pope has been described in various publications and continues to be a hotly debated issue. See, for instance, Numbers, *Galileo Goes to Jail*; Livio, *Galileo and the Science Deniers*.

46. One has to guard against simplistic explanations, not only in cosmology, but also in other fields of study, such as medicine; see Ferngren, *Medicine and Religion*.

accepted by Christians of different persuasions.[47] The joy of discovering the many mysteries in the vast universe God created is certainly compatible with Christianity. But what about the practical applications of such newly found knowledge? For example, genetics and DNA sequencing promise not only a better understanding of the human body but also a potential cure for a large number of diseases. At the same time, many Christians are—for good reasons—strongly against any procedures that would lead to human cloning or the creation of designer babies. This tension between promise and peril can often place believers in a difficult dilemma. Certainly, we want to acknowledge our limitations as created beings and refrain from the temptation of "playing God."[48] However, if treatments could enable a blind person to see or a quadriplegic to walk again—should Christians not be at the very forefront of such progress?

The problem is that the opportunities technology creates can be a force for good, but they can also be a source of temptation. Dealing with this dilemma brings us back to a tension Jesus expressed when he recognized that his followers are in this world, but not of the world (John 13:1; 15:19; 16:33; 17:6–18).[49] Given this delicate position as followers of Jesus, believers will do well to heed the following advice given by the apostle John: "Do not love the world or anything in the world. If anyone loves the world, love for the Father is not in them. For everything in the world—the lust of the flesh, the lust of the eyes, and the pride of life—comes not from the Father but from the world" (1 John 2:15–16). Undoubtedly, the technologies of the Fourth Industrial Revolution can be extremely attractive, even seductive. However, as John reminds us, the world (and all its gadgets, one might add) will pass away, "but whoever does the will of God lives forever" (v. 17).

Given this tension, I attempt to choose a middle path in this book, but one that is bending toward optimism. When presenting a technology and its future possibilities, I also highlight some of the dangers and possible negative side effects of this innovation. This is crucial, because as Christians we should always maintain a critical distance to everything

---

47. A particularly influential voice within the evangelical world in this regard was Arthur F. Holmes (1924–2011), a professor who taught philosophy at Wheaton College for several decades. In books like *All Truth Is God's Truth* (1977), Holmes argued eloquently for Christians to embrace a broad education within a Christian framework.

48. For this complex topic, see, for example, Sandel, *Case against Perfection*; Clarke et al., *Ethics of Human Enhancement*; Davies, *Editing Humanity*.

49. The apostle Paul prescribes a similar approach to the world (1 Cor 7:31), so Malet, "Believer in the Presence of Technique," 74.

this world has to offer, acknowledging that final redemption only lies with the fullness of God's kingdom, when Christ returns in glory. In addition, we also need to be aware of the following principle formulated by the media scholar and critic John M. Culkin (1928–93): "We shape our tools and thereafter our tools shape us."[50] That is to say, the tools humans craft for themselves are never simply neutral objects. Yes, they can usually be used for either good or evil, but beyond that they also create their own dynamics, which often leads to unintended consequences that may only be discovered when it is too late, and the damage is already done.[51]

Christians can have a variety of positions regarding how to engage with technology—or disengage from it. A helpful theological framework for exploring these possibilities is found in H. Richard Niebuhr's *Christ and Culture*. In this Christian classic, Niebuhr presents the following five views regarding how Christians can relate to this world: (1) Christ against culture, (2) Christ of culture, (3) Christ above culture, (4) Christ and culture in paradox, and (5) Christ transforming culture.[52] I think the first position ("Christ against culture") has merit when relating to technology, by calling for a prophetic critique of the powers of this world and the courage to be different.[53] However, in this volume, I mostly embrace the fifth position, the conversionist view, which hopes for the renewal and transformation of all things.

For this reason, the chapters of this book tend to highlight the potential of certain technologies and developments, because I believe these might have some redemptive qualities we can already experience in the here and now, in this age of tension between the first and the second coming of Christ.[54] Each chapter's theological reflection is followed by a few discussion questions, as well as suggestions for further reading. Some of the sources I list agree with what I have proposed in the chapter,

50. Quoted in Dyer, *From the Garden to the City*, 36.
51. Shatzer, *Transhumanism and the Image of God*, 6–8, 17, 21, 112–13.
52. Niebuhr, *Christ and Culture*, xliii–lv.

53. Carl Mitcham makes a good point as well in his analysis of Niebuhr's framework, arguing "for the first and fourth alternative theologies of the Christ-technology relationships as being the most adequate for our time." Mitcham, "Technology as a Theological Problem," 9.

54. Eschatology, or the study of the last things, is of course a vast field. A good starting point for understanding the "already" but "not yet" principle are publications by George Eldon Ladd (1911–82) like *Presence of the Future*, 10–11. For a contribution of pentecostalism to give people hope in the here and now, see Cox, *Fire from Heaven*, 111–16.

while others disagree. I have also included secular authors who clearly have a completely different worldview from what I believe as a Christian, but I list them nonetheless because I consider them to be important conversation partners. My hope is to create opportunities for readers to further engage with the topics and questions under discussion, whether they concur with my cautiously optimistic framework or not. Given the complexities of the topics presented in this volume, I welcome dissent and hope my book will inspire many fruitful and lively discussions.

The following nine chapters cover a wide range of areas that will be impacted by various technologies of the Fourth Industrial Revolution. These are areas such as medical care, the job market, education, entertainment, and—in the last chapter—the possibility for humans to become a multiplanetary species, thanks to advances in space travel. In the first chapter, however, I address the area of mobility and autonomous vehicles. I chose this topic as a starting point not because I want to imply self-driving cars and trucks are the most important technology of the Fourth Industrial Revolution, but because autonomous vehicles are a good example of how a variety of technologies (including AI and image processing technologies) need to come together in order to create new opportunities.[55] In addition, at the time of writing (in the year 2024), self-driving cars are already a hot topic and something that many people can relate to, for example, because their own vehicle may already have some capabilities for autonomous driving. In that sense, the future has already begun. So, fasten your seat belt and enjoy the ride, as we are about to explore the potential of the Fourth Industrial Revolution!

DISCUSSION QUESTIONS

1. Before coming across this book, had you heard about the Fourth Industrial Revolution? If so, in what context?

2. Winston Churchill (1874–1965) famously said, "We shape our buildings, and afterwards our buildings shape us."[56] What other examples can you think of regarding the principle that we (as humans) make ourselves tools, but then these tools also shape us?

---

55. For those interested in the technical details of a variety of cutting-edge technologies and discoveries, I recommend the podcast by Lex Fridman, an AI researcher working at MIT. E.g., Thrun, "Flying Cars, Autonomous Vehicles."

56. Quoted in Kelly, *Best Little Stories*, 408.

3. In your opinion, what should be the church's stance toward technology?
4. As a Christian, are you rather optimistic or pessimistic when it comes to the use of novel technologies like AI? Explain how you came to this conclusion.

SUGGESTIONS FOR FURTHER READING

- Klaus Schwab, *The Fourth Industrial Revolution* (2017). A classic text explaining what the Fourth Industrial Revolution is and why it is important—still highly relevant.
- Yuval Noah Harari, *Homo Deus: A Brief History of Tomorrow* (2018). A dystopian perspective on a future driven by data, written by a public intellectual with Jewish roots and an atheistic worldview.
- Ray Kurzweil, *The Singularity Is Near: When Humans Transcend Biology* (2005). A utopian view on the power of AI surpassing human intelligence within a few decades.
- John C. Lennox, *2084: Artificial Intelligence and the Future of Humanity* (2020). A Christian mathematician and philosopher of science warns of possible negative consequences related to AI.
- Tony Reinke, *God, Technology, and the Christian Life* (2022). Presents a biblical foundation for evaluating technology; written from a Reformed perspective, balanced, and yet providing a largely optimistic viewpoint.
- John Dyer, *From the Garden to the City: The Place of Technology in the Story of God* (2022). An accessible theological reflection on technology, first written when the author served as the director of web development at Dallas Theological Seminary.

1

Mobility

A NOTEWORTHY CAR RACE took place in the Mojave Desert in California on March 13, 2004. One million dollars in prize money for the fastest car to complete a particular circuit would wait for the winner and, with so much at stake, various teams were competing. Given these parameters, there seemed to be nothing unusual about this race—except for one crucial detail: not a single driver was present, only cars.[1] This unconventional event was funded by the Defense Advanced Research Projects Agency (DARPA), a government agency that organized the DARPA Grand Challenge recognizing autonomous vehicles would play an important role in the future and that it would therefore be beneficial to encourage private companies to develop such cars. Remarkably, at the 2004 challenge none of the participating teams was able to finish the course, and so nobody claimed the prize money. However, one year later, in 2005, the engineers had learned some important lessons, doubled their efforts, and competed again. This time, several self-driving cars were able to finish the track, with the team from Stanford University coming in first.[2]

---

1. As the *New York Times* described the subsequent event in 2005: "In a Grueling Desert Race, a Winner, but Not a Driver"; similarly, the *Washington Post* announced: "A Big Finish with No One at the Wheel." Davies, *Driven*, 108.

2. The DARPA challenge is told in fascinating detail by Lawrence D. Burns, former corporate vice president of research, development, and planning at General Motors. Burns, *Autonomy*, 14–65.

Fast forward twenty years or so, and it is a different world. Nowadays, self-driving cars are beginning to become part of daily life, as the following examples show.

- Waymo, a subsidiary of Alphabet/Google, is already offering driverless rides to the public in cities like Phoenix and San Francisco—with plans to expand to Los Angeles and Austin as well.[3]
- In China, Didi Chuxing, which is larger than Uber in terms of daily rides offered, is the domineering ride-sharing company. Didi Chuxing is already testing autonomous vehicles in Jiading, a district of Shanghai, and hopes to expand into several other Chinese cities as well soon.[4] Baidu, the Chinese equivalent of Google, was even planning to operate one thousand driverless taxis by the year 2024 (a goal which it did not achieve at the time of writing).[5]
- In the second half of 2020, Tesla became the world's most valuable carmaker, despite the relatively small number of cars the company produced at that time (Table 3).[6] However, many investors rewarded Tesla for its future potential due to being far ahead in various areas, which includes Autopilot, its software for autonomous driving.[7]
- Not to be outdone, other carmakers are investing in this promising area as well. For instance, General Motor's Cadillac offers Super Cruise, Mercedes the Drive Pilot, Volvo's system is called Pilot Assist, and Nissan has the ProPilot Assist.[8]

---

3. O'Dowd and Hagan, "Take a Ride through Phoenix."
4. McGrath, *Autonomous Vehicles*, 247–48.
5. Kharpal, "Baidu Pushes."
6. Klebnikov, "Tesla Is Now." At the time of writing (April 2024), Tesla's value had fallen, but it was still the largest car maker by market capitalization, followed by Toyota and Porsche. Companies Market Cap, "Largest Automakers."
7. Such technology comes with a price, of course; in 2023, Tesla's self-driving package cost $15,000. Porter, "Tesla Raises Price."
8. Threewitt, "10 Cars."

Table 3. The Ten Largest Car Companies
by Market Capitalization in 2021

	Name	Market Capitalization	Country
1	Tesla	811.96 billion USD	United States
2	Toyota	204.70 billion USD	Japan
3	BYD	108.04 billion USD	China
4	Volkswagen	103.68 billion USD	Germany
5	NIO	89.62 billion USD	China
6	Daimler	81.49 billion USD	Germany
7	General Motors	77.91 billion USD	United States
8	BMW	55.23 billion USD	Germany
9	Volvo	51.81 billion USD	Sweden
10	Hyundai	50.54 billion USD	South Korea

In addition, self-driving technologies are applied not only to cars, but also to the trucking industry. Startups like Waymo, TuSimple, and Embark have considered entering the market, while Aurora, Kodiak Robotics, Einride (a Swedish company), and Tesla are anticipating making substantial progress soon. Traditional manufacturers like Daimler and Volvo are competing in this important market as well, which will possibly lead to revolutionary changes in the transportation sector.[9] As in previous industrial revolutions, much of this transformation is driven by technological innovation. These advances brought about by technology have, in turn, economic, political, and social implications. However, understanding the technological developments is essential and foundational, so it is worthwhile looking at them in more detail.

Engineers have been wanting to build self-driving cars for a long time, but until recently achieving this feat seemed like a distant dream. Already in 1939, at the New York World's Fair, General Motors presented a vision of the future aptly called Futurama, a vision that included "the first self-driving car, which was an electric vehicle guided by radio-controlled electromagnetic fields generated with magnetized metal spikes embedded in the roadway."[10] In popular imagination, autonomous vehicles also appeared on television and in movies. One example was the 1980s series *Knight Rider*, in which a crime fighter played by David Hasselhoff was

---

9. Clevenger, "Who's Still in Autonomous Trucking?"; Bishop, "Big Dawgs in Automated Trucking."

10. Gringer, "History of the Autonomous Car."

assisted by an AI-powered car that not only was able to fly (at least a little bit, using its "turbo boost"), but could also drive short distances by itself.[11] Similarly, James Bond was able to remotely maneuver his BMW 750iL in the movie *Tomorrow Never Dies* (1997).[12]

While imagination regarding self-driving cars was vivid and enthusiastic, several key elements were missing in order to turn this vision into reality. One of the crucial components missing was computing power—lots of it. The ability to process vast amounts of data is essential because there are so many things happening around a car in a real-life traffic situation. It is one thing to develop a computer software that can beat the smartest human beings at a game like chess, for example.[13] After all, what happens on a chess board is subject to strict rules, is therefore predictable, and can be calculated. But to develop a machine that drives better than a human surely seems like an insurmountable challenge. That is, unless a computer program comes to the point at which it can process more pieces of information, even in a complex environment like traffic, than any human ever could. With microprocessors (chips) that can execute trillions of operations per second and keep getting faster, such performance levels may soon become a reality.[14]

However, a self-driving car not only needs to be able to process and interpret gigantic amounts of data within milliseconds; it first needs to collect the relevant data necessary to drive safely. For human drivers, this happens primarily through their eyes, which are truly amazing features. The recent progress in the self-driving endeavor has only become possible because of advancements in the areas of sensors and camera technologies. The advantages a camera system has compared to a human driver are remarkable. To begin with, humans only have two eyes, which means they can only look in one direction at any given point in time (mostly forward, but then people also need to check their mirrors or are tempted to use their smartphone, which is one way accidents happen). By contrast,

---

11. Baldwin, "K.I.T.T."

12. Hard, "Most Incredible."

13. The performance of computers in games is an important measurement on how far AI has come. A memorable milestone in human history was reached in 1997, when IBM's Deep Blue defeated the chess legend Garry Kasparov, and in 2016, when the Go world champion Sedol Lee lost against AlphaGo (a program with self-learning capabilities developed by Google's DeepMind). Lee, *Birth of Intelligence*, 48.

14. The performance of such chips is now measured in teraflops (with "tera" standing for a trillion, or one million million, and FLOPS signifying "floating operations per second"). See, for example, Bos, "Tesla's New HW3."

a self-driving car might have eight or more cameras, enabling it to constantly look in every direction—and all this without blinking, even once.[15] Furthermore, cameras can also have higher resolution, see farther than the human eye, and be equipped with special night-vision capabilities. In addition, besides using cameras, self-driving cars are able to examine their surroundings by taking advantage of ultrasonic sensors, radar, and LiDAR (light detection and ranging), which uses laser light pulses.[16]

Another key technology that is making self-driving cars a reality is high-speed networks like 5G, because these enable the fast exchange of data between various entities equipped with microchips. The G in 5G stands for *generation* and is another example of how fast information technologies have developed in recent years. Mobile networks started with 1G, when Nippon Telegraph and Telephone first offered this service to the citizens of Tokyo, Japan, beginning in 1979.[17] An important milestone was reached with 3G, which came over twenty years later and enabled people to connect to the internet. Now, with 5G, consumers can download a movie in around thirty-five seconds, something that might have taken over forty minutes on 4G.[18]

Granted, this kind of downloading capability is an impressive performance, but the real advantage of 5G lies somewhere else: It enables machines to communicate with each other at lightning speed. As Asha Keddy, a vice president of Intel's Mobile and Communications Group, recognized already in 2016, "With 5G, we will be moving from a user centric world to one of massive machine type communications where the network will move from enabling millions to billions of devices—an era that will connect these devices intelligently and usher in the commodification of information and intelligence."[19]

Humans have limited capacity when it comes to processing information, which is why, at some point, a faster network does not create a noticeable difference for consumers anymore. By contrast, machines will benefit from being able to exchange large data packages among themselves with fewer and fewer delays, which is called reduced latency—something

---

15. The Tesla Autopilot, for example, has eight surround cameras. Tesla, "Advanced Sensor Coverage."

16. McGrath, *Autonomous Vehicles*, 111; Ondruš et al., "How Do Autonomous Cars Work."

17. Galazzo, "Timeline from 1G to 5G."

18. Fisher, "5G Speed."

19. Quoted in West, *Future of Work*, 44.

that will become more obvious in the future, when 6G and 7G will come along (assuming the networks will be called by these names then).[20] The point is that faster networks like 5G enable the internet of things (IoT), and one concrete application of the IoT is self-driving cars that can constantly communicate with each other. On the micro-level of a particular traffic situation, this could help to avoid accidents. On the macro-level, this may revolutionize traffic flows, even to the point that traffic jams might become a thing of the past, as cars choose the optimal routes and drive at the most reasonable speed to avoid congestions.[21]

Throughout this chapter, the focus is mostly on self-driving cars and trucks, because the automobile industry is such a crucial factor in the world economy. However, different technologies will impact other forms of autonomous transportation as well. For instance, accidents caused by human error are not only a phenomenon on roads. In the shipping industry, it is estimated that 70 to 90 percent of maritime accidents are due to human error.[22] It is therefore likely autonomous ships would reduce the risk of accidents considerably once the necessary technology has been sufficiently tested and refined. To some extent, this is already happening; Norway, for example, is experimenting with an autonomous and electric ferry that will be operating based out of the city of Trondheim, and the *Yara Birkeland* was designed to "be the world's first zero-emission autonomous container ship."[23] Similarly, transportation by rail will also see increased levels of automation because autonomous trains have many advantages, improving "safety, performances and quality of service while reducing investment and operational cost and saving energy."[24]

Besides changing traffic on roads, rails, and waterways, the technologies of the Fourth Industrial Revolution are also bound to revolutionize transportation in other ways, such as in the air. General Motors, for instance, is working on entering the air taxi business by offering an eVTOL, a "sleek, electric vertical take-off and landing aircraft" powered

20. Violino, "What 5G Promises for IoT."

21. For this specific area of interconnectivity, experts also speak of the internet of vehicles (IoV). Mahmood, *Connected Vehicles*.

22. Porathe et al., "At Least as Safe," 417–25. This study also points out that automation can create new types of risks, which can cause new kinds of accidents.

23. Reddy et al., "Zero-Emission Autonomous Ferries." The first autonomous ferry to operate was a project by Rolls Royce in cooperation with the Finnish ferry operator Finferries that began service in Turku, Finland in 2018. Sawers, "Rolls-Royce Demonstrates."

24. Collart-Dutilleul et al., *Reliability, Safety, and Security*, xiv.

by four rotors.[25] Other companies that would like to venture into this lucrative market include Toyota, Hyundai, Volocopter, EHang, and Uber, as well as the world's dominant airplane manufacturers, Boeing and Airbus.[26] Granted, some of these models sound more like science-fiction and may only become a reality in the 2040s, or even later. However, in Dubai, discussions have already become quite concrete since its Road and Transport Authority (RTA) and Dubai Air Navigation Services (DANS) signed a memorandum of understanding (MOU). The purpose of this MOU is part of "Dubai's smart self-driving strategy, which aims to convert 25 percent of all travel in Dubai into self-driving flights through various means of transport by 2030."[27] On a less spectacular level there are, of course, air transport strategies for the delivery of physical goods, such as drones.[28] As more and more goods are delivered by drones, this will likely make important contributions as well by reducing the number of vehicles on the road, thereby leading to less congestion, fewer accidents, and less pollution.[29]

Technologies like 5G, advanced camera systems, and data-processing AI have made autonomous vehicles a real possibility. Consequently, this is something that will probably become a reality in the 2030s and 2040s, even if progress will be gradual (see also the distinct levels of autonomous driving listed in Table 4).[30] Despite technological and regulatory challenges, these developments toward autonomy will be almost irresistible, because they might be able to bring about the dawn of a new automobile age: one in which driving becomes safer, cleaner, and more efficient—advantages that are discussed in more detail below, in the theological section of this chapter.[31]

25. Paukert, "GM Surprises."
26. Hornyak, "Flying Taxi Market."
27. Wray, "Flying Taxi Trials in Cities."
28. Players in this field include Matternet, Wing (a division of Alphabet, the parent company of Google), Zipline, Flytrex, DroneUp, UPS Flight Forward, and Manna ("an Irish drone delivery company beginning operations in Texas"). Wolf, "Who Are."
29. "On an environmental level, autonomous drones can significantly reduce the number of delivery trucks and vans on the road. And because they're fully-electric, they have the potential to be powered by renewable energy—creating 100% emission-free deliveries." Matthew, "Are Automated Drone Deliveries."
30. Based on a description by the Society of Automotive Engineers (SAE). SAE International, "SAE Levels of Driving Automation."
31. Such a vision would point to "a world in which emerging technological trends allowed for cars that didn't take up unnecessary real estate, didn't belch greenhouse gases, and didn't sit idle nearly all day." Davies, *Driven*, 170.

Table 4. The Five Levels of Autonomous Driving

Level	Description
Level 0	No Automation: The car has no automated support systems; the driver must take care of everything.
Level 1	Driver Assistance: The car has basic assistance features, such as adaptive cruise control (ACC); the driver is still in full control of the vehicle.
Level 2	Partial Automation: The car can sometimes drive by itself, staying in its lane; the driver is needed to respond to sudden changes in the traffic flow.
Level 3	Conditional Automation: The car's systems are able to perform all driving functions; however, the driver needs to be always ready to take over.
Level 4	High Automation: The fully autonomous car can handle most situations; the driver can take care of other things during the drive.
Level 5	Full Automation: The car is autonomous under all conditions; people do not have to take any action, and the vehicle may not even have a steering wheel.

To some observers, fully self-driving cars may still seem like a distant fantasy, but it is highly likely commercial applications will be hitting the road quite soon, as far as the transportation of goods is concerned. Such commercial applications may come in stages and may therefore not depend on fully autonomous solutions. One possibility would be to organize trucks in convoys, where three semis drive on the highway, but only the one in front is being supervised by a human driver (an approach called truck platooning).[32] Human drivers could also be employed to drive trucks within the city and to load and unload them, while the long stretches on the freeway would be automated.

The crucial point to realize is that there is a lot of money to be made here (or lost, for those who fail to innovate). In the United States, trucking is big business, as trucks form the core of the American logistics system. In 2022, for example, "The trucking industry generated $940.8 billion in gross freight revenues," accounting for "80.7% of the nation's freight bill."[33] After using (autonomous) trucks, deliveries within cities, in particular to cover the last mile that reaches the consumer, could then be arranged by smaller vehicles, such as the ones being designed by Nuro, to help deliver Domino's pizzas, or by using drones—something Amazon started to offer through its new service "Prime Air."[34]

32. Bishop, "U.S. States Are Allowing."
33. American Trucking Associations, "ATA American Trucking Trends."
34. Holley, "Domino's Will Start"; Palmer, "Amazon Wins FAA Approval"; Chen, "11 Photos of Amazon's New."

Second, apart from delivering goods, autonomous solutions will also be developed to transport people. Again, this may not happen overnight, but considering the technological progress that has been made, it seems only a matter of time until there will be fully autonomous taxis. The traditional taxi industry was already revolutionized through the arrival of car-sharing services like Uber and Lyft, and it looks like it is going to be disrupted again.[35] The reason is similar to what was outlined above: The economic incentives are substantial, because—up to now—the driver's salary is such a large component of the cost of operating any kind of taxi or car-sharing service. According to the research firm Frost & Sullivan, drivers make up to 80 percent of the total cost per mile for a non-autonomous ride-sharing service.[36] By contrast, a fleet of fully autonomous cars would have a much lower cost base (not having to pay any drivers), which means these companies would be able to offer their services at a lower price, thereby exercising considerable pressure on their competitors.

Third, as autonomous commercial deliveries and ride-sharing services become more prominent, a growing number of consumers will also opt for buying a self-driving car. There is currently some pushback from those who emphasize part of the pleasure of having a car is the sense of freedom and independence that comes through being in control. It is certainly conceivable that twenty, thirty years from now people will still choose to steer a car themselves, especially when driving down a scenic route.[37] However, the reality is many people use their vehicle primarily for their daily commute, which can be a grueling and soul-crushing experience. Since several years, the average time Americans spend commuting is almost an hour every day.[38] The commute would be a completely different experience if people were able to check their email, watch the news, or play computer games while on their way to and from work.[39] All these activities are considerably more fun (and more productive) than staring intensely at the road ahead while being stuck in stop-and-go rush

---

35. Together with ride-sharing services also offered through a fleet of bicycles and e-scooters, this approach to transport is known as "micromobility." Standage, *Brief History of Motion*, 182–83.

36. Shetty, "Uber's Self-Driving Cars."

37. E.g., Torchinsky, *Robot, Take the Wheel*; Webster et al., *Never Stop Driving*; Crawford, *Why We Drive*.

38. DePillis et al., "Most Americans."

39. However, whether people will be productive while using an autonomous vehicle remains to be seen, so the argument by Singleton, "Discussing the 'Positive Utilities,'" 50–65.

hour traffic. For this reason alone, the gradual advance of self-driving cars will probably be unstoppable.

Granted, there are formidable technical, legal, and regulatory challenges ahead when it comes to autonomous transportation solutions. One particularly complicated question is related to who bears responsibility when an autonomous vehicle causes an accident. Is the driver (if there is one) at least partially responsible? The manufacturer that produced the car? Or the company that supplied the self-driving software?[40] Even though these are complex problems, it is likely a solution will be found, especially if it can be demonstrated that self-driving cars cause far fewer accidents than human drivers do. Autonomous vehicles will also be a blessing to people who are not able to drive due to a disability, or to seniors who cannot drive anymore.[41] Keeping in mind these advantages and challenges related to autonomous driving, it is now time to evaluate this technology from a theological point of view.

A CHRISTIAN PERSPECTIVE ON MOBILITY

Several of the technologies and developments associated with the Fourth Industrial Revolution can be highly controversial, especially for Christians. When it comes to self-driving cars, there are valid concerns, but there is also much to be said in favor of this innovative technology and the way it will transform people's lives. In the following, I make the argument autonomous vehicles will, potentially, be (1) safer, (2) cleaner, and (3) more efficient. At the same time, new technologies carry their own

---

40. Another issue with ethical implications is the problem of a machine evaluating a situation where human lives are at stake, a variation of the trolley problem. However, due to the complexity of traffic situations, the question is not simply whether an autonomous car will run over a child on the road or abruptly turn to the side and crash into a group of several adults, for instance. Rather, autonomous cars in such a situation "will very quickly compute the probabilities and potential outcomes of alternative actions and take the one deemed best. The actions will be more complex, such a [sic] blow the horn, put on the brakes, swerve a little to the other lane and see if the advancing car is stopping, if not then swerve back again, check and see if the children have reacted to get out of the way, etc. And do this all in 2–3 seconds." McGrath, *Autonomous Vehicles*, 98.

41. Self-driving vehicles might also be advantageous for children and teenagers, who are too young to acquire a driver's license. In fact, compared to previous generations, young people today are already less eager to be able to drive or to own a car: "Driving is no longer seen as a fun thing, and teenagers aren't rushing to get their driver's licenses when they turn 16." Dhawan, *Autonomous Vehicles Plus*, 37. Several advantages of autonomous cars are also highlighted by Herger, *Last Driver's License Holder*.

risks and often have unintended consequences. For instance, self-driving cars could be hacked and then used as a weapon, and traffic in our cities may actually increase as robot-taxis offer rides at more affordable prices and therefore attract more customers. Still, I believe the benefits outweigh the risks, and that the transition to autonomous vehicles is something to look forward to.

First, self-driving cars and trucks will be safer. Just this argument by itself should be enough to get Christians excited, considering Christianity is a life-affirming faith. In the foundational texts of Gen 1 and 2, we read how God created life and an environment in which humans could flourish. In contrast to all other creatures, God "the Father has life in himself" (John 5:26a); and just as with God is "the fountain of life" (Ps 36:9), so it is the Spirit who "gives life" (John 6:63), while Jesus is "the life" (14:6c) and came that we "may have life, and have it to the full" (10:10).[42] God's life-bringing mission became necessary because death entered the world due to the fall (Gen 3), and humans now live in an era of restoration, even though the final redemption of all things still lies in the future.

Since we, as Christians, affirm God gives life to all things (1 Tim 6:13b) and that, in particular, God is the one who gives life and breath to all people (Acts 17:25b), we should always look for ways to save human lives and do our best to avoid the unnecessary and untimely death of people. Unfortunately, human lives are wasted daily on our streets and highways because deadly traffic accidents happen every day. In the past few years, traffic deaths in the United States alone have amounted to over forty thousand casualties per year.[43] Granted, gradual progress has been made due to new initiatives, regulations, and innovations (such as airbags), which is why this number is down from a high in 1979, when 51,093 people were killed in fatal crashes.[44] However, to put these numbers into perspective: In all of the wars combined that the United States has fought, beginning in 1775, over a million Americans have been killed, but since Ford started mass-producing cars in 1913, more than 3.5 million have lost their lives in traffic accidents.[45]

---

42. For the importance of life as a theological concept in the context of mission, see World Council of Churches, "Together towards Life."

43. Adkins, "Small Decrease."

44. IIHS, "Fatality Facts 2021."

45. Scranton Law Firm, "Death from War." Or, to put it in a more global perspective: "An estimated 60 million people were killed in motor vehicle crashes in the twentieth century. That's more than all of the military *and* civilian deaths during World War II." Townsend, *Ghost Road*, 9 (emphasis in the original).

Most of these deaths are due to human error, with intoxication, reckless driving (particularly speeding), and distracted driving being the most common factors why human drivers cause accidents.[46] By contrast, a fully autonomous car would be 100 percent alert at all times, follow traffic regulations consistently, and would not be affected by emotional outbursts like road rage. Therefore, the AI-driven car may soon be superior to any human driver, which is why it is anticipated that traffic casualties could be reduced by 90 percent or more once autonomous vehicles become the norm (naturally, this would only be the case if the remaining technological issues can be solved).[47]

In addition to thousands of deaths, car-based transportation as it is set up in the United States today also leads to millions of serious injuries each year.[48] In America, there are over six million accidents in a typical year, and many of these cause injuries, sometimes severe injuries, such as people losing limbs, losing their eyes, or becoming paralyzed. It seems that, as a society, we have become paralyzed when it comes to addressing these issues. Somehow, we have accepted such carnage is the price we pay for being able to drive wherever we want, whenever we want. In this context, it is also worth remembering there are massive economic interests behind the car industry, including the industries that specialize in when things go wrong. As the technology consultant Michael E. McGrath points out in *Autonomous Vehicles: Opportunities, Strategies, and Disruptions*,

> It's important to acknowledge that there are many companies, organizations, and people who benefit from auto accidents. This includes many law firms and trial lawyers, insurance companies, courts, auto repair businesses, etc. A significant reduction in accidents will affect them. While it's disappointing, their organizations are lobbying to postpone autonomous vehicles to delay this benefit to society.[49]

Consequently, unmasking these special interests and fighting for a new approach to transportation could become an important justice issue for Christians in the coming decades.

---

46. Meyer, "Top Five Causes."

47. At this point, it looks like self-driving technology is already causing less accidents, compared to average human drivers, but this issue is still being debated. Brahambhatt, "Settling the Debate." For the failures of autonomous cars in this regard, see Marx, *Road to Nowhere*, 132–39.

48. Sagen, "Car Accidents."

49. McGrath, *Autonomous Vehicles*, 25.

While the examples I gave above mostly focus on the United States, traffic fatalities are a truly global problem. As the World Health Organization (WHO) highlights, "approximately 1.19 million people die each year as a result of road traffic crashes."[50] To put it differently, every single day almost 3,700 people are killed in incidents involving motorized vehicles. Tragically, more than half of these fatalities occur among the most vulnerable road users that may not even have a car—traffic participants like pedestrians, cyclists, and motorcyclists.

In addition, 93 percent of traffic deaths worldwide occur in low- and middle-income countries, which is a disproportionately high number, considering these countries only account for 60 percent of the world's vehicles. So severe is this problem that road accidents are "the leading cause of death for children and young people 5–29 years of age."[51] These numbers are tragic, revealing a deeply flawed and unjust system. But things do not have to remain this way. Increasingly, we have the technology at our disposal to change things. Some may not like the disruptions such a move might entail. However, as Christians, we should stand up for the protection of human life and therefore be proactive in working toward a future in which safer vehicles and traffic systems will become the new norm.

Having said that, self-driving vehicles may cause new problems, including the loss of human life. Autonomous cars rely heavily on software, and this software could be hacked by a variety of actors, including malevolent hackers, criminals, and terrorists.[52] Hackers could manipulate self-driving cars in such a way they cause chaos in our cities and unprecedented traffic jams. Criminals may be able to steal cars without having to drive them. However, even more alarming is the possibility that terrorists could take control of entire fleets of autonomous vehicles and start driving them into crowds of pedestrians or causing massive head-on collisions on freeways, which would lead to severe injuries and, potentially, thousands of casualties.[53]

In such a scenario, the gains of having fewer fatal traffic accidents caused by human error would be reversed. This ambivalence is not only true of autonomous vehicles, but of technology in general. In a fallen world, technology creates both opportunities and threats, and with every

50. World Health Organization, "Global Road Safety."
51. CDC, "Global Road Safety."
52. Kermorgant and Siary, "Is the Law Ready," 94–96.
53. Schwartz, *No One at the Wheel*.

step humanity seems to take forward, there are also trade-offs, imbalances, and negative side effects, a dynamic John Dyer describes well in *From the Garden to the City: The Place of Technology in the Story of God*.[54] Similarly, Tony Reinke writes, "The Gospel of Technology promises to simplify our lives and give us more free time, stronger relationships, added security, and better societies."[55] However, in the end people are often left with "more complex lives, less free time, increased loneliness, added insecurities, and amplified social inequality."[56]

With regards to self-driving cars, these trade-offs and downsides related to security issues will not be easy to solve. As one group of researchers puts it, "Autonomous vehicles (AV) are vulnerable to many kinds of cyberattacks. The software driving fully AV will have more than 100 million lines of code, so it is impossible to predict the security problems."[57] Tackling these problems will require a concerted effort coming from the manufacturers of autonomous vehicles, as well as involving regulatory bodies, such as the National Highway Traffic Safety Administration (NHTSA). As Javed Ali, an expert on counterterrorism explains, the "NHTSA has laid out its current efforts on autonomous vehicle cybersecurity by describing various protection measures focused on intrusion detection, incident response and intelligence and information-sharing."[58] Cybersecurity is a major theme related to technologies of the Fourth Industrial Revolution, a topic to be further discussed in chapter 6. Only if these security challenges of self-driving vehicles can be adequately addressed, they could become an innovation that saves human lives.

A second reason why autonomous cars might be a step in the right direction is because they are moving toward electrification and are therefore contributing to a cleaner environment.[59] Some of the self-driving technologies offered today are part of traditional cars with combustion engines, but with all the software and sensors involved the trend is clearly pointing toward battery-driven vehicles that are more like a gadget or

---

54. Dyer, *From the Garden to the City*, 132–34.
55. Reinke, *God, Technology, and the Christian Life*, 179–80.
56. Reinke, *God, Technology, and the Christian Life*, 180.
57. Linkov et al., "Human Factors."
58. Ali, "Opinion."
59. These two technologies are interrelated because "autonomous vehicles are technology-based platforms, and electrically powered cars are much more compatible than internal combustion engines (ICE) to being operated by software. Electric motors are more responsive to control and easier to integrate into an autonomous platform." McGrath, *Autonomous Vehicles*, 119.

computer, rather than a car as traditionally understood. As one author writing about autonomous vehicles describes it, "When I first drove the Tesla Model S, I thought of it as a computer on wheels"; however, he then realized Tesla's cars "can be better thought of as a battery on wheels."[60]

Granted, if an electrical vehicle is charged at a network that depends on fossil fuels, then this does not make much of a difference in terms of protecting the environment (the whole question of energy production and consumption is a topic in itself, which is examined in greater detail in chapter 8). In addition, it also must be acknowledged that the current supply chain of lithium batteries creates its own set of environmental problems, as well as issues related to child labor and unsafe working conditions. This is because a large portion of the necessary raw materials for batteries, such as cobalt, are currently imported from countries like the Democratic Republic of Congo (DRC), which is troubled by corruption, instability, violence, and occurrences of modern-day slavery.[61]

Nonetheless, there is a possibility more and more people will not only drive an electrical car with improved battery solutions but will also have solar panels installed on their home's roof, using this energy source to charge their vehicles. Such an arrangement would noticeably improve people's quality of life—at the end of the day, nobody likes to breathe in the fumes of cars and buses when walking, jogging, or biking next to a road with a lot of traffic. If all vehicles driving on city roads were electric, the surrounding air would be much cleaner and quite similar to what it is like in the countryside.[62] Plus, bearing in mind how silent electric vehicles are, it would also be much less noisy. Since noise pollution is a very real health problem, just like smog is, autonomous transportation could make a considerable contribution to a better environment. As such, this technology may be commendable from a public theology perspective, as it would enable society to better care for both creation and human beings.

Third, self-driving cars could lead to more efficient traffic flows, particularly once most vehicles are autonomous and can communicate with each other. Less congestion and fewer traffic jams mean more quality of

---

60. McKenzie, *Insane Mode*, 8. Compare Kevin Kelly, who speaks of a "computer on wheels" or "rolling computer" that will become an "internet car" and therefore a "connected car." Kelly, *Inevitable*, 111–12.

61. Rapier, "Environmental Implications."

62. Hamish McKenzie puts it this way: "we humans have better ways to power our lives than to burn a dinosaur-era compaction that dirties the air and skanks up the chemistry of the atmosphere." McKenzie, *Insane Mode*, 8.

life for everybody living in cities, and more free time for those who need to use the road to go places.[63] Some people may also give up private car ownership altogether, considering how convenient and cost-efficient autonomous car-riding services may become one day. Since currently the average car in America is driven less than an hour a day, cars could be used much more efficiently if they were constantly driving. Consequently, cities could be redesigned because there would be less need for roads and parking spaces. In Seattle, for instance, "which is in dire need of new affordable housing, 40% of the land area is currently used for parking."[64] To varying degrees, this is a nationwide issue; there are currently around one billion parking lots in the United States. Certainly, America's cities would look remarkably different if this incredibly high number could be reduced.[65]

Unfortunately, precisely due to these advantages of self-driving cars, cities could become even more crowded. Basic economics states that the demand for a product or service increases when its price decreases. If autonomous vehicles really become that affordable, it is quite possible overall traffic would increase, as these robotaxis would then also be used by people who previously were not driving (such as children, teenagers, and people with various disabilities).[66] Except for charging, robotaxis may also be on the road 24–7, driving around in search for customers, without taking any breaks for rest and sleep like human drivers do. Given these potential challenges caused by autonomous vehicles, mobility in the twenty-first century will have to combine a whole range of innovative technologies, including self-driving cars, but also delivery drones, air taxis, infrastructure for bicycles, advanced tunnel systems, hyperloops, supersonic airplanes, high-speed trains, and innovative forms of public transport.[67]

Rethinking transportation and mobility may also be necessary considering how many American households have more than one vehicle, and that the car has become an idol for many. Cars are an expression of autonomy and liberty, but also a status symbol that communicates the wealth and social standing an individual possesses. However, as followers of Jesus we would do well to pay more attention to his many warnings regarding materialism and the accumulation of possessions (Matt

---

63. Reducing congestion is a major benefit highlighted in Winston and Karpilow, *Autonomous Vehicles*, 29–77.

64. Peters, "Here's How Much Space."

65. McGrath, *Autonomous Vehicles*, 29, 269.

66. Grush and Niles, *End of Driving*, 194–95.

67. E.g., Klepeis, *Future of Transportation*.

6:19–34; 16:26; 19:16–30; Mark 10:17–31; Luke 6:20–26; 12:13–34; 14:33; 16:19–31; 18:18–30). Since, as Christians, our identity and sense of self-worth lie in Christ and not in our worldly possessions, reevaluating how we view cars could become a major step toward a deeper level of discipleship.

At the same time, like all material goods, owning a car can increase people's opportunities to exercise personal agency, practice hospitality, and become a blessing to others. Particularly in American culture, the car is an important cultural icon, symbolizing independence and freedom. Well-meaning politicians and city planners may want to restrict private car ownership for a variety of reasons, but when faced with such initiatives it is crucial to remember the saying that the road to hell is paved with good intentions. The technological innovations of the Fourth Industrial Revolution, such as autonomous cars, must be used in a way that enhances the choices people have, rather than reducing them.

I believe autonomous vehicles will bring about several positive changes Christians can embrace. At the same time, every technological innovation comes with its own downsides and dangers, and it is quite possible that a future dominated by self-driving cars will not bring about the advantages highlighted above. Personally, I am optimistic some of the technical challenges will be solved, such as increasing the safety and security of autonomous vehicles, to protect them from hackers. Nonetheless, even if these technical challenges can be adequately addressed, there is yet another downside of self-driving cars and trucks that has serious social and economic implications: the loss of jobs. As a society, we must think about all the different people who earn their living by driving, including professional truck drivers, taxi drivers, and Uber and Lyft drivers—all these people would lose their jobs if driverless trucks and cars became the norm, which is a serious problem indeed. This is such an important topic that it warrants its own discussion, which is why, in the following chapter, we turn to questions related to work and unemployment.

DISCUSSION QUESTIONS

1. When, do you think, will autonomous vehicles become part of everyday life in the United States? What about other countries?
2. What are some of the risks and opportunities associated with self-driving cars?

3. In your opinion, how could the design of our cities change by taking advantage of new mobility solutions?

4. What considerations should Christians take into account when it comes to choosing different modes of transportation?

SUGGESTIONS FOR FURTHER READING

- Tom Standage, *A Brief History of Motion: From the Wheel, to the Car, to What Comes Next* (2021). A fascinating history of human transportation, highlighting current developments, as well as future implications.

- Hamish McKenzie, *Insane Mode: How Elon Musk's Tesla Sparked an Electric Revolution to End the Age of Oil* (2018). A history of Tesla, written by a journalist who worked in communications for this company for a period of time.

- Lawrence D. Burns, *Autonomy: The Quest to Build the Driverless Car—And How It Will Reshape Our World* (2018). An informative history about the development of self-driving cars, written by a former GM executive.

- Michael E. McGrath, *Autonomous Vehicles: Opportunities, Strategies, and Disruptions* (2021). A helpful overview on various aspects of autonomous vehicles, written by a management and technology consultant.

- Matthew B. Crawford, *Why We Drive: Toward a Philosophy of the Open Road* (2021). A philosopher-mechanic makes a passionate case for driving as an expression of people's skill, independence, and freedom.

- Paris Marx, *Road to Nowhere: What Silicon Valley Gets Wrong about the Future of Transportation* (2022). Highlights the downsides of electric cars and autonomous vehicles, pointing to the possibilities of public transport instead.

2

Work

DURING THE EARLY DAYS of the 2020 presidential election cycle, one of the candidates within the Democratic party was the entrepreneur and philanthropist Andrew Yang. Yang did not get very far in terms of attracting votes, but his platform and political message were unique and innovative.[1] Yang was the only candidate who made the Fourth Industrial Revolution a major theme in his campaign, specifically by pointing out that countless workers might lose their jobs in an age dominated by AI and sophisticated robots. The solution, according to Yang? Offering a universal basic income (UBI). Following this plan, every American adult would receive one thousand dollars per month from the government, thereby enabling them to have a sense of security and thrive, even while going through periods of unemployment or underemployment.

One of the specific examples Yang highlights in his book *The War on Normal People: The Truth about America's Disappearing Jobs and Why Universal Basic Income Is Our Future* is the plight of truck drivers. To understand why this is such a powerful example, some numbers might be helpful. In the United States, there are currently around 3.5 million truck drivers. Trucking is an extremely important industry in terms of employment, so much so that, in twenty-nine states, being a truck driver is the

---

1. On February 11, 2020, it was reported that, "Presidential candidate Andrew Yang dropped out of the 2020 Democratic race after finishing well behind top-tier candidates in the Iowa caucus and New Hampshire primary." Dzhanova and Calia, "Democrat Andrew Yang."

most common job.² In addition, a significant number of people make a living by supporting these truck drivers, by working at gas stations, truck stops, motels, etc. That, explains Yang, is another 7.2 million jobs.³

However, trucks and taxis are just one example of how recent technologies like self-driving vehicles are affecting future employment opportunities. Besides transportation, jobs will be lost in other industries as well, thereby affecting a wide range of occupations. Several studies are sounding the alarm in this regard, as the following examples demonstrate.

- Two researchers from Oxford University, Carl Benedikt Frey and Michael A. Osborne, caused quite a stir in 2013 when they predicted up to 47 percent of jobs in the United States could be lost to automation.⁴
- The consulting company McKinsey calculated that, worldwide, four hundred million to eight hundred million jobs could be lost to automation by the year 2030; and that the United States "could lose between 16 million and 54 million jobs between 2016 and 2030."⁵
- A study by Oxford Economics (from 2019) focused more specifically on the impact of robots, claiming that they "could take over 20 million manufacturing jobs around the world by 2030."⁶ While these sophisticated machines increase productivity for the companies that install them, "As a result of robotization, tens of millions of jobs will be lost, especially in poorer local economies that rely on lower-skilled workers. This will therefore translate to an increase in income inequality," the study warned.⁷

A certain number of job losses due to advances in machinery have been a reality for quite some time now. Robots, in particular, have been employed by the automobile industry since the 1960s.⁸ However, things might be different this time, especially considering the technologies of

---

2. Yang, *War on Normal People*, 43.
3. Yang, *War on Normal People*, 45.
4. For some perspective on this often-cited study, see Rinehart and Edwards, "Understanding Job Loss Predictions."
5. Manyika et al., "Future That Works," §19.
6. Taylor, "Robots Could Take Over," §1.
7. Taylor, "Robots Could Take Over," §5.
8. "One of the first industrial robots, Unimate, invented by George Devol, was put to work by General Motors in 1961." Schwartz, *Work Disrupted*, 26.

the Fourth Industrial Revolution, such as AI, will not only affect blue-collar workers but white-collar workers as well.

Traditionally, machines have been used primarily to replace or augment the physical strength humans can bring to a task by using their muscles. A steam-engine powered locomotive can transport infinitely more weight than any human ever could, even with the help of strength-enhancing tools, such as a ricksha or a wheelbarrow. Similarly, a tractor can pull a larger plow, thereby enabling a farmer to cultivate crops on a larger piece of land. In this sense, the tractor is similar to the advantage an ox brings about in farming. Throughout history, humans have always been aware certain kinds of animals (like elephants or buffaloes) are physically stronger than they are. The advent of machines and engines that are stronger than both animals and humans was therefore not much of a surprise.

However, humans have habitually considered themselves the most intelligent beings on Earth. For a long time, the idea that a machine could surpass not only the physical but also the cognitive abilities of humans seemed unfathomable.[9] With the advent of AI, super-fast computers, and the collection of immense amounts of data, this is now beginning to change. For instance, AI-powered programs equipped with sophisticated vision technologies may soon not only be able to drive vehicles, which is traditionally a blue-collar job, but will also be adept at interpreting medical images and evaluating legal documents—thereby putting white-collar jobs, such as doctors and lawyers, at risk.

The reality is all kinds of repetitive and predictable tasks will be increasingly automated, because anything that has to do with processing copious amounts of information can be done much quicker by computers. The work of radiologists who specialize in diagnosing cancer by interpreting images created by advanced machines like CTs and MRIs may therefore soon be disrupted. After all, "a radiologist can review 20,000 films a year . . . while algorithms could allow the review of millions, or even billions of images."[10] At this point, the performance of radiologists and AI in reading images are comparable, but capabilities of the latter will continue to get better and better. However, this does not mean radiologists will become redundant; instead, there could be a positive

---

9. Accordingly, besides the "Fourth Industrial Revolution," this era also has been called the "second machine age." Brynjolfsson and McAfee, *Second Machine Age*, 9–11.

10. Schwartz, *Work Disrupted*, 32.

development as "doctors will have more time to spend providing context and empathy to patients, rather than wading through the data."[11]

But what about general practitioners; what about the family doctor who fulfills an important social function? For now, their jobs seem safe, but further down the road AI-powered machines may be able to not only deal with cognitive tasks but to skillfully engage with human emotions as well. Furthermore, even a general practitioner needs to primarily deal with the collection and interpretation of data. With this example of the general practitioner in mind, the bestselling Israeli historian Yuval Noah Harari is worth quoting in full when he writes in *Homo Deus: A Brief History of Tomorrow*,

> Even doctors are fair game for the algorithms. The first and foremost task of most doctors is to diagnose diseases correctly, and then suggest the best available treatment. If I arrive at the clinic complaining of fever and diarrhoea, I might be suffering from food poisoning. Then again, the same symptoms might result from a stomach virus, cholera, dysentery, malaria, cancer or some unknown new disease. My physician only has a few minutes to make a correct diagnosis, because that is all the time my health insurance pays for. This allows for no more than a few questions and perhaps a quick medical examination. The doctor then cross-references this meagre information with my medical history, and with the vast world of human maladies. Alas, not even the most diligent doctor can remember all my previous ailments and check-ups. Similarly, no doctor can be familiar with every illness and drug, or read every new article published in every medical journal. To top it all, the doctor is sometimes tired or hungry or perhaps even sick, which affects her judgment. No wonder that doctors sometimes err in their diagnoses or recommend a less-than-optimal treatment.[12]

By contrast, an AI-empowered device like IBM's Watson (which first acquired widespread fame in 2011 by winning the game show *Jeopardy!*) could become a medical specialist by being linked to a databank that includes "every known illness and medicine in history."[13] So far, Watson's performance in the medical field has not been very impressive, but in the future a similar machine could be developed that would be familiar with all the personal medical data of a particular individual and, in contrast to

11. Schwartz, *Work Disrupted*, 32.
12. Harari, *Homo Deus*, 317–18.
13. Harari, *Homo Deus*, 319.

any human doctor, would never be sick, tired, or irritated, but patiently explain everything the patient desires to know.

As this example demonstrates, even jobs that currently enjoy high social status because they require sophisticated qualifications may be at risk in the age of the Fourth Industrial Revolution. As AI-driven machines become increasingly powerful, they will be faster and more precise in performing many tasks that until now have been the domain of well-educated middle-class workers and professionals. In addition, lower-class jobs that traditionally required human interaction are in danger as well. For example, Andrew Puzder, the former CEO of CKE Restaurants, the parent company of Carl's Junior and other fast-food restaurants, "praised digital devices over human workers" when he explained regarding the former: "They're always polite, they always upsell, they never take a vacation, they never show up late, there's never a slip-and-fall, or an age, sex or race discrimination case."[14]

Accordingly, various recent publications and articles have highlighted what kind of jobs might be in danger of automation. Examples in this category (listed here in alphabetical order) include accountants, administrative staff (such as secretaries), agricultural workers, bankers, bookkeeping clerks, cashiers, construction workers, couriers, customer service representatives, dentists, doctors, food service workers, journalists, lawyers, legal clerks, manufacturing workers, pharmacists, retail workers,[15] security guards, service workers (like receptionists), soldiers, taxi drivers, teachers, telemarketers,[16] traders, truck drivers, and warehouse workers.[17]

This is quite an impressive list, covering a wide range of occupations. To be sure, not all these jobs will disappear overnight; more often than not the transition will be gradual. To take truck drivers as an example: The average truck driver in the United States is male and around fifty years old, and may therefore have a hard time adapting to a new job, whether as a software engineer or a caregiver for the elderly.[18] However, currently their jobs are quite secure—in fact, logistics companies have thousands of vacancies to fill, because turnover is rather high and there are not enough young people interested in becoming truck drivers

---

14. West, *Future of Work*, 3.

15. Doyle, "Is Your Job at Risk." Aside from self-checkout stations, another reason fewer retail workers will be needed is because of the growing importance of online shopping.

16. Needle, "What Jobs."

17. Ford, *Rise of the Robots*, 12–17; Oppenheimer, *Robots Are Coming!*, 14–15.

18. Yang, *War on Normal People*, 43.

anymore.[19] For autonomous trucks to become a reality at a significant scale, ten to fifteen years of addressing technological and regulatory challenges may well be ahead of us, and by that time a large portion of American truck drivers will be ready for retirement.[20]

In this scenario, self-driving trucks would not be a threat to people's jobs, but rather a technology-based solution to fulfill a crucial task which fewer and fewer people are willing to perform. In addition, technologies tend to create new jobs, not only in entirely new sectors, but also within the very same industry and occupation.[21] One example of this phenomenon is the arrival of ATMs. When ATMs were first introduced in the 1970s, one would have been tempted to think that this would destroy thousands of bank teller jobs, since now customers were able to withdraw and deposit money by themselves, without the help of another human being. However, the opposite occurred: ATMs caused cost-savings for banks, enabling them to open more branches, where they now needed to employ a larger number of bank tellers who would interact with their clients, going beyond such standardized tasks as simply handing out cash.[22]

In fact, since ATMs first "appeared on the scene, the number of human bank tellers in the United States has roughly doubled, according to Boston University economist James Bessen."[23] This is because the latter now fulfill different roles, namely "learning to assist customers with loans, open new accounts, market financial products, troubleshoot, and more—jobs that machines were unable to do."[24] However, given new developments that go beyond ATMs (such as internet banking and easily accessible online trading platforms), it is quite possible the number of bank branches and of the employees needed to staff them will decrease in the near future.

As this example of the banking landscape illustrates, the risk of job losses is real, especially when one considers how fast new technologies are developing, making it difficult for people to keep up with the changes. In such an environment, what kind of jobs might be promising

19. This issue became a widely discussed challenge during the supply chain problems that arose at the end of 2021. Ngo and Swanson, "Biggest Kink"; Semuels, "Truck Driver Shortage."

20. That truck drivers will still be needed in the foreseeable future is highlighted in several studies, such as Center for Global Policy Solutions, *Stick Shift*; Leonard et al., "Autonomous Vehicles, Mobility, and Employment."

21. This is one of the main points highlighted in Autor et al., *Work of the Future*, 4–5, 7.

22. Schwartz, *Work Disrupted*, 14–15.

23. Schwartz, *Work Disrupted*, 14.

24. Schwartz, *Work Disrupted*, 14.

occupations for decades to come? Here are some examples: (1) jobs that drive technological innovation—such as designing, building, and servicing robots; (2) jobs based on human creativity, like musicians, artists, and artisans that specialize on customized products; (3) jobs that consist primarily of leadership skills, such as being a CEO, manager, or coach; (4) jobs requiring dexterity and a human touch, like being a nurse or a physical therapist.[25]

As work environments and employment opportunities change, employees will have to demonstrate greater flexibility and a willingness to keep learning, as they accept the idea that they will probably have several careers over the course of their lives. At the same time, employers and managers will have to make adjustments as well, creating a new kind of work environment that enables them to attract the best possible talent to contribute to the success of their organization. The futurist and bestselling author Jacob Morgan has been exploring these themes for a number of years, and the following overview highlights some of the major shifts that are currently redefining the nature of work (Table 5).[26]

Table 5. The Changing World of Work

	Traditional Paradigm	*Future Paradigm*
Motivation	employee engagement	employee experience
Qualification	hard skills	soft skills
Office environment	set hours and location	flexibility
Leadership style	managing	coaching and mentoring
Relationship to machines	humans act like robots	humans work with robots
Social order	traditional hierarchies	flatter structures
Type of workforce	static workforce	dynamic workforce
Innovation model	factory	laboratory
Work and free time	work-life balance	work-life integration
Significance of knowledge	knowledge is power	perpetual learning is power
Time horizon	long-term employment	focus on projects and tasks
Decision-making	decisions based on intuition	decisions based on data
Retirement age	retire at age sixty-five	retire when dead

25. Compare Martin Ford who sees potential for jobs in three categories: (1) genuine creativity, (2) complex human relationships, and (3) highly unpredictable jobs. Mahdawi, "What Jobs."

26. Morgan, "This Is."

Authors like Morgan are optimistic technologies like AI will primarily change how people work, rather than eliminating the need for human workers altogether. One reason is that, even if machines outperform humans in certain fields, people may still prefer a person to perform a particular job. As the British economist Daniel Susskind describes in *A World without Work*, "Throughout life, we can point to certain tasks—crafting furniture, tailoring a suit, preparing a meal, caring for one another in old age and ill health—where we value the process behind them, and in particular the fact that they are done by human beings, rather than just the outcome that is achieved."[27] While many products and services will become affordable and therefore accessible to the masses, the wealthy will be able to pay for more personal solutions. Accordingly, Susskind observes certain new kinds of jobs are already available today, namely "strange but reasonably well-paid roles that rely almost entirely on the patronage of the most prosperous in society: bespoke spoon carvers and children's playdate consultants, elite personal trainers and star yoga instructors, craft chocolatiers and artisanal cheesemakers."[28]

The problem with this arrangement is that it leads to an unequal society, since "what is emerging is not just an economic division, where some earn much more than others, but a status division as well, between those who are rich and those who serve them."[29] In addition, not many people will be able to work full-time as musicians, personal trainers, or artisanal cheesemakers, because the number of people who are willing and able to pay for these extravagant products and services is limited. What kind of jobs will then be available for the average person who does not have any outstanding skills or qualifications? One trend is more and more people will have to work in the gig economy, something we have already begun to experience with the arrival of ride-sharing platforms like Uber and Lyft.[30] Many people appreciate the kind of flexibility and independence these jobs offer. However, the downside is these arrangements do not offer benefits like health insurance and overtime pay, and

27. Susskind, *World without Work*, 123–24.
28. Susskind, *World without Work*, 110.
29. Susskind, *World without Work*, 110.
30. Workers for these platforms are also called "clickworkers" and often suffer from a "lack of job security and few, if any, labour protections." Berg and De Stefano, "Employment and Regulation for Clickworkers," 180. Besides Uber and Lyft, other examples include Amazon Mechanical Turk (https://www.mturk.com), Upwork (https://www.upwork.com), TaskRabbit (https://www.taskrabbit.com), and Clickworker (https://www.clickworker.com).

people often have to work at several jobs simultaneously to make ends meet.

In light of these developments, Susskind warns: "Karl Marx spoke of workers as the 'proletariat,' adopting the ancient Roman term for members of the lowest social class; today, though, the term *precariat* is gaining ground instead—a word that captures the fact that more and more work is not just poorly paid, but also unstable and stressful."[31] Crucially, questions related to work are not only economic in nature; there is an important psychological component as well. This is because humans do not only go to work to earn a living; if this were the case, millionaires and billionaires would embark on perpetual vacations—but almost none of them do that; most of them keep working, often more than forty hours a week. Besides a salary and benefits, a job also provides people with meaning, status, camaraderie, and a sense of pride.

For many people, their work gives them a sense of identity, so much so that their job may even be the primary factor determining who they are as a person. After all, one of the first questions people ask when meeting somebody new is to inquire what they do for a living. Consequently, if the Fourth Industrial Revolution leads to a world with fewer jobs, more unstable jobs, and the need to frequently change jobs, then this would not only have financial implications for people but affect their sense of well-being too. Technological unemployment could become a major crisis for modern society as it would deeply affect people on a personal level.[32]

At the same time, innovative technologies also bear in them the potential for a better life for a larger number of people. First of all, the Fourth Industrial Revolution may create unprecedented amounts of wealth, as innovations like AI and genetic engineering will bring forth not only new products, but entirely new industries that will possibly go beyond anything we can imagine today.[33] And while this newly created wealth may at first be concentrated in the hands of a few privileged

---

31. Susskind, *World without Work*, 109 (emphasis in the original).

32. The term "technological unemployment" was first used in the 1920s and was then popularized by the economist John Maynard Keynes (1883–1946) in the 1930s. Schatzberg, *Technology*, 159–61.

33. A good starting point to examine the potential of future industries are the analyses by the company ARK Invest (https://ark-invest.com), founded by Catherine Wood. See, for instance, ARK's "Big Ideas 2024" report, which explores the potential of technologies like AI, Bitcoin, precision therapies, electric vehicles, robotics, reusable rockets, and 3D-printing.

individuals and corporations, we could, over time, see an improvement of the social situation for the majority of the population—similar to what eventually took place after the previous industrial revolutions.[34]

Second, regarding the nature of work, one needs to acknowledge that many jobs people perform today are unsafe and unfulfilling. This sobering reality has been described as "3D" jobs, which stands for jobs that are dirty, dangerous, and demeaning.[35] In spite of the hardships associated with them, these jobs are usually in the category of low-paying manual work and are often performed by marginalized groups in society, such as immigrants. Considering the working conditions of blue-collar workers like oil rig drillers, coal miners, garbage collectors, sewage cleaners, and meat processors—would it not add immensely to these people's quality of life if machines took over their jobs while they could find work in a cleaner and safer environment?

In addition to the already mentioned "3D" of undesirable work one could add another *d*, considering that many jobs society currently offers are also quite dull, causing people to be easily bored or irritated.[36] One could think, for instance, of customer service hotline representatives, security guards, parking lot attendants, data entry specialists, and cashiers—since all these people are created in the image of God, might they long to do something more creative? Could the Fourth Industrial Revolution have more interesting careers in store for them, for example as healthcare workers, cybersecurity experts, or virtual reality designers? These kinds of questions point to both peril and promise when it comes to the impact novel technologies might have on employment opportunities. As Christians, we therefore need to respond to this challenge of our time and start thinking about the implications of work and unemployment from a theological point of view.

---

34. See also Kelly, who writes, "It's hard to believe you'd have an economy at all if you gave pink slips to more than half of the labor force. But that—in slow motion—is what the industrial revolution did to the workforce of the early 19th century. Two hundred years ago, 70 percent of American workers lived on the farm. Today automation has eliminated all but 1 percent of their jobs, replacing them (and their work animals) with machines. But the displaced workers did not sit idle. Instead, automation created hundreds of millions of jobs in entirely new fields." Kelly, *Inevitable*, 49.

35. Low, *Economics Primer*, 71.

36. Townsend, *Ghost Road*, xiv, 119.

A CHRISTIAN PERSPECTIVE ON WORK

In recent years, there has been a growing awareness that, besides evangelism and discipleship, participating in the *missio Dei* also means contributing to the common good and doing so informed by a biblical basis.[37] Equipped with such a broad vision, I believe the church has something valuable to offer when it comes to questions related to work and employment in the context of the Fourth Industrial Revolution. In the following, I am suggesting three key areas in which believers could make a tangible difference. (1) Christians need to continue investing in education, particularly in postsecondary education, so that people will be able to acquire new qualifications and skills that will enable them to find well-paying jobs. (2) Times of transitions and great technological change often lead to an increase in inequality in society, which is why the church must get involved in discussing policies that can empower those living and working on the margins. (3) Even so, educational opportunities and innovative policies cannot solve some of the deepest issues humans struggle with. Ultimately, believers need to help people to find their identity in being sons and daughters of God, giving them a sense of belonging that is independent of the social status they currently may or may not have.

Given that, in the Fourth Industrial Revolution, people will have to acquire new skills in order to find gainful employment, I submit the first response required of the church has to do with investing in education. Throughout church history, education has always been one of the strong areas of Christian engagement. A commitment toward offering a broad education (for every child, not just for the elites) became especially crucial in the aftermath of the Protestant Reformation. The German reformer Martin Luther (1483–1546), for instance, emphasized the need for both boys and girls to be educated (a rather revolutionary proposition in those days), so that they could be instructed in the faith and become productive citizens.[38] Since then, Protestants have continued to promote education for the masses, particularly so that people would be able to read the Bible for themselves.[39] In addition, John Amos Comenius (1592–1670), a Czech theologian and pedagogue, proposed a

---

37. A classic explanation of the concept of *missio Dei* is given by the South African theologian and missiologist David J. Bosch (1929–1992) in Bosch, *Transforming Mission*, 398–402.

38. Androne, *Martin Luther*, 39–41.

39. An emphasis on mass education and mass printing is one of the main arguments made in Woodberry, "Missionary Roots of Liberal Democracy," 244–74.

number of innovations when it came to teaching children, so much so that Comenius is often considered the "father of modern education."[40]

However, Christians not only got involved in primary and secondary education, but also were innovative in conceptualizing higher education, by inventing what would become the modern-day university. Within the Roman Catholic tradition, these efforts came out of the monasteries and cathedral schools of the Middle Ages, but eventually Protestants became involved as well.[41] After all, Luther was himself a university professor, and John Calvin (1509–1564) founded an academy in Geneva, Switzerland, that soon became a center of theological thought, attracting students from all over Europe. While most of the early modern universities were founded in European countries, the global missions movement also led to the founding of universities on other continents, such as the University of Santo Domingo (in the Dominican Republic, founded in 1538) and the University of Santo Tomas, which was established in Manila, the Philippines, in 1611.

Most of the first universities were built on Christian foundations, and by offering degrees in disciplines like theology, medicine, and law they were cutting-edge for many centuries, offering the finest and most advanced education that was available anywhere in the world.[42] In the United States, Christian colleges were founded that emphasized communal living and a liberal arts curriculum, thereby displaying a commitment to form the whole person through education. Unfortunately, much of this Christian heritage in American higher education has been lost, even though there are still a number of colleges and universities that are holding fast to a faith-based education.[43] However, where does Christian higher education stand today when it comes to teaching the subjects of the future? The kind of subjects that will enable people to find jobs?

---

40. Mangalwadi, *Book That Made*, 215.

41. Raines and Leathers, *Economic Institutions of Higher Education*, 17–21.

42. Medieval education was based on the Roman trivium (grammar, rhetoric, and logic) and quadrivium (geometry, arithmetic, astronomy, and music). Furthermore, "The university usually had four faculties. The arts were the general course for all. Theology, law, and medicine were more advanced studies." Cairns, *Christianity through the Centuries*, 235.

43. The classic volumes on Christian higher education in the United States are Marsden, *Soul of the American University*, and Burtchaell, *Dying of the Light*. For more recent publications on the subject, see Schuman, *Seeing the Light*, and Carpenter et al., *Christian Higher Education*.

As the world of work is changing, the educational opportunities offered by the church will have to change as well. Education is such a crucial topic for the Fourth Industrial Revolution that it will be discussed more thoroughly in the next chapter, so at this point I am going to limit myself to three suggestions. First, Christians need to embrace research, particularly in the natural sciences (like physics, chemistry, and biology). Traditionally, Christian colleges and universities have done well in teaching what is already known, but this needs to be amplified by making new efforts in discovering what is yet unknown.[44] Second, Christian colleges and universities should be innovative in terms of the majors they offer to their students, prioritizing areas of study that have a lot of potential for growth in terms of future employment opportunities—areas such as cybersecurity, biomedical engineering, software engineering, computer science, information and data sciences, robotics and automation, AI, and nanotechnology.[45] Third, Christian institutions of higher education need to look beyond traditional students in their early twenties and offer educational opportunities to people of all ages, facilitating and encouraging an approach to life-long learning that will empower people to adapt and enable them to stay employed.

Besides investing in innovative forms of education, the church can also make a contribution by advocating for structural changes that will lead to a more just and free society. As indicated above (in the first section of this chapter), the dystopian view that sophisticated machines will take over all our jobs is most likely too pessimistic, and therefore not realistic.[46] It is much more probable that new technologies will create more jobs than they destroy, mirroring a similar development to what has taken place in previous industrial revolutions. However, one of the biggest problems of technology-driven growth is the growing inequality in society, as it is primarily the rich (and especially the super-rich) who are benefiting from these developments. This phenomenon has already started to unfold in the context of the Third Industrial Revolution. As a study by an MIT economist suggests, tech innovations since the 1980s

---

44. Glanzer and Carpenter, "Conclusion," 305.

45. Several websites highlight certain degrees and their future potential for gainful employment, such as: Bachelors Degree Center, "30 Best College Majors."

46. For this kind of dystopian view, see, in particular, Harari's warnings about a "useless class." Harari, *Homo Deus*, 322–32; *21 Lessons for the 21st Century*, 28–34. Compare Topf, "'Useless Class' or Uniquely Human?," 17–38.

have benefited highly skilled workers, but not low-skilled workers.[47] The income gap is even more obvious when comparing the earnings of CEOs with that of regular employees: Around 1980, "the CEOs of America's largest firms earned about 28 times more than an average worker; by 2000, that ratio stood at an astounding 376 times."[48]

The following four additional facts demonstrate how serious the problem of growing inequality has become:

- The Gini Coefficient measures relative inequality within a country. While some developed countries like France and Greece have seen a decreasing Gini Coefficient since the 1980s, most developed countries (including Sweden, New Zealand, and the United States) have seen a notable increase in inequality levels.[49]
- Although productivity has steadily gone up in the United States since the Second World War, hourly wages pretty much stagnated in the 1970s and 1980s, while only slightly improving since the 1990s.
- Income shares of the top 1 percent have risen dramatically between 1981 and 2016, particularly in the United States, but also in countries like Denmark, Ireland, and the UK.
- At the top of the top things are even more extreme in America: "from 1981 to 2017, the income share of the top 0.1 percent increased more than three and a half times from its already disproportionally high level, and the share of the top 0.01 percent rose more than fivefold."[50]

These dynamics were exacerbated further by COVID-19, which was declared a pandemic from March 2020 to May 2023.[51] Understandably, it would be difficult to raise wages during times of economic decline. But why have wages for working people stagnated even while productivity has increased? One explanation is that much of this economic growth has been produced by automated machines. The owners of these machines therefore become wealthier, while the bargaining power of the human workforce has decreased, since they are not contributing that much to the output anymore. One way to illustrate this dynamic is to compare some of

47. E.g., Dizikes, "Study Finds."
48. Susskind, *World without Work*, 141.
49. Susskind, *World without Work*, 136–37.
50. Susskind, *World without Work*, 138.
51. Stantcheva, "Inequalities in the Times of a Pandemic," 1–37.

the most prominent companies in the 1960s with those of the digital age, particularly with regards to employment numbers. While companies like AT&T and General Motors each employed over half a million people in their heydays, today's tech giants can create much greater value with far fewer employees (Table 6).[52] In addition, some smaller IT companies were valued extremely high while they had very few employees. WhatsApp, for instance, was valued nineteen billion dollars in 2014, but only had fifty-five employees at the time, and when Facebook bought Instagram for one billion dollars (in 2012) it merely employed thirteen people.[53]

Table 6. Largest US Companies and Their Employee Numbers

Year	Company	Market Cap	Workforce
1964	AT&T	$254 billion	758,611 employees
	GM	$201 billion	660,977 employees
	Standard Oil	$140 billion	147,000 employees
2024	Microsoft	$3.14 trillion	220,000 employees
	Apple	$2.66 trillion	161,000 employees
	Nvidia	$2.25 trillion	29,600 employees

The problem is that companies offering digital solutions gravitate toward a "winner takes all" environment, in which they create new kinds of monopolies that often exercise not only considerable economic but political power as well. They exercise all this power while creating a relatively small number of jobs, which is concerning because traditionally the middle class in developed countries have been able to secure both their income and their benefits (such as health insurance, as well as a pension) through well-paying jobs. Now, "If countries end up in a situation in which many people are unemployed or underemployed for significant periods of time, their workers will need some way to receive health care, disability, and pension benefits outside of employment."[54]

In light of such developments, one of the suggestions that has been made is the already mentioned universal basic income (UBI). Proponents of this solution are not only found among politicians, such as Andrew Yang, but also among techno-billionaires like Richard Branson,

---

52. Tartar, "Hiring Gap"; Companies Market Cap, "Market Capitalization of Apple."
53. Espindola and Wright, *Exponential Era*, 155.
54. West, *Future of Work*, 136.

Mark Zuckerberg, and Elon Musk.[55] In addition, the idea is also popular among conservative and libertarian thinkers, like the economist Milton Friedman (1912–2006), which is why it may be possible to achieve bipartisan support for this innovative approach. More recently, Charles Murray made the case that paying every adult in the US thirteen thousand USD per year (which would include three thousand dollars for mandatory health insurance) would be a comparable cost to what the US is currently spending on social matters.[56] In this model, UBI could become a simple approach to replace a whole plethora of welfare programs, thereby reducing the administrative burden of government. In addition, UBI takes away the stigma of welfare, because everybody receives it, and as such it also does not create incentives that hinder people from taking up regular work.

Nevertheless, any kind of welfare or investment program has its limitations because it only deals with the financial but not the psychological dimensions of employment and unemployment. In the biblical worldview, work is part of what God ordained for human beings to flourish; in this sense, work is part of paradise (Gen 2:15), not of the fall. What changed with the fall was that now the ground (not work itself) was cursed, making it difficult for people to earn a living (Gen 3:17–19). Any kind of work, whether in the field, in a factory, or in an office, tends to have difficult, exhausting, and frustrating dimensions. However, in the grand scheme of creation, fall, and redemption, Christians have the hope and expectation that work can be redeemed, at least to some extent, while living in this age of tension, between the first and the second coming of Christ.

In the biblical understanding, Christians do not merely have a job that helps pay the rent; rather, Christians have a calling, which is why their work becomes part of their vocation. Within this framework, believers fulfill a priestly function in their work, becoming a blessing to their fellow human beings and contributing to the beautification of God's creation.[57] As believers we can therefore affirm the value of work as a constant of God's plan for humanity, something that will continue to be an important part of the human experience, even if many tasks may soon

---

55. Schatt, *Still Room for Humans*, 157.

56. Murray, *In Our Hands*, 7–15.

57. Many Christians are demonstrating a growing desire to see their work (their jobs) as part of God's kingdom work in this world—a vision expressed in publications like Volf, *Work in the Spirit*; Keller, *Every Good Endeavor*; Lutz and Unruh, *Equipping Christians for Kingdom Purpose*.

be automated due to the advances the Fourth Industrial Revolution is bringing about.

We can be confident that work will not disappear. But at the same time, we need to realize that work will radically change, which is why the church should help people prepare for those changes. "As computers can complete more tasks, people may increasingly move from completing tasks to the more human capabilities, such as problem-solving, communicating, interpreting, addressing unexpected challenges, asking questions, and managing human (and human and machine) relationships."[58] In light of this development, one of the most crucial tasks Christians have in the twenty-first century in terms of being salt and light is to enable people to work alongside highly competent and capable machines, while still affirming the uniqueness of human beings.[59]

However, the reality is that people sometimes lose their jobs, even if they have great qualifications and even if they value their work as part of God's calling on their lives. It is therefore essential Christians provide a framework for people that affirms their dignity and gives them a stable sense of identity, independently of whether they are currently employed, underemployed, or unemployed.[60] One of the unhealthy developments of modernity is that a person's job often becomes their primary source of identity and sense of self-worth. It is important to realize this has not always been the case; rather, "this job-focused construct is a recent notion in human life. For much of recorded history, jobs were not the be-all and end-all of human existence. People understood their identity as more closely linked to family, ethnic group, religion, neighborhood, or tribe."[61]

The church can offer an alternative, more comprehensive vision of rooting one's identity in God, rather than in any specific task. As Os Guiness explains in *The Call: Finding and Fulfilling the Central Purpose of Your Life*, "If we ever limit our calling to what we do, and that task is taken away from us—we suddenly find ourselves unemployed, fired, retired,

---

58. Schwartz, *Work Disrupted*, 15.

59. As Kelly puts it, "You'll be paid in the future based on how well you work with robots. Ninety percent of your coworkers will be unseen machines. Most of what you do will not be possible without them." Kelly, *Inevitable*, 60.

60. Regarding not being gainfully employed or underemployed, Ben Witherington reminds us, "it is a huge mistake to evaluate the merits or worth of one's work on the basis of whether one is remunerated for it, much less on the basis of *how much* one is remunerated for it." Witherington, *Work*, 31 (emphasis in the original).

61. West, *Future of Work*, 150. Being created in God's image provides human with a unique dignity, as well as a priestly calling: Kilner, *Dignity and Destiny*; Swann, *Imago Dei*.

or pronounced terminally ill—then we are tempted to depression or doubt."[62] To avoid this kind of crisis, believers need to realize that "calling should not only precede career but outlast it too. Vocations never end, even when occupations do. We may retire from our jobs but never from our calling. We may at times be unemployed, but no one ever becomes uncalled."[63]

As the twenty-first century continues to unfold, Christians have the unique opportunity to invite people into a deeper understanding of the human self, one that may only be partially related to having paid work. We have a lot of to offer in this regard: a sense of belonging (by offering community, through the church), a sense of identity (as people see themselves as valuable members of the body of Christ), and a sense of destiny (being part of a royal priesthood that will one day reign and rule with Christ). As things around us keep changing, often at a rapid pace, we can proclaim the good news of a God who is unchanging, and of an indestructible kingdom that cannot be shaken (Dan 2:44, 7:18, 22, 27; Heb 12:28). Since people will have to constantly adapt and reinvent themselves in terms of their work, Christians can make a significant contribution by providing pastoral care and guidance, contributing to people's mental stability by offering community and spiritual practices that bring about a sense of peace and joy.

Particularly in times of uncertainty and whenever the intrinsic value of certain people is being questioned, the church of Jesus Christ has a powerful witness in this world by affirming the tremendous dignity of every single person, based on the fact that they are created in the image of God (Gen 1:26–28; 5:1; 9:6; Jas 3:9). The *imago Dei* is a powerful antidote against the poison of racism, misogyny, and any other form of discrimination; it protects the elderly and the unborn, the disabled and the depressed, as well as anybody who is unable to work or has difficulty finding employment, be it temporarily or permanently.

Besides being created in God's image, believers have an additional sense of identity and security in that, through the redeeming work of Christ, they have been adopted into God's family, thereby becoming sons and daughters of God (Matt 5:9; Luke 6:35–36; 20:34–36; John 1:12–13; 11:52; Rom 8:14–29; 9:6–8; 2 Cor 6:18; Gal 3:26–29; 4:1–7; Eph 1:5; Phil 2:15; 1 John 3:1–2, 9–10; 5:1–2; Rev 21:7). In other words, we are royalty,

---

62. Guiness, *Call*, 229.
63. Guiness, *Call*, 230.

and this is something that will never change throughout the course of our lives, independent of what we do. Outward circumstances may alternate, and in the era of the Fourth Industrial Revolution they may change more frequently and more unexpectedly than most of us would wish for. However, through Christ, there are certain inward realities that will always remain the same, thereby creating a sense of stability that can help us to navigate the constant changes in the environment surrounding us.

While believers can enjoy life from a position of rest, having secured their identity in Christ, this does not mean they are called to a life of passivity. Quite the contrary, Christians are called to a life of ongoing redemptive activity while they dwell here on Earth. As mentioned above, one of the most strategic areas for Christians to get actively involved in during the Fourth Industrial Revolution is the realm of education. Such an engagement will have to include primary, secondary, and higher education. While education will empower people to cope with a changing world, educational institutions will also go through technology-driven changes—which is the topic we will examine in the following chapter.

DISCUSSION QUESTIONS

1. According to your estimation, will AI create more jobs than it destroys? Or are we moving toward widespread technological unemployment?
2. How does UBI compare to traditional attempts of building a social safety net for people?
3. Ben Witherington offers "the following as a Christian definition of work: *any necessary and meaningful task that God calls and gifts a person to do and which can be undertaken to the glory of God and for the edification and aid of human beings, being inspired by the Spirit and foreshadowing the realities of the new creation.*"[64] What are your thoughts regarding this definition of work?
4. What are some of the elements of a biblical understanding of work? How is a believer's work related to their vocation or calling?

---

64. Witherington, *Work*, xii (emphasis in the original).

SUGGESTIONS FOR FURTHER READING

- Charles Murray, *In Our Hands: A Plan to Replace the Welfare State* (2016). An argument for UBI, from a libertarian/conservative point of view.

- Andrew Yang, *The War on Normal People: The Truth about America's Disappearing Jobs and Why Universal Basic Income Is Our Future* (2019). Presents Yang's vision as he was running for president of the United States.

- Jeff Schwartz, *Work Disrupted: Opportunity, Resilience, and Growth in the Accelerated Future of Work* (2021). A practical, solution-oriented guide to how the world of work is changing, by a consultant working for Deloitte.

- Daniel Susskind, *A World without Work: Technology, Automation, and How We Should Respond* (2020). Warns of widespread technological unemployment, written by an Oxford economist and former policy advisor to the British government.

- Ben Witherington III, *Work: A Kingdom Perspective on Labor* (2011). A biblical theology and ethics of work, written by a renowned New Testament scholar teaching at Asbury Theological Seminary.

- Os Guiness, *The Call: Finding and Fulfilling the Central Purpose of Your Life* (2003). Presents a vision of living fully for God's glory, which includes (but is not limited to) a person's job.

3

Education

To THRIVE IN THE era of the Fourth Industrial Revolution, people will need skills and qualifications. However, the challenge will be "to prepare students for a world in flux," as the educator Cathy N. Davidson explains in her thought-provoking book *The New Education*.[1] With so much information already available on the internet and personalized tutoring robots on the horizon, it is unclear what kind of role traditional teachers will play in the future, if any. On the other hand, the COVID-19 pandemic has demonstrated both the inevitability and the limitations of technology in education. During this time, many parents grew tired of teaching their children at home the whole day, while students experienced fatigue as they had to participate in one Zoom call after another. Given these recent experiences, what is the way forward in education?

As the world is changing toward an economy increasingly powered by AI and other innovative technologies, education will have to change as well. Most children growing up in the new millennium are digital natives; one of the primary tasks of educators will therefore be to teach them how to take advantage of technological tools in their journey of learning.[2] Already today, these tools include tablets, smartphones, and laptops students have at their disposal, enabling them to constantly be

---

1. So the subtitle of Davidson, *New Education*.
2. Digital natives are those who were born after 1980; in addition, "Unlike most Digital Immigrants, Digital Natives live much of their lives online." Palfrey and Gasser, *Born Digital*, 1, 4. For education, this means teachers need to increasingly develop a partnering approach in their teaching, so Prensky, *Teaching Digital Natives*.

online in order to access and exchange information (as well as getting increasingly distracted, and maybe even harmed by cyberbullying and damaging online content).³

Children naturally learn through play, something that can be powerfully promoted through using technology. As John Goodwin, the CEO of The Lego Foundation, elaborates, "Evidence suggests that learning through play happens when the activity is experienced as joyful, helps children find meaning in what they are doing or learning, involves active, engaged, minds-on thinking, as well as iterative thinking (experimentation, hypothesis testing, etc.) and has opportunities for social interaction."⁴ He continues by highlighting "learning through play with technology, including hybrid play," which combines digital and physical experiences.⁵ These approaches to learning are valuable because they provide "opportunities for young learners to acquire knowledge across a variety of contexts while developing a range of holistic skills, such as cognitive, creative, physical, social and emotional skills."⁶

Goodwin then mentions three concrete examples of how children can have valuable learning experiences through play: (1) coding platforms like Scratch, a free and open source environment that was started in 2007 to celebrate children's creativity and collaboration and now operates in 196 countries; (2) games like Minecraft where children can build and explore vast virtual worlds; and (3) plays focusing on robotics, such as Lego Mindstorm, which enables children to use a variety of components to build their own robots.⁷

With all this talk about innovation it is important to realize where our current education system has come from. To a large extent, the traditional school system was designed to prepare people for the factory floor; what was needed were large numbers of young people who had learned to behave, stay in line, and start working at the ring of a bell.⁸ Showing up on time, following instructions, and getting used to an eight-hour day

---

3. See also the extensive research conducted by Smith et al., *Digital Life Together*.
4. Goodwin, "Learning through Play," §6.
5. Goodwin, "Learning through Play," §6.
6. Goodwin, "Learning through Play," §6.
7. See the websites of the coding platform Scratch (https://www.scratchfoundation.org), the education section of Minecraft (https://educommunity.minecraft.net/hc/en-us), and Mindstorm, a product series of Lego (https://www.lego.com/en-us/themes/mindstorms/about).
8. Rose, "How to Break Free."

were deemed essential for preparing young people for the world of work, and so that is what schools did. The factory of the industrial age was built on standardization and mass production, which was powered by the conveyor-belt. This "production line mentality" has influenced our schools, and even though the working environment has changed substantially in the past few decades, the education system has, in some ways, recently moved even more toward these traditional structures by placing such an overemphasis on standardized testing.[9]

Instead of the monotony of the factory floor or the office cubicle that characterized much of the previous industrial revolutions, the new world of work has more resemblance with a laboratory.[10] A laboratory is characterized by a radical commitment to innovation; it is powered by collaborating experts who have the courage to constantly try out new things, and this kind of spirit of wanting to discover new solutions also needs to characterize the educational institutions of the future. Here are some suggestions regarding what schools that prepare students for the age of the Fourth Industrial Revolution could look like:

- Throughout our educational landscape, we must strengthen the STEM subjects and accept the reality that "every worker in the future will need some technical skills."[11]

- At the same time, we also need a renewed focus on human qualities. Even though machines are mastering many tasks typically performed by humans, people are still more adept at creative endeavors, imagination, critical thinking, social interaction, and physical dexterity. The educational system of the future needs to develop these inherent abilities in humans, so that they are equipped to partner with machines, rather than trying to compete with them.[12]

- In addition, we must encourage creativity, experimentation, and entrepreneurship. A source of inspiration regarding the latter could be South Tapiola High School, one of the best schools in Finland, which has one of the best education systems in the world. At this school, the "Young Entrepreneurship Programme gives students the

---

9. Robinson, "Changing Education Paradigms"; compare Robinson and Aronica, *Creative Schools*, 183.

10. For the contrast between factory and laboratory in the workplace, see Morgan, "Lab, the Factory."

11. Marr, "8 Things."

12. Marr, "8 Things."

- opportunity to work in groups to create a business of their own, then enter their ideas in national competitions."[13]

- Last but not least, we should prepare students for a world in which they will need to balance their own cultural identity with a global outlook. On one hand, young people today are growing up in an interconnected world, especially as far as technological realities are concerned. At the same time, there is also social, political, and economic backlash against an unbridled globalization (a kind of McDonaldization, if you will) that threatens to erase culturally specific treasures and traditions. To navigate these sensibilities, students will need intercultural competencies that empower them to succeed in pluralistic and complex environments.

As these points illustrate, training and educating people in the context of the Fourth Industrial Revolution must include the development of both hard skills and soft skills. A good indicator for this necessity is the networking website LinkedIn, which lists the top soft and hard skills needed for the workplace of the future as follows (Table 7).[14]

Table 7. Becoming Future-Ready:
The Top Five Soft Skills and Hard Skills

	Soft Skills	Hard Skills
1	Creativity	Blockchain
2	Persuasion	Cloud computing
3	Collaboration	Analytical reasoning
4	Adaptability	Artificial intelligence
5	Emotional intelligence	UX design

However, our schools and universities will change not only regarding what they teach but also with regards to how students are taught. Increasingly, learning will be powered by new technologies that can be applied to the world of education, such as virtual reality (VR) and augmented reality (AR). The most prominent application of the latter is probably the game *Pokémon Go*, which became a sensation in 2016. *Pokémon Go* is played outside, in the real world, with players using their

13. Fleming, "How Can We Prepare Students," §11.

14. As listed by Schwartz, *Work Disrupted*, 79. Besides competencies, young people will also need credentials (which is why the college degree is not dead), connections, and cash, as explained by Malia Krauss, *Making It*.

smartphones to find certain virtual characters in a particular physical place, for which they get points.[15]

AR could become a much more prominent feature in people's lives once AR smart glasses become more common through which people can access and control data. In contrast to smartphones, users can do so without having to use their fingers to touch a screen, thereby freeing their hands for other activities. Examples for this technology include Bose Frames, Ray-Ban Stories, Amazon Echo Frames, and Razer Anzu.[16] Granted, at this point smart glasses do not seem to be very successful items (the first Google Glass, for instance, was discontinued as a consumer product in 2015).[17] Currently, it is difficult to anticipate to what extend people will embrace such wearable products. In any case, it is noteworthy that, already in 2017, Mark Zuckerberg "called virtual and augmented reality the next major computing platform capable of replacing smartphones and traditional PCs."[18]

While technologies like VR and AR are exciting for any kind of learner, they hold particular promise for students with special needs. Imagine a child sitting in a wheelchair, putting on a VR headset and then being able to visit the Grand Canyon, a volcano, a theme park, the moon, or a museum on the other side of the world. Another example is children with autism who enjoy using tablets, computers, and technology in general because the logical and predicable structure of how software is programmed suits them.[19] In addition, advances in technologies like voice recognition will give more opportunities for learners who have difficulty using traditional channels of input, such as the keyboard and the mouse, for example because they are visually impaired or unable to use their hands.

Voice recognition has already become mainstream technology in devices like Amazon's Alexa, Apple's Siri, and Google's Assistant. Smart speakers are becoming a staple in many households, which is why more people are becoming accustomed to the idea of interacting with a machine in ways that are similar to human interaction. Granted, what these machines are currently able to accomplish (performing tasks like turning

---

15. Musha Doerr and Occhi, *Augmented Reality of Pokémon Go*; Henthorn et al., *Pokémon Go Phenomenon*.

16. E.g., Martindale, "Best Smart Glasses of 2024."

17. Weidner, "Why Google Glass Failed."

18. Anderson, *Virtual Reality*, 11.

19. Anderson, *Virtual Reality*, 38.

on the light or playing a song) is not particularly impressive. However, these devices will continue to become better and more sophisticated, which will also have important pedagogical implications. Recently, progress has been made so that these devices are "now able to be affect-sensitive and pick up on excitement, boredom, anger or confusion in the people they are working with."[20] This is possible because "increasing use is being made of data generated by facial recognition, eye-tracking and other biometric techniques of mood detection."[21]

The technologies of the Fourth Industrial Revolution will make it possible to move away from the traditional classroom and its most common form of instruction: the lecture. Rather than just processing information by listening to the teacher talk, students will increasingly have the opportunity to engage with different types of intelligence (including kinesthetic-body smart, musical, intrapersonal, interpersonal, musical, visual-spatial, naturalistic, existential, logical-mathematical, and verbal-linguistic intelligence).[22] In addition, students may also want to use different sensory avenues to learn. This is crucial because, while many students are visual learners, learning opportunities can also be created by engaging with other senses, such as hearing, taste, smell, and haptic.

Increasingly, the classroom will be used for interaction, discussion, and exploration. This paradigm shift is encapsulated in the concept of the "flipped classroom," where students acquire information on their own (for instance, by watching instructional videos) and then come together in the classroom to discuss what they have discovered.[23] In addition, the maker movement is gaining momentum, which places a premium on not only visually or verbally processing information but putting knowledge to the test by building and making things, thereby empowering students to not only be part of a consumer culture but to become creators as well.[24]

---

20. Selwyn, *Should Robots Replace Teachers?*, 61.

21. Selwyn, *Should Robots Replace Teachers?*, 61.

22. Alaniz and Wilson, *Naturalizing Digital Immigrants*, 72. Alternatively there is a model of four couplets with eight aptitudes, namely: logical/linguistic, personal/social, cultural/physical, and spiritual/moral. Seldon, *Fourth Education Revolution*, 101.

23. Bergmann and Sams, *Flip Your Classroom*; Walker et al., *Flipped Classrooms with Diverse Learners*.

24. The maker movement takes place in a variety of spaces, such as libraries, as well as mobile innovation labs that cooperate with local schools (especially public schools among low-income communities), a vision pursued by STE(A)M Truck (https://www.steamtruck.org).

This focus on creativity can be expressed through traditional avenues, such as music, drama, cooking, and artisanry (like woodworking and pottery). However, innovative technologies create new opportunities in this regard. As the authors of *Invent to Learn: Making, Tinkering and Engineering in the Classroom* explain,

> Today, the availability of affordable constructive technology and the ability to share online has fueled the latest evolutionary spurt in this facet of human development. New tools that enable hands-on learning—3D printers, robotics, microprocessors, artificial, virtual and augmented reality, e-textiles, "smart" materials and new programming languages—are giving individuals the power to invent. We're not just talking about adults. Children of all ages can use these tools to move from passive receivers of knowledge to real-world makers. This has the potential to completely revolutionize education as we know it.[25]

In the future, these technologies may increasingly be made available through the offerings of tech giants that are creating their own divisions for education, such as Google for Education, Apple Teacher, and Amazon Ignite.[26] Given the technical know-how and financial capabilities these corporations possess, teachers and students can look forward to a time when more resources for learning will be available to them than ever before.

Besides the increased use of various technology-based applications, this generation may also experience the arrival of robots in the classroom. Neil Selwyn, a professor of education, classifies such robots in the following four categories:

- "Classroom teacher" robots which "are usually designed to act in the dual role of authority figure and as an explicit source of knowledge."[27]

- Humanoid robot teachers that, so far, "have tended to be highly realistic in appearance but rather less autonomous in their actions."[28]

---

25. Martinez and Stager, "Maker Movement"; compare Martinez and Stager, *Invent to Learn*.

26. See the websites of these corporations like Google (https://edu.google.com), Apple (https://www.apple.com/education/k12/apple-teacher), and Amazon (https://ignite.amazon.com).

27. Selwyn, *Should Robots Replace Teachers?*, 30.

28. Selwyn, *Should Robots Replace Teachers?*, 32.

- Companion and peer robots that function as tutors; one version are table-top devices such as Sota, which is only twenty-four centimeters tall but "can hold the attention of students, detect student identities at the beginning of class, discern silences to enable turn-taking, and simulate approval or disapproval by changing eye colour."[29]
- Care-eliciting robots like the PARO seal that can be petted, which has proven to be especially helpful for children with autism.[30]

As these examples demonstrate, technology carries with it the tremendous opportunity to address a wide range of educational needs. There is no school or system that will be right for every single student in the country, or even a city. The good news is education in the age of the Fourth Industrial Revolution can become much more personalized than it currently is. Historically, education has always been more personalized for the elites—one just has to think of the private tutors in ancient Rome (known under the titles of *magister*, *grammaticus*, and *rhetor*) who educated the next generation of rulers by teaching them in their homes.[31] For more ordinary people, education still happened through personal interactions, albeit on a lower level. As an article about tutoring expounds, "It could be argued that tutoring was the very first form of instruction. Children were trained one-on-one by parents, other relatives, and members of the village who had particular specialized skills. The apprenticeship model reigned for several millennia before we encountered the industrial revolution and classroom education."[32]

As mentioned above, this kind of education inspired by the First Industrial Revolution emphasized approaches like memorization and standardization.[33] Now, however, with the aid of technology, personalized education may become the new normal again, which will be the case as AI-powered tutors find their way into people's homes.[34] This might not

---

29. Selwyn, *Should Robots Replace Teachers?*, 34.

30. Selwyn, *Should Robots Replace Teachers?*, 36.

31. Other terms for teachers included "*litterator*, *praeceptor*, and *professor*," who were supplemented by specialist teachers, "such as the *calculator*, the professional mathematics instructor." Maurice, *Teacher in Ancient Rome*, xiv, 1.

32. Graesser et al., "Instruction Based on Tutoring," 410–11.

33. One way to describe this shift would be to say that education is moving from massification (of the industrial age) to post-massification. Tight, "Mass Higher Education," 93–108.

34. In an early treatment about the what, how, and why of intelligent machine tutors, Beverly Park Woolf explains, "the earliest intelligent tutor was implemented in

happen in the next few years, but as AI continues to make progress, especially in terms of the ability to understand written texts, things will change dramatically—especially once this cognitive ability covers both texts dealing primarily with facts (like textbooks and encyclopedias) and written works that focus on human emotion, such as novels and poetry.[35] An AI-empowered tutor that has read and internalized every single Wikipedia article, every science book, every poem (no matter in which language it was composed), and every journal article that is publicly available—such a device would be quite an amazing personal teacher indeed, if it were able to discuss this knowledge with a human in meaningful ways.[36]

Much of what I have described above might soon be applied in primary and secondary school settings, but higher education will have to change as well. In fact, the higher education scene is already changing, for example through the arrival of massive open online courses (MOOCs), a mode of instruction first offered by the University of Manitoba (Canada) in 2008.[37] Through MOOCs people from all around the world have the opportunity to access first-class course materials, often for free, such as offered by Stanford University in California.[38] However, MOOCs have their limitations as well; in this kind of learning format, it is hard for students to stay motivated, and consequently the completion rates of most courses are quite low. As Justin Reich explains in *Failure to Disrupt: Why Technology Alone Can't Transform Education*, "the challenges of learning at scale are not merely technical in nature."[39] Rather, a decisive factor in learning has to do with its social dimension, as evidenced in receiving coaching from an expert and experiencing peer support.[40]

---

the 1970 Ph.D. thesis of Jaime Carbonell, who developed Scholar, a system that invited students to explore geographical features of South America." Park Woolf, *Building Intelligent Interactive Tutors*, 18.

35. An interesting development in this regard has been the progress that the programmers of ChatGPT have recently achieved. Trumbore, "ChatGPT."

36. Granted, this level of tutoring can only be achieved in a more distant future, after AI has made more progress toward understanding the human condition in general. Currently discussed topics related to AI and education include automated grading, gamification, intelligent tutoring systems providing automated personalized feedback, social and teachable robots, adaptive math software, and MOOCs. Bittencourt et al., *Artificial Intelligence in Education*.

37. Rollins, "What's a MOOC?"

38. It was in 2011, when Stanford offered the "Introduction to AI" online class for free, that MOOCs became a prominent topic. Shah, "Capturing the Hype."

39. Reich, *Failure to Disrupt*, 8.

40. Reich, *Failure to Disrupt*, 46.

In most countries, the majority of universities are public institutions which are financed and managed by the government. In the United States, the Ivy League schools are private institutions backed up by multi-billion-dollar endowments, endowments that are sometimes larger than the gross domestic product (GDP) of entire countries.[41] As described above, outstanding universities like Stanford and MIT offer MOOCs, and tech giants like Apple and Amazon are pressing into the market of education through the products and services they offer. Clearly, some very rich and powerful entities are controlling much of education today, and thereby exercising considerable influence over how our children and youth are being shaped. In this kind of environment, it is imperative for followers of Jesus to remember he is calling us to be salt and light, to exercise a positive and noticeable influence in this world (Matt 5:13–16). With this principle in mind, we now turn to evaluating the area of education from a Christian point of view.

A CHRISTIAN PERSPECTIVE ON EDUCATION

Historically, education has always been one of the strong points of the church. I therefore hope Christians can capitalize on these past experiences while also increasing their present investment and commitment in innovative ways, so they can prepare people for a future that will be shaped by the Fourth Industrial Revolution.[42] Entire books could be written on the why and how of Christian education in the twenty-first century, but in the following I limit myself to three points. (1) Believers can make a difference whenever they utilize technology to make education more accessible; for instance, by being innovative in the kind of education offered to children with special needs. (2) Every local church should aspire to not only be a place of worship that is primarily used on Sundays, but also to become a center of education which people can use throughout the week, enabling and encouraging them to embark on a quest of lifelong learning as part of their discipleship journey. (3) Christians should avoid the extremes of both technophobia and technophilia. Accordingly,

---

41. E.g., Segal, "Harvard Is Wealthier." US universities with large endowments include both private and public institutions, with Harvard, Yale, and Stanford occupying the top spots; see Wood, "15 National Universities."

42. For a historical perspective, see, for example, Van Engen, *Educating People of Faith* and chapter 7 ("Christianity's Imprint on Education") in Schmidt, *How Christianity Changed the World*, 170–93.

some of what the church offers should wholeheartedly embrace novel technologies (such as organizing coding boot camps), but at the same time God may also be calling the faith community to offer alternatives in which people can enjoy screen-free experiences in an environment that is completely offline.[43]

First, regarding making education available on the margins, this is an area where Christians can make a tangible difference by offering customized educational solutions to people with special needs. One such group are the deaf, who present a particular missional challenge, considering salvation comes by *hearing* the good news of Jesus Christ (Mark 4:9–25; Luke 8:18, 11:28; John 8:47; Acts 15:7; Rom 10:13–15, 17; Gal 3:2, 5; 1 Thess 2:13; Rev 1:3). As a number of mission leaders and ministries have recently emphasized, the deaf are among the largest unreached people groups in the world.[44] There are an estimated two hundred fifty to three hundred million deaf people worldwide, and in many cases the number of evangelical believers among them is less than 2 percent (which is often used as a threshold to define when a people group is considered unreached).[45] The popular Christian database Joshua Project, for instance, lists the deaf as a distinct people group in 216 different countries, and in many cases it is not even known to which extent they have been reached with the gospel or not.[46] Numerous ministries have begun to respond to this challenge by developing tools to communicate the good news, as well as by trying to understand more deeply how deaf people learn, and what is important for them when it comes to processing information in ways they feel comfortable with.

For centuries, Christians have been committed to education because they wanted people to be able to understand the gospel, read the Bible for themselves, and take advantage of additional resources that can help believers to grow in their faith. In addition, a commitment to human flourishing also needs to translate into investments in education in general, because education is a key factor for people to be able

---

43. For a discussion of both technophobia and technophilia in the context of education, see in particular, chapters 3 and 4 in Davidson, *New Education*, 75–132.

44. King, "'Person Standing in the Gap,'" 124; Herzog, *Social Contexts of Disability Ministry*, 106.

45. Entinger, "Deaf"; Door International, "Reaching the Largest." The World Health Organization (WHO) highlights that "over 5% of the world's population—or 430 million people—require rehabilitation to address their 'disabling' hearing loss." World Health Organization, "Deafness and Hearing Loss."

46. Joshua Project, "Deaf."

to do well, especially in today's society. That is why the challenge to expand educational opportunities to every human being continues. The deaf, mentioned above, are just one example, but there are also other people with physical limitations in need of particular pedagogical approaches, such as the blind. In addition, children in Western countries are increasingly diagnosed with behavioral challenges, whether it is attention-deficit/hyperactivity disorder (ADHD) or being somewhere on the autism spectrum.[47]

As mentioned above, developments like AR and VR provide opportunities to engage students in new and exciting ways. In addition, technologies related to big data and AI can provide more customized solutions to learning, thereby providing the best possible educational experience not only for children with special needs, but also for highly gifted children who feel underchallenged in a traditional classroom.[48] In the area of discipleship and mentoring, Christians have always emphasized the power of one-on-one relationships and small groups. Examples include Moses investing in Joshua and Elisha learning from Elijah. Jesus called his apostles as individuals, and while he also interacted with the masses, he made it a priority to invest extra time into a small circle of just three followers (Peter, John, and James), while giving a special assignment to the Twelve. Similarly, the apostle Paul worked together with others in teams, while also placing a high priority on investing in individuals, such as Titus and Timothy. This personal approach of passing on knowledge and wisdom stands in stark contrast to the type of mass education that became common in modernity, particularly in the industrial age of standardization. In a postmodern and postindustrial age, Christians now have the opportunity to encourage forms of learning that are individualized and communal at the same time, which more closely resemble the examples and principles displayed in Scripture.

Examining the biblical foundations for education is important because churches can have a great missional impact by becoming centers of learning.[49] There are too many church buildings that are mostly

---

47. For example, one in ten children in the US are now affected by ADHD. Shaban, "ADHD in Children." See also Bock and Stauth, *Healing the New Childhood Epidemics*.

48. Several recent publications address the needs of gifted children: Castellano and Frazier, *Special Populations in Gifted Education*; Jolly et al., *Parenting Gifted Children*; Danielian et al., *Teaching Gifted Children*.

49. Having said that, the relationship between the church and Christian institutions (such as schools) can be complex. See, for instance, Stone, "Churches and Christian Schools"; Doriani, "Should Churches."

used on the weekends, while they are basically empty from Monday to Friday. Considering many churches have not only a sizable auditorium but also several support buildings and a large parking lot, this is a tremendous underusage of valuable real estate resources. Fortunately, many churches already have a kindergarten, run a primary school, or may even have established an entire K-12 system.[50] For the church to be relevant in knowledge-based societies, this kind of work is to be commended and needs to be continued and expanded.[51] However, what about the thousands of congregations that currently mostly focus on their Sunday morning services and do not have any kind of educational commitments yet? What kind of transformative effect would it have on the nation if every single congregation in America were engaged in some kind of educational activity? According to the National Congregational Study survey there are some three hundred eighty thousand churches in the United States.[52] Granted, many smaller churches may not have the necessary resources to build up a full-fledged school in the traditional sense. But by combining homeschooling initiatives with innovative technologies, even small congregations would be able to offer a high-quality experience to students. What an incredible opportunity for churches to bring transformation to their communities and to be relevant in a post-Christian environment by offering one of the things people in the twenty-first century will need most: education.

Increasingly, these offers in the area of education will have to address not only the needs of children and youth but all age groups, as the church facilitates a culture of lifelong learning. Churches ought to be known as centers of learning, places where people cannot only find a sanctuary but also a library, as well as programs and workshops that help them to adapt to an ever-changing environment. Some Christians may not see education as a primary responsibility of the church, possibly because they have gotten used to the idea this is something the government will take care of. Historically, the nation state has indeed had an interest in forming future

---

50. For organizations promoting Christian schools, see the Association of Christian Schools International (ACSI, https://www.acsi.org), the American Association of Christian Schools (AACS, https://www.aacs.org), and the more specific focus of the Association of Classical Christian Schools (ACCS, https://classicalchristian.org).

51. The recent growth of Christian schools has also been noticed by secular observers: Graham, "Christian Schools Boom."

52. Goshay, "'Difficult Days Are Ahead.'" Others count three hundred thousand religious gatherings, including not only churches, but synagogues, temples, and mosques as well. Chaves, *American Religion*, 56.

factory workers and soldiers, but these might be interests that contradict what Christian parents want for their children, namely, to be primarily disciples of Jesus and agents of the countercultural kingdom of God.[53]

Biblically speaking, it is first and foremost the parent's responsibility to train their children and to raise them in the fear of the Lord (Deut 4:9; 6:6–9; Prov 1:8; 22:6; Eph 6:4; Col 3:21; 2 Tim 3:14–15). Especially with the advent of excellent online materials, homeschooling is becoming a viable option for more and more parents (a process that was accelerated by the COVID crisis). However, building entire institutions—whether high schools, vocational schools, liberal arts colleges, or research universities—goes beyond what any family can accomplish; here the church needs to step in. Individuals, couples, and families can be a light for Christ on the individual level, but to be a shining city on a hill, to be a force for good on the societal level, is the task of the church.[54]

One of the areas where the church can make the most tangible and visible impact is education. The necessity to offer an alternative to the public school system may become more obvious in the years ahead. Already today, many inner-city schools are failing, and they are failing those who would need an uplift the most—such as African American and immigrant communities. Often times, the only schools offering a decent education are charter schools or some other form of private initiative that creates some much-needed competition. School choice is a paramount priority for anyone who is concerned about these societal developments, so much so that school choice has been called the civil rights issue of our time.[55] Besides failing schools, another problem is many educational institutions are so dominated by a culture of progressivism they have become centers of indoctrination, rather than centers of learning.[56]

In such an environment, it is more important than ever that Christians offer a prophetic alternative to the public education system. The idea of a value-free education is an illusion. Every teacher teaches with a particular worldview in mind, and every school communicates a certain set of priorities to its students, both through what is taught and through what

---

53. Lee, *Unexpected Blessing*; Platt, *Counter Culture*.

54. The imagery of a city on a hill goes back to Jesus's words in the Sermon on the Mount (Matt 5:14); it was famously used by the English Puritan John Winthrop (1588–1649), as well as by President Ronald Reagan (1911–2004). Rodgers, *As a City on a Hill*, 2; Van Engen, *City on a Hill*, 3–11.

55. Garcia, *School Choice*, 55, 81–83.

56. Rice Hasson and Farnan, *Get Out Now*, xii; Whittington, *Speak Freely*.

kind of topics are neglected or avoided.[57] Christian schools are intentional about what they teach and promote an integration of faith and learning, so that parents and students know what to expect and can make a choice regarding whether they want to be part of this educational experience or not.

However, presenting a Christian worldview is not enough. Believers also need to teach the right kind of subjects, preparing young people for promising careers. Increasingly, this will mean Christian institutions have to offer technology-related subjects. This would include teaching subjects like cybersecurity and computer science at the college or university level. Of course, not everybody has the time and money necessary to attend college. This is where coding boot camps come in. One example is the Bethel School of Technology (or Bethel Tech), which is part of Bethel, an influential church in Redding, California. According to the school's academic catalog, Bethel Tech aspires "to build a faith-based tech school as the first of its kind."[58] Students can choose from UI/UX design, full stack development, data science, and cybersecurity. Graduates are in demand, and the average starting salary for a junior developer apparently is sixty-six thousand dollars. However, the school's "greatest desire is to see our students serve companies with excellence, in both skill and character by representing the love of Christ to everyone, everywhere."[59]

While embracing and teaching technology is crucial, it is also important for Christian schools to enable their students to develop a critical distance toward recent technological developments. This is not a contradiction, as one of the challenges of the Fourth Industrial Revolution will be to avoid both technophobia and technophilia. To combat the latter, faith-based institutions should offer their students times and spaces in which they can unplug from their devices and learn in a screen-free environment. Digital natives grow up with smartphones and iPads, which also means that glancing through articles and watching videos comes more naturally to them than reading entire books. Here Christian schools could augment their educational experience by teaching students the joy of holding a book in one's hands, turning its pages (made of paper), and fully engaging with the author's world by reading the entire volume, from cover to cover.[60]

57. Romanowski and McCarthy, *Teaching in a Distant Classroom*, 29–90.
58. Bethel College, "Catalog," 10.
59. Bethel College, "Catalog," 10.
60. Losing the art of reading in a world dominated by the internet has been highlighted by Carr, *Shallows*; Ryken and Mathes, *Recovering the Lost Art of Reading*; Prior, "Technology of Reading," 187–201.

Such deep reading that invites deep thinking could be encouraged in reading rooms in which no electronic devices are allowed. Besides creating screen-free spaces, students also need to have designated times away from technology. Here the idea of the Sabbath has immense potential to bring relief from the constant distraction provided by text messages, email, and all sorts of notifications. Schools could encourage a Sabbath from technology, in which students focus on their relationship with God and their fellow human beings instead (Gen 2:2–3; Exod 20:8–11; Deut 5:15; Neh 13:15–22; Isa 58:13–14; Jer 17:21–27; Luke 4:16). For example, teachers and professors could make sure their assignments and deadlines are arranged in such a way that students can take a break from Saturday evening to Sunday evening, thereby encouraging a twenty-four-hour period in which people can disconnect from the internet and connect with their Creator instead. A more radical step could be to block access to the school's email and its online learning system during this twenty-four-hour period, so that even professors and administrators will not be tempted to work on the day when they should be resting.

In addition, the idea of the Sabbath-rest could be transferred to an entire institution. While most Christian schools will need to rely heavily on technology, a small number of educational institutions could carve out a niche for themselves by offering a screen-free environment to their students. At such a school, students would have to lock away their devices when they arrive, and the classrooms would have no computers, not even for the teachers. Instead, the focus would be on tangible experiences like building things with one's hands, learning how to play an instrument, deep reading, group discussion, and formal debates.[61]

This kind of scree-free environment could also be a model for small Christian colleges that emphasize a traditional liberal-arts education and focus on teaching interpersonal skills. The curriculum would be based on some form of the Great Books tradition, where teachers and students come together to read the works of exceptional thinkers and then discuss what they have discovered. Granted, the number of students who would attend such an institution would be relatively small. However, this kind of campus could also function as a retreat center for other people—such as students from a regular university who would like to recharge in a different kind of environment. These screen-free campuses could also become

---

61. I began to explore some of these ideas in Topf, *Pentecostal Higher Education*, 229–32.

a sanctuary for people wanting to undergo a digital detox, or maybe even break free from an internet addiction.

The internet has become almost omnipresent; we need technology to enrich our educational endeavors, and often times the education offered will prepare people for a life of work in technology-related occupations. Precisely for this reason it is so crucial Christians create times and spaces in which people can take a break from technology. This is even more important considering technological innovations dominate not only our schools and workplaces, but the world of play as well—with that in mind, we now turn to entertainment as the topic of the following chapter.

DISCUSSION QUESTIONS

1. What is your view on homeschooling? To what extent has your view on homeschooling been shaped by your own experience or people whom you know personally?
2. What educational possibilities could be achieved through virtual reality (VR)?
3. What advantages and disadvantages do you see in students being taught by an AI-powered robot?
4. How could Christian colleges and universities become more competitive in offering technology-related subjects?

SUGGESTIONS FOR FURTHER READING

- Alvin J. Schmidt, *How Christianity Changed the World* (2004). Highlights the many blessings brought forth by the Christian faith, with the seventh chapter focusing on education.
- David I. Smith et al., *Digital Life Together: The Challenge of Technology for Christian Schools* (2020). Based on an in-depth study, the researchers describe how educators, parents, and students experience technology in a Christian school setting.
- Michael Collender and Jonathan Shaw, *Wiser Than the Machine: The Value of Classical Christian Education in an Age of Artificial*

Intelligence (2024). Describes recent developments in AI (such as ChatGPT) and formulates a Christian response.

- Jaime Donally, *The Immersive Classroom: Create Customized Learning Experiences with AR/VR* (2021). Provides concrete examples regarding how learning can be enhanced through the use of innovative technologies.

- Neil Selwyn, *Should Robots Replace Teachers? AI and the Future of Education* (2019). Introduces some thought-provoking issues in just 159 pages, written by a professor of education from Melbourne, Australia.

- Anthony Seldon, *The Fourth Education Revolution: Will Artificial Intelligence Liberate or Infantilise Humanity?* (2018). Argues for the responsible use of AI in education, written by a British scholar, educator, and author.

4

Entertainment

IN THE FALL OF 2023, the finals of the online game *League of Legends* World Championship (also known as "Worlds") were held in Seoul and Busan, South Korea. Remarkably, more than six million viewers watched the event, thereby creating "record-breaking media value" within the world of gaming.[1] Worlds is an annual competition in which two teams fight each other over a map, with the goal of destroying the opponent's base, which is called Nexus. At its top levels, this computer game has become so competitive that professional teams compete against each other, and star players are able to achieve considerable fame and fortune. As this example of Worlds demonstrates, gaming has become big business. It has also gained recognition as a sport—although esports were not officially part of the 2024 Olympics in Paris, France, there are conversations on whether they could become part of the games later, thereby further underscoring the significance of these new platforms.[2]

According to William Collis, author of *The Book of Esports: The Definite Guide to Competitive Video Games*, the "Big Five" of esports can be divided into the following main categories: (1) first-person shooters (FPSs), (2) battle royale games like *Fortnite*, (3) multiplayer online battle arenas (MOBAs) in which players need to "destroy opposing forces and overwhelm the opposing team's fortified base," (4) collectible card games, and (5) fighting games like the classic *Street Fighter* which "feature two

---

1. Hitt, "2023 League of Legends."
2. Crowl, "Esports Olympics."

players dueling with martial arts on a 2D or 3D plane."[3] In addition, there are other popular computer and video games (such as *Grand Theft Auto* and *Minecraft*) that are part of how people are increasingly spending their free time in the twenty-first century (Table 8).[4]

Table 8. The Top Ten Bestselling Video Games of All Time

	Game	Release Year	Copies Sold
1	Tetris	1984	520 million
2	Minecraft	2009	300 million +
3	Grand Theft Auto V	2013	195 million +
4	Wii Sports	2006	82.9 million
5	PlayerUnknown's Battlegrounds	2017	75 million
6	Mario Kart 8 Deluxe	2014	69.04 million
7	Red Dead Redemption 2	2018	61 million +
8	The Elder Scrolls V	2011	60 million +
9	The Witcher 3	2015	50 million +
10	Overwatch	2016	50 million

Computer games are not limited to nerds and a selective group of teenage boys anymore; they have become entertainment for the masses. Whether people play on their laptops, use a game console like Sony's PlayStation or Microsoft's Xbox, or play on their mobile phones, games have become part of mainstream culture, similar to other popular pastimes like music, sports, and movies.[5] In fact, in 2020, global video game revenue grew to one hundred eighty billion USD, thereby "making the videogame industry a bigger moneymaker than the global movie and North American sports industries combined" (which brought in one hundred billion USD and seventy-five billion USD, respectively).[6]

What makes video games such a fascinating leisure activity? One factor is that, compared to other forms of entertainment, the consumer plays a more active role. Television was the big innovation of the post–World War 2 era, overtaking the radio as the primary form of entertainment in the 1950s.[7] However, watching television is a passive way of spending

3. Collis, *Book of Esports*, xii–xiii.
4. Sirani, "10 Best-Selling Video Games."
5. A review of game consoles is given by Vazharov, "7 Best Video Game Consoles."
6. Witkowski, "Videogames Are a Bigger Industry," §2.
7. In the United States, the peak time for watching TV was reached in 2009–10,

one's free time—and people are not even able to publish their comments, the way viewers can on video platforms like YouTube. By contrast, in a video game, the players are actively involved, and they can also hone their skills and measure their progress as they learn how to master a particular game. In addition, video games can have a strong social component as well. More and more games are played online, thereby facilitating social interactions through chat and other interactive features.

Another reason why the gaming industry has become so large is because it has increasingly gone mobile.[8] Nowadays, when people wait in line, commute to work, or have any other kind of downtime, they instinctively reach for their smartphones in order to be entertained, thereby avoiding even brief periods of boredom. Many people will check their emails, read the news, and text with friends on such occasions. However, increasingly people also turn to games on their phones when they are bored. These offers may not be particularly sophisticated, and yet games such as *Candy Crush* provide entertainment for millions of people, which is why a review of the most downloaded mobile games states, "Nothing has grabbed hold of middle-aged moms, teens, and anyone looking to kill time quite like match-three puzzle games."[9] As this quote demonstrates, video games are a form of entertainment that has now gone mainstream, capturing the imagination (as well as the time and money) of millions of people.

While playing games on computers and gaming consoles is already quite exciting considering the excellent graphics available today, things are destined to become even more interesting once virtual reality (VR) offers become more common and more elaborate. To enjoy VR experiences, the user puts on a headset that completely covers their eyes, thereby creating a more immersive experience, compared to looking at a traditional screen. A variety of VR headsets are now available, including Meta Quest Pro, HTC VIVE XR Elite, Sony PlayStation VR, HP Reverb G2, and Apple Vision Pro.[10] At the time of writing, the latter costs three thousand five hundred USD, while most of the other headsets are in the hundreds of dollars—so they are not exactly inexpensive. However, VR

---

when Americans watched almost nine hours every day. That number has gone down somewhat since then but, still, "The thing that Americans do most often with their free time is not cooking or exercising or hiking or any other seemingly salutary activity. No, Americans watch TV." Madrigal, "When Did TV Watching Peak?"

8. Shaw and Chess, "Reflections on the Casual Games Market," 283–84.
9. Marsh et al., "Most Downloaded Mobile Games," §33.
10. Stein, "Best VR Headset of 2024."

headsets are a growing market, with products like Oculus Quest 2 having thousands of five-star reviews on Amazon and reviewers saying things like, "Best thing I ever bought for myself! Great VR experiences to be had in this! For exercise, doing 3D art, amazing visual puzzle games."[11] Another reviewer, a senior citizen, states:

> This thing is awesome! I am 73 years old and I absolutely love it, I have to do some of these things seated because I will fall down so I bought myself a 360° swivel chair just so I can have as much fun as possible! I put this headset on for 20 minutes or so and it revives my entire day! I like the games [and] I like the meditation applications, the immersive experiences.[12]

It is to be expected VR offers will become more complex and more varied as the technology continues to advance and social acceptability of wearing a headset of some form increases. Consequently, these technologies will be used not only for games, but for other applications as well, such as education (as mentioned in the previous chapter of this book).[13] In addition, many workplaces might also benefit from their employees using VR headsets as they perform their tasks. People may begin using virtual reality and mixed reality in daily life as well, for example, when doing online shopping, at a museum, or even while walking through a city. Eventually, we might be heading toward smart cities in which every street sign, every historical plaque, and every landmark building is connected to the internet, ready to interact and provide additional information with a variety of devices that people might be wearing.[14]

Alternatively, things might turn out quite differently, and VR may not become popular at all. Wearable devices may never become mainstream, possibly because the average consumer finds them too intrusive or too cumbersome. However, it is worth remembering when mobile phones first arrived in the 1980s, they were so heavy and prohibitively expensive that they were mostly perceived as a status symbol for a small number of yuppies. Today, just forty years later, the smartphone has conquered the world, to the point that, for most people, it is difficult to

---

11. Pagw4a, "Best thing ever!," April 8, 2021, reviewing Amazon, "Oculus Quest 2."

12. Amazon, "Oculus Quest 2."

13. Remarkably, "the education sector is one of the top industries for VR and AR investments, according to the '2019 Augmented and Virtual Reality Survey Report' by Perkins Coie and the XR Association." Gnanadurai et al., "Exploring Immersive Technology," 2.

14. Cronin and Scoble, *Infinite Retina*, 99–105, 307–20.

imagine life without their iPhone (or an equivalent device). It is quite possible a similar market penetration lies ahead of us in the area of VR and wearable devices.[15]

This seems to be the view of Mark Zuckerberg, the founder of Facebook, who believes that, "in the future, we'll probably still carry phones in our pockets, but I think we'll also have glasses on our faces that can help us out throughout the day and give us the ability to share our experiences with those we love in completely immersive and new ways that aren't possible today."[16] Remarkably, Zuckerberg made this statement back in 2015, several years before he announced in 2021 that his company would henceforth be called Meta. With this rebranding initiative Zuckerberg demonstrates he is serious about capitalizing on the metaverse, a concept that "originates from *Snow Crash*, a dystopian novel from the 1990s in which people flee the crumbling real world to be fully immersed in a virtual one."[17] By contrast, Zuckerberg's vision is to promote a "utopian idea that will unlock an entirely new economy of virtual goods and services."[18] One of the main attractions of the metaverse would be that people can create full-bodied avatars of themselves through whom they can interact with others in a variety of 3D-environments.

Granted, not everybody feels this optimistic about spending time in virtual worlds, partially for very practical reasons. One of the concerns with VR headsets is people get dizzy while using them. However, products like the KAT treadmill are designed to stabilize VR users, while at the same time enabling them to move in all directions, including squatting down.[19] Using this kind of treadmill while being in an immersive VR experience could lead to a considerable amount of physical exercise, thereby addressing one of the main critiques of other forms of entertainment, such as watching TV. The vision for the future of VR is to make it a multi-sensory experience. Traditional video games focus on video and audio, but advanced VR could include touch as well. In addition, new technological developments like the tracking of eye and hand movements,

---

15. See also this comment by Kelly: "Yes, these glasses look dorky, as Google Glass proved. It will take a while before their form factor is worked out and they look fashionable and feel comfortable." Kelly, *Inevitable*, 105.

16. Spoonauer, "AR Goggles Will Replace Phones," §3.

17. Heath, "Mark Zuckerberg," §8.

18. Heath, "Mark Zuckerberg," §8.

19. See also KAT VR's website (https://www.kat-vr.com).

as well as recognition of the user's changing facial expressions, will make VR a more interactive experience.[20]

In view of such developments, virtual reality might become especially fascinating in relation to adult entertainment, at least for some people. Regrettably, the sex industry has always been eager to exploit the opportunities technology has offered. As *The Guardian* reports describing the early days of the internet, "In the 1980s, the internet was frequented by three types of people: government officials, university scholars, and porn seekers. The three were not necessarily mutually exclusive."[21] When examining the history of the internet, one is confronted with the reality that it was pornography producers who drove important innovations, such as the need for greater bandwidth, e-commerce (secure online transactions), and streaming videos online, long before YouTube or Netflix were invented.[22] It is therefore to be expected that the sex industry will also become an important driver when it comes to promoting technologies like VR.[23]

In addition, consumers might turn to an even more realistic experience by seeking the companionship a sex robot can provide.[24] The problematic aspects of sex robots are similar as those associated with pornography. Just like the latter, the sex robot industry leads to the objectification of women and is therefore profoundly sexist. In addition, as customers engage with sex robots, they may also engage in violence or other forms of abusive behavior. The obsession with certain sexual fantasies could then spill over into the real world. On the other hand, the proponents of sex robots argue, these dolls could bring at least some degree of sexual satisfaction and emotional connection to those who otherwise have no access to it—for example, people with disabilities, soldiers serving in remote locations, or people who, for psychological reasons, find it difficult to pursue a romantic relationship with another human being.[25]

The debates surrounding sex robots become more complex when one imagines that, one day, an AI may become so sophisticated it could

---

20. Reed et al., *Adventure Games*, 176.
21. Brooks, "Porn Pioneers," §11.
22. Jacona, "Porn Industry."
23. In fact, "it is said that pornographers have always been at the forefront of every communication technology"—including books, various kinds of images, and recording devices for recording movies, such as VHS and DVDs. Dyer, *From the Garden to the City*, 129.
24. Devlin, *Turned On*.
25. McArthur, "Case for Sexbots," 38–40.

be declared to be a self-conscious being of some sort. In that case, the rights of such a being would have to be protected and respected, some ethicists argue.[26] However, consciousness is a tricky issue, and there is no indication machines will become self-aware anytime soon, certainly not in the next ten or twenty years. What we will see in the coming years and decades are increasingly sophisticated forms of entertainment, including the creation of virtual worlds that will be extremely fascinating and captivating, which is why they require a response from us as Christians.

A CHRISTIAN PERSPECTIVE ON ENTERTAINMENT

In the Garden of Eden, God ordained for humanity to work, but the Creator also instituted the Sabbath rest, which invites us to think about a theology of what we do with our free time. In the following, I propose three areas of reflections related to entertainment. (1) We have been influenced by the Protestant work ethic, which is important, but what about the value of activities like serving, volunteering, and playing? (2) The church needs to draw boundaries as people explore new forms of entertainment; one example is the plight of pornography that is destined to become even more serious with novel offers like virtual reality and sex robots. (3) Churches and Christian organizations will have to upgrade their IT infrastructure in order to offer compelling content to communicate the gospel in an increasingly virtual world.

Particularly within Protestant Christianity, believers like to emphasize the importance of work—and rightly so, considering God ordained for humans to be agents of transformation. As already discussed in chapter 2, work is an important part of the human existence, which is why Christians should be interested in questions related to employment, as well as offering the kind of education that enables people to find jobs (see chapter 3). But does this mean life is supposed to be all work, and no play?

While the Bible certainly places an emphasis on the value of work and being productive, this is balanced by prescribing times of rest and celebration as well. This fundamental principle is also anchored in the creation accounts of Gen 1 and 2. Just as Adam and Eve were to imitate God's

---

26. Issues related to the consciousness of machines (or some form of free will) are discussed by various authors in *Robot Sex*, including: Danaher, "Symbolic-Consequences Argument," 103–31; Petersen, "Is It Good for Them Too?," 155–68; Hauskeller, "Automatic Sweethearts for Transhumanists," 208–13.

creativity by cultivating the Garden of Eden, they were also expected to follow God's example of resting on the Sabbath, thereby creating a healthy rhythm of six days of work and one day of rest. This arrangement is so foundational that the Sabbath rest even forms part of the Ten Commandments God gave to Moses at Sinai (Exod 20:8–11; Deut 5:12–15).

The Sabbath creates not only room for rest but also a space of protection for those who could otherwise easily be exploited. Accordingly, even servants and slaves were invited to join in the divinely ordained rest, thereby indicating there is something more imperative than work: worship. In fact, prioritizing worship over work is fundamental to the exodus narrative, which is arguably the most foundational story of redemption in the Hebrew Bible (Exod 20:2; Lev 11:45; Num 15:41; Deut 6:20–23; Josh 24:5–17; Judg 6:8–9; 1 Sam 10:18; 1 Kgs 8:51–53; Ps 78:42–52; Jer 32:20–21; Ezek 20:5–10; Dan 9:15; Hos 13:4). The Israelites were enslaved in Egypt, and their taskmasters worked them ruthlessly. However, God was determined to rescue them from this dire existence, and so the Lord sent Moses to challenge Pharaoh by declaring, "Let my people go, so that they may worship me" (Exod 7:16; 8:1, 20; 9:1, 13; 10:3).

Based on this experience of liberation, animals were to rest, too, and so was the land. While humans and animals could rest on the seventh day, the land was to rest in the seventh year. This makes sense from a productivity point of view: Soil needs time to recuperate, especially in a context when, unlike in modern-day agriculture, no synthetic fertilizers were used. However, in the biblical narrative the theological significance of this arrangement is even more pertinent. The Sabbath rest demonstrates there is something more important than work, something more important than the profits labor creates for the landlord, yes, even something more important than producing food, so people will have something to eat. The Sabbath is a reminder that God is the ultimate source of all provision. God gave the land to Israel, and when they failed to honor the Lord and what he had given to them, God took their land away, by sending the Israelites into exile (Exod 23:10–12; Lev 25:2–6; 26:27–35, 43; 2 Chr 36:21; Neh 10:31).

In our day and age, people take it for granted that they have a free weekend, which is why they can easily forget how revolutionary the concept of a universal Sabbath is. The Sabbath is one of the most important contributions of the Judeo-Christian tradition that has profoundly shaped the way people think about work and free time all over the world. One can fly almost anywhere in the world today and find that many workplaces and offices are closed on Saturdays and Sundays—but it was not always this way. In the Roman Empire, for instance, there was no weekly day of rest; slaves and workers were able to take a break during holidays and public festivals, but not on a weekly schedule.[27]

Even in the Islamic tradition, which does have Friday as its holy day, there was traditionally a different view of free time. As Jonathan Bloom and Sheila Blair explain, "Unlike Jews and Christians, who celebrate a weekly Sabbath, or day of rest, Muslims deem it necessary only to stop work during the time of communal prayer, not for the entire day."[28] For example, "a shopkeeper might only put a stick or a cloth across the entrance to his shop to signal that it was closed while he went to the mosque for prayer. Only in modern times has the Thursday-Friday 'weekend' emerged in some Muslim countries such as Iran and Kuwait as an equivalent to the Saturday-Sunday weekend celebrated in the West."[29]

Secular societies that rejected the Christian narrative also tried to develop alternatives to the Sabbath. For instance, the Soviet Union under Stalin attempted to introduce a five-day rhythm in 1929. Under this system, workers would get one random day off, so that 80 percent of the work force would always be working. However, this system turned out to be profoundly frustrating, since "most people did not have the same rest day as their spouses, or friends, or family."[30] In addition, machines broke down frequently—because "when a system works 24 hours a day, every day, there's no real time to repair or maintain them."[31] Given these shortcomings, this idea was soon abandoned and, after another try with a six-day week, the Soviet Union eventually returned to the traditional seven-day week.

The sabbath demonstrates that God values for all human beings to have regular days of rest, to be able to enjoy themselves. Apart from setting aside time for worship, there is also a theological case to be made for the value of play, because it rejuvenates us and creates opportunities for human interaction. When we play, we become more like children, which is something Jesus encouraged us to do in order to enter the kingdom

---

27. Joshel, *Slavery in the Roman World*, 174–75, 192, 199, 205.

28. Bloom and Blair, *Islam*, 109. However, "only such determinedly 'secular' countries such as Turkey and Indonesia follow global practice and place the weekend on Saturday and Sunday." Sedgwick, "Islam and Popular Culture," 286.

29. Bloom and Blair, *Islam*, 109.

30. Nosowitz, "Why Can't We," §14.

31. Nosowitz, "Why Can't We," §14.

of God (Matt 18:1–4; 19:14; Mark 10:14–15; Luke 18:16–17). It is also noteworthy that "most depictions of the *future* kingdom of God describe that age . . . in terms of joy, song, dance and even play."[32] In light of such a vision, believers should make it a priority to create meaningful ways for people to spend their free time together.

Another major theme related to spending one's free time and seeking out entertainment for relaxation has to do with setting healthy boundaries. Online entertainment can be incredibly attractive, which is why churches need to teach their members to evaluate it critically, and to ask questions like: "At what point does a tool, even one with undisputed benefits, cross the line and become a master? At what point does what is lost supersede what is gained?"[33] One offer whose enslaving character is rather obvious is pornography. In a society that so heavily relies on the internet, porn is now always readily available, and this has become a real issue for the church too.[34] Traditionally, pornography has been seen as an issue that is primarily affecting men, but increasingly women are experiencing this as a struggle as well. In the era of the Fourth Industrial Revolution, questions related to adult entertainment might become even more vexing through the introduction of sex robots.

In some sense, sex robots might be less exploitative than the production of porn, which is often associated with human trafficking and other abusive situations. By contrast, a robot cannot be abused in an ethical sense because it has no feelings; it just looks like a human but is not in itself an image-bearer. On the other hand, there still remains the challenge Jesus formulated in the Sermon on the Mount when he said, "anyone who looks at a woman lustfully has already committed adultery with her in his heart" (Matt 5:28). In making this and similar statements, Jesus was moving beyond the outward behavior of humans and turning his attention on the heart instead, focusing on the inner condition of a person.

Within such a framework that focuses on the transformation of the human heart, the ministry of the church can be one of liberation and deliverance because it points to an alternative to the tyranny of sin. As Derek Prince (1915–2003) rightly recognizes, "your body makes a wonderful servant, but a terrible master," and this is certainly true in the area of

---

32. Edgar, *God Who Plays*, ix (emphasis in the original).
33. Byrd DeRegibus, "On Human Transcendence," 140.
34. E.g., Perry, *Addicted to Lust*; Ortlund, *Death of Porn*.

human sexuality.[35] As prominent examples like Tiger Woods have shown, being addicted to sex can overpower a person, almost destroying their lives.[36] From a secular point of view, the main concern with pornography or prostitution is the exploitative nature of these industries. However, when artifacts like sex toys or robots are being used, it is more difficult to explain why people should stay away from these forms of entertainment. Christians can offer an alternative here, by opposing a culture that is saturated with sex and pointing to a lifestyle that focuses on loving God and loving others instead (Matt 22:34–40; Mark 12:28–34; Luke 10:25–37).

Faced with the possibility of increasingly sophisticated sex robots, one of the reactions has been a call for them to be banned, to prohibit the manufacturing and selling of such humanoids.[37] However, it seems to me that a ban would be the wrong approach, mainly for two reasons. First, from a libertarian point of view, we should be wary of giving governments too much power. If certain people want to engage in activities that do not hurt anybody, then there should be room for doing so in a free society. Second, sex robots may contribute to the social good in some ways, for example by providing companionship for people who would otherwise be lonely, or by creating an outlet for those who would otherwise be tempted to live out their harmful sexual fantasies in the real world (particularly by abusing more vulnerable members of society, such as women and children).

Rather than looking to government to solve this problem through new regulations, I believe it is the role of the Christian community to point people to a different kind of lifestyle. In a sex-saturated culture, believers are called to live holy lives, and this must include voluntarily staying away from what the sex industry has to offer, whether in the form of traditional online pornography, more elaborate VR experiences, or sex robots. In the context of this conversation, it is important to highlight sex robots are not only about sex, but about companionship as well.[38] As these machines become more advanced, it is quite possible some people, especially men, will enter into some form of relationship with them, possibly because they find such an arrangement more convenient, compared to a traditional marriage. In contrast, Christians could become known as

---

35. Prince, *Fasting*, 35.
36. Childs, "Tiger Woods May Be."
37. Danaher et al., "Should We Campaign Against," 47–72.
38. For a discussion between two female computer scientists on this topic, see: Open to Debate, "Agree to Disagree: Sex Robots?"

those who value spending time with people, and who prioritize getting married and having children, thereby modeling what God had originally in mind for Adam and Eve as they were living in the Garden of Eden in rich, shalomic relationships.[39]

Finally, if churches want to be a prophetic voice in society, they will have to compete in terms of what kind of content they produce for people to consume. Much of what drives the modern economy is the attention for eyeballs—the more often people go online and the longer they stay on a particular website, the more money can potentially be made.[40] Of course, churches and Christian organizations could decide to simply not participate in this game of competing for people's attention. However, Christ has given his followers the Great Commission, through which they are invited to go and seek out the lost (Matt 28:18–20; Mark 16:15–18; Luke 24:46–49; John 20:21–23; Acts 1:8). As Douglas Wilson explains, "Christians should go with our life-transforming message, and where should we go? *Where the people are*. And where people gather today is online. And when we go there, we should not go to them with a truncated gospel. Rather, we must proclaim a gospel that encompasses everything—all of Christ for all of life."[41]

The vast majority of Christian churches and ministries have already adapted to the information age by making it a priority to have a well-maintained website. In 1985 both dot com and dot org domains were created, and corporations started to register their domain names, with companies like Xerox (in 1986) and Apple (in 1987) being among the first.[42] Many churches did not even think about having an internet presence back then, but today maintaining an attractive website is considered a must for most Christian institutions. Once it became clear websites were part of how people looked up information, most churches made sure they had a respectable internet presence.[43] And while early websites primarily provided information in the form of text, it is increasingly crucial websites display photos and videos as well, because people are

---

39. See also Topf, "Technology as a Modern-Day Tower of Babel."

40. Agrawal, "Competition for Online Eyeballs." For a Christian perspective, see Reinke, *Competing Spectacles*.

41. Wilson, *Ploductivity*, 106 (emphasis in the original).

42. Raphael, "Internet's 100 Oldest."

43. A church website is also crucial for outreach, considering that, in 2019, "17 million Americans who don't regularly attend church visited a church website." Musonda, "Church Online Statistics for 2021."

now responding primarily to visual stimulation. In fact, one could argue that, in the twenty-first century, a church or ministry without a website is virtually nonexistent (pun intended). This kind of dynamic became even more true during COVID, when it proved more important than ever to be able to connect with people remotely.

I suggest this trend is going to continue in relation to VR and AR. Just like it is unthinkable for a church or Christian ministry to have no website today, so ten or twenty years from now it might be of similar importance to offer some kind of immersive experience in order to convey the message of the gospel or what a particular ministry has to offer. A historical perspective may be of help here to encourage churches to continue engaging with novel technologies in order to spread the gospel. Jennifer Powell McNutt provides valuable missiological insights when she explains,

> The good news of Jesus Christ is a universal message that does not change, but the transmission of the message often requires contextual innovation. Today, for the church to do that effectively, it must reach audiences in the places where minds and hearts can be shaped using modes that can effectively mobilize people's attention. During the time of Paul, the Roman roads paved the way. In the medieval period, it was due to monastic centers. During the time of the Reformation, it was through the printing press. In the recent past, pastors have taken to the radio, television, and now the podcast.[44]

Among these technologies, the internet has its own dynamic and significance. As the missiologist Al Tizon states, "The internet is not just another means of communication, but a hyper-medium that subsumes, links, and enhances all previous media."[45] Consequently, "the question for the church is not, 'How do we share the gospel through the internet,' but rather, 'How do we share the gospel *in* internet.'"[46] Understanding the internet as an actual place with its own cultural dynamics and challenges is likely to become an even more obvious reality once the metaverse becomes more common. Understandably, many Christians feel skeptical toward new developments like the metaverse, and it is certainly appropriate to critique the shift toward virtual worlds. However, rather than focusing

---

44. Powell McNutt, "Partnering with Pastors," 234.
45. Tizon, "Reconciling All Things," 10.
46. Tizon, "Reconciling All Things," 10 (emphasis in the original).

on the negative effects, it might be more strategic to primarily see the opportunities these novel technologies may have to offer for the church.

One example for such an optimistic approach is Jeff Reed from The Church Digital who sees exciting possibilities when it comes to virtual reality and mixed reality.[47] He believes the lines between the physical and the digital will become increasingly blurred. Specifically, Reed suggests Christians can identify the following four opportunities in the metaverse.

A New Environment for Church Services

VR and AR would enable Christians to create more immersive worship experiences during Sunday mornings. Many churches already use projectors to make announcements, display song lyrics, and highlight Bible verses during a sermon. All this flow of information could become even more compelling by creating a 3D environment that is both informative and interactive.[48]

A New Education Tool for Discipleship

A disciple of Jesus is primarily a student, and what we as the church want to teach people could become so much more exciting by using the tools of the metaverse. For instance, a Bible study about Paul's missionary journeys could be enhanced as participants use a VR set to be right there, joining the apostle as he travels to ancient Ephesus, Athens, and Rome.

A New Mission Field to Invest In

Reaching out to gamers and other individuals who are excited about the metaverse will become an important missional task in the years to come. As Christians, we are called to go where people are, and if people are increasingly spending time in virtual worlds, then we need to be present in those digital spaces as well.

---

47. Church.digital, "Episode 188: The Future Church." For a more balanced and detailed discussion, see Bock and Armstrong, *Virtual Reality Church*.

48. The four points are taken from the YouTube message cited above, but Jeff Reed also has his own website (https://thechurch.digital).

A New Community Worthy of a Church

There is tremendous value in having church in a physical building, as has traditionally been the case. However, more and more communities are being formed in virtual spaces, and arguably these should have an expression of the body of Christ as well. Some ministers are already experimenting in this direction, such as Bishop D.J. Soto and his VR Church, where 80 to 85 percent of attendants tend to be atheists and agnostics, meaning that his virtual church services are an opportunity to reach the unchurched.[49]

Another example of how the metaverse can create opportunities for Christians is Cornerstone Church of Yuba City, California. As their lead pastor, Jason Poling, explains, 75 to 80 percent of the people who join their virtual services are de-churched, meaning individuals who have been hurt by previous church experiences.[50] By coming together in a virtual environment, these people may be able to reconnect with their faith in new ways. Whatever the specifics may look like for a particular church or ministry, the fact is technology is shaping the way people spend their free time, and Christians need to recognize the opportunities this shift entails. Another crucial area that is radically changing due to technological innovations is healthcare, and so that will be the theme of the following chapter.

DISCUSSION QUESTIONS

1. In your opinion, should churches participate in the metaverse? Why or why not?
2. What are some of the arguments and counter-arguments regarding the question whether sex robots should be banned or not?
3. What are some of the theological foundations for arguing that life should not only be about work?
4. As Christians, how should we spend our free time?

---

49. See also the website of Virtual Reality Church (https://www.vrchurch.org).

50. The website of Cornerstone Church (https://www.cornerstoneyc.com) includes a section titled "Metaverse Church."

SUGGESTIONS FOR FURTHER READING

- Ben Witherington III, *The Rest of Life: Rest, Play, Eating, Studying, Sex from a Kingdom Perspective* (2012). A biblical and theological reflection on the Christian life outside of work.

- Michael Maley, *Video Games and Esports: The Growing World of Gamers* (2020). Presents a broad range of issues related to video games, including critical voices.

- Barak Lurie, *Rise of the Sex Machines* (2019). Describes various factors why sex on demand will become increasingly popular and who will resist this trend, written by a Christian lawyer who is passionate about Judeo-Christian values.

- John Danaher and Neil McArthur, eds., *Robot Sex: Social and Ethical Implications* (2018). Presents a variety of viewpoints regarding sex with robots.

- Leslie Shannon, *Interconnected Realities: How the Metaverse Will Transform Our Relationship with Technology Forever* (2023). An optimistic introduction to the possibilities provided by the metaverse, written by a Silicon Valley–based trend scout and futurist.

- Andy Crouch, *The Tech-Wise Family: Everyday Steps for Putting Technology in Its Proper Place* (2017). Proposes boundaries when it comes to technology use, encouraging alternative ways of spending time together.

5

Healthcare

FEW THINGS ARE MORE devastating than to watch how the life of a loved one is being diminished by an incurable disease. There are many examples that could be told in this regard, but in the following I turn to one described by Robert A. Freitas Jr. in his essay "Welcome to the Future of Medicine."[1] In this essay, Freitas tells how his maternal grandfather, Irving Lincoln Smith, "died in 1935, at the age of 39" and that the death of the breadwinner caused extreme economic hardship for his family, considering these were the heydays of the Great Depression. Smith died of encephalitis, an inflammation of the brain that causes "a pounding headache, unending nausea, stiff muscles, then drowsiness, coma, and sometimes death."[2] Tragically, penicillin had already been discovered by Alexander Fleming (1881–1955) several years earlier, in 1928. However, only ten years later, in 1938, more research was conducted, demonstrating "penicillin was an effective treatment for some bacterial forms of encephalitis."[3]

The point Freitas desires to make is that his grandfather's death could have been avoided if already existing scientific knowledge had been turned into concrete medical applications more quickly, and that this is a challenge continuing to this day. "Each of us similarly has friends and loved ones we care deeply about—children, spouse, parents, and friends.

---

1. Freitas, "Welcome to the Future of Medicine," 67–72.
2. Freitas, "Welcome to the Future of Medicine," 67.
3. Freitas, "Welcome to the Future of Medicine," 68.

Two of them die every second, somewhere on Earth, totaling 52 million worldwide annually."[4] These are sobering numbers but, Freitas goes on to say, "almost all of these deaths are, in principle, medically preventable—not by the methods of present-day medicine, but by a new form of medicine, called nanomedicine, that now lurks on the technological horizon."[5]

Freitas's affectionate description of his grandfather is deeply moving, as is the hope he has for the future of medicine and his refusal to simply accept that millions die each year of causes that could be prevented. In the age of the Fourth Industrial Revolution, new developments in healthcare are going to change the way we perceive the human body and how we address and cure medical conditions. In this chapter, I address three aspects of this upcoming revolution: (1) healthcare will become more personalized, preventive, and data-based; (2) it will employ new instruments, such as nanorobots; and (3) as scientists learn more about the genetic make-up of humans, new interventions might enable humanity to find novel treatments or to avoid certain diseases in the first place.

First, healthcare in the Fourth Industrial Revolution will be increasingly based on data, thereby making the practice of medicine more preventive and more personalized. To understand why this is such an important paradigm shift, it may be helpful to first look at healthcare as it is widely practiced today. Contemporary medicine is subject to massification, and in that sense is very much a child of the industrial era with its conveyor belt mentality. As renowned cardiologist Eric Topol has pointed out in publications like *The Patient Will See You Now* and *Deep Medicine*, this tendency toward massification is visible in various key areas, including the use of medication.

Pharmaceutical companies often spend billions of dollars to research a new medication, and from this perspective it is understandable that they expect a return on their investment by selling their product to large numbers of people. Doctors are part of this dynamic because they like to prescribe medications that promise tangible results. Combine this with widespread chronic diseases like diabetes and an advertising culture constantly promoting medications on TV, and the result is "mass medicalization."[6] As Topol explains referring to a statistic from 2010, "In the United States alone, there is a $29-billion market for the sea of

---

4. Freitas, "Welcome to the Future of Medicine," 68.
5. Freitas, "Welcome to the Future of Medicine," 68.
6. Topol, *Creative Destruction of Medicine*, 22.

anti-diabetic medication" (a number that grew to over forty-nine billion dollars in 2019).[7] However, within this market, "the most commonly used drug, metformin, doesn't even work in about 25 percent of patients."[8] For other medications, the discrepancies are even more drastic: with Abilify, a medication to treat schizophrenia, 75 percent of patients "do not have the desired or expected benefit."[9] And with Crestor, a treatment for high cholesterol, only one in twenty (or 5 percent) are clinical responders. Given these disappointing numbers, what is needed is a more customized approach to drug selection, one that takes into account the gene risk variants present in a particular individual.

Similarly to medication, screening is applied to large segments of the population as well, usually simply by identifying a (more or less arbitrary) threshold in terms of age. Unfortunately, this "mass-screening model . . . is enormously expensive and leads to an untold number of false positive results and more unnecessary biopsy procedures."[10] For instance, "mass screening for early detection of cancer is one of the most accepted rituals of health care in the United States."[11] However, among women in their fifties who are screened yearly for breast cancer by undergoing a mammography, only 0.05 percent avoid a breast cancer death, while more than 60 percent "will have at least one false positive result," which then can lead to unnecessary procedures like biopsies, surgery, and radiation.[12] This approach causes Topol to ask, "how can we possibly be viewed as all having the same risk profile, given the differences in our biology and environmental exposures?"[13]

In light of these shortcomings, Topol envisions a different kind of medicine, one that is radically personalized and democratized. The basis for this hyperpersonalized approach to healthcare will be data, "the full gamut from sensors, images, labs, and genomic sequence, well beyond an electronic medical record. We're talking about lots of terabytes of data about you, which will someday accumulate, from the womb to tomb, in

---

7. Topol, *Creative Destruction of Medicine*, 213. For more current data, see IMARC, "United States Diabetes Market."

8. Topol, *Creative Destruction of Medicine*, 213.

9. Topol, *Deep Medicine*, 36.

10. Topol, *Creative Destruction of Medicine*, 163.

11. Topol, *Creative Destruction of Medicine*, 28.

12. Topol, *Deep Medicine*, 31.

13. Topol, *Creative Destruction of Medicine*, 28.

your personal cloud, stored and ready for ferreting out the signals from the noise, even to prevent an illness before it happens."[14]

Besides medication and screening procedures, another crucial aspect of modern medicine consists of the high-tech machines available for diagnosis and treatment. From precision instruments for surgery to MRIs and CTs, it is utterly amazing what a medical team can achieve today, given the right tools.[15] However, powerful as these tools may be, they also are subject to limitations. One of these limitations is that humans are operating these devices, and humans are prone to make mistakes. To avoid mistakes, many steps of operating these machines are already automated, and this is something that may increase in the future.

In fact, we may even witness entire surgeries performed by robots. One example of this that took place already was a surgery performed by a dentist robot in Xian, China, in 2017, implanting "two 3D printed teeth into a woman's mouth."[16] Granted, this particular procedure may have been more of a publicity stunt. Nonetheless, robots already play a vital role in the operation room, and this trend is likely to accelerate in the coming years. This does not mean surgeons will become redundant. However, it does mean the best surgeons will be those who have learned to work alongside the most advanced machines.

Once a robot takes over the actual physical procedure, supervised by the human surgeon, this creates several advantages. For instance, aging surgeons in their seventies could still be orchestrating complex operations based on their many years of experience, even when their motoric skills and eyesight are not what they used to be. Not having to hold the knife anymore that cuts open the patient may also decrease nervousness and stress in surgeons, thereby freeing them from turning to unhealthy coping mechanism, such as alcohol consumption (which is significant considering alcoholism is a serious problem among surgeons, but obviously this would not be an issue for surgical robots).[17] Nonetheless, even a surgery performed by a robot is still a highly invasive procedure, no matter how sophisticated and well-trained the machine might be. The

14. Topol, *Patient Will See You Now*, 5.
15. LaGratta, "CT vs MRI."
16. De La Bastide, "Chinese Robot Just Performed."
17. According to a survey conducted in 2010, 15.4 percent of responding surgeons struggled with alcohol, with the percentage higher among female surgeons (25.6 percent), compared to males (13.9 percent). Oreskovich et al., "Prevalence of Alcohol Use Disorders." Compare Barber, "Drug and Alcohol Rehab for Doctors."

real revolution in healthcare will come about through advances in nanotechnology, when robots will be so tiny they can participate in the human blood flow, and join other cells to rebuild damaged tissue, make a targeted delivery, or fight off malignant intruders.[18]

Several areas of application in biomedicine can be envisioned for nanorobots, such as directed drug delivery, precision surgery, medical diagnosis, and detoxification.[19] Granted, much of this sounds like science fiction, and progress has been relatively slow. A basic problem that needs to be solved is transportation. Since nanodevices and microrobots are far too tiny to carry any kind of battery, a different solution must be found, which could consist of either an off-board power generation (magnetic or ultrasound) or an on-board power generation (chemical and biohybrid).[20] In addition to the transportation problem, there is still a wide range of other technical challenges that need to be addressed before a nanorobot could make a tangible difference in the healthcare field.[21]

Fortunately, important milestones have already been reached. For instance, in 2018 professors at the University of Texas in San Antonio built what was then the smallest medical robot: a tiny device, just one hundred twenty nanometers (nm) in length, that "can push miniscule payloads and enter the membranes of cells, abilities that they hope will make it useful for medical applications."[22] To put the size of this robot into perspective: a bacterium is around one thousand nm, "far too large to enter cells or tiny blood vessels."[23] Given this kind of advancement, it will be exciting to see how a variety of nano-sized elements (such as sensors) could be used going forward to monitor people's health on an ongoing basis. Through a healthcare app this information could then be transmitted directly to the person's smartphone, thereby empowering patients by giving them direct access and control over their personal data.

Another technology that could bring about significant changes on how healthcare is done are 3D printers.[24] 3D printers are currently mostly

---

18. Fischer, "How Nanorobots Are Used."

19. Li et al., "Micro/Nanorobots for Biomedicine." Several technical challenges must be overcome before this innovative technology can be put to use: Kostarelos, "Nanorobots for Medicine."

20. Soto et al., "Medical Micro/Nanorobots."

21. Li et al., "Micro/Nanorobots for Biomedicine."

22. Grifantini, "State of Nanorobotics in Medicine," §18.

23. Grifantini, "State of Nanorobotics in Medicine," §17.

24. In fact, 3D printing could be used to manufacture the kind of microrobots

used in manufacturing, for example in the aerospace and automotive industry.[25] Now, what if a 3D printer could be programmed in such a way that it would not produce something made of metal or plastic, but would be able to "print" a human organ? This possibility caused quite a stir a number of years ago, namely at the TED talk given by the surgeon Anthony Atala in 2011, who made it sound as if it would soon be possible to print entire organs, even complex ones, such as a human kidney.[26] However, the sample he showed during his talk was just a mold, without blood vessels or any internal structures, so it was not actually a functioning organ.[27]

This is not the first time technologies of the Fourth Industrial Revolution create excitement, which is then soon followed by disillusionment. More than fifteen years later, after Atala's thought-provoking TED talk, we are nowhere near being able to simply print out the organs transplant patients all around the world are so eagerly waiting for. Nonetheless, progress has been made. Already in 2010, a regenerative-medicine company based in San Diego called Organovo was able to print human blood cells.[28] In addition, even if producing a fully functioning organ still lies in the future, 3D printing can be used for a number of applications that may be less spectacular but can still make a real difference in the lives of patients.

- For instance, organoids can be produced that mimic human anatomy to such a degree they can be used for drug testing.[29]
- 3D printing can also provide custom-made products, such as orthopedic implants, dental implants, and joint replacements.
- Customized prostheses and orthoses can be manufactured in more cost-efficient ways, which is especially crucial for children who quickly outgrow these much-needed devices.[30]
- 3D printing could also be used to produce customized medication with just the exact doses for a particular patient. Multiple treatments could be combined into one drug, thereby creating a "polypill,"

---

mentioned above. Hastings, "Fish-Shaped Microrobots to Deliver Chemotherapy."

25. Awari et al., *Additive Manufacturing*, 169–72.
26. Atala, "Growing New Organs."
27. Topol, *Creative Destruction of Medicine*, 139.
28. Bullock, "Sir, Your Liver Is Ready."
29. Nawrat, "3D Printing in the Medical Field." See also Labios, "Super Productive 3D Bioprinter."
30. Formlabs, "Introduction to Medical 3D Printing."

which would make things much easier for patients who, until now, have to take a large number of different pills every day.[31]

- Another application is to produce more precise or more versatile medical supplies, including bandages, surgical instruments, infusion pumps, and pacemakers. For example, when surgical instruments are produced by 3D printers, they are sterile and can be made exceedingly small and precise, so that "these instruments can be used to operate on tiny areas without causing unnecessary extra damage to the patient."[32]

- In addition, 3D printing can be employed for preparatory work, such as when a surgeon reproduces the spine of a patient, in order to practice an upcoming surgery. These patient-specific surgical models help "physicians prepare better for surgeries, leading to drastically reduced time and cost in the operating room while improving patient satisfaction, lowering anxiety, and reducing recovery time."[33]

Besides taking advantage of new kinds of hardware, innovation in healthcare is also coming about through accessing new levels of information about the human body. People's DNA entails the complete information regarding the genetic makeup of a person, which includes information about any possible malfunctioning of particular body parts, as well as people's risk levels regarding certain illnesses. Deciphering (and interpreting) the human genome has therefore become a top priority. A historical milestone was reached in 2000 when, as part of the Human Genome Project, the first survey of a human's entire DNA was completed. Inspired by this progress, then President Bill Clinton proclaimed enthusiastically, "More than 1,000 researchers across six nations have revealed nearly all 3 billion letters of our miraculous genetic code. I congratulate all of you on this stunning and humbling achievement."[34] Clinton then went on to say,

> With this profound new knowledge, humankind is on the verge of gaining immense new power to heal. Genome science will have a real impact on all our lives and even more on the lives of

31. Pew, "What Is Medical 3D Printing?"
32. Nawrat, "3D Printing in the Medical Field," §14.
33. Formlabs, "Introduction to Medical 3D Printing," §6.
34. NIH, "June 2000 White House Event," §7.

our children. It will revolutionize the diagnosis, prevention and treatment of most, if not all, human diseases.

In coming years, doctors increasingly will be able to cure diseases like Alzheimer's, Parkinson's, diabetes and cancer by attacking their genetic roots. Just to offer one example, patients with some forms of leukemia and breast cancer already are being treated in clinical trials, with sophisticated new drugs that precisely target the faulty genes and cancer cells, with little or no risk to healthy cells. In fact, it is now conceivable that our children's children will know the term cancer only as a constellation of stars.[35]

To be sure, these are moving and compelling words pointing to a more hopeful future. However, similarly to what has been the case in other instances, the hype has not been quite able to live up to the promise. Since Clinton delivered his congratulatory speech, not that much has happened in the realm of concrete applications based on the human genome, but there are promising developments. To begin with, the cost for analyzing the human genome has come down substantially, thereby making this kind of information more accessible. In the early days, even just uncyphering a small portion of the human genome was a massive and expensive undertaking. Even in 2007, several years after the milestone mentioned above, deciphering the entire genetic information of one human being still took four years and cost one hundred million USD.[36] Since then, new machines have been developed to aid in this task. In 2018, the Rady Children's Hospital in San Diego was able to produce "a fully sequenced and interpreted genome in only 19.5 hours," and today a genome sequencing can be performed for a few hundred dollars.[37]

So far, it is not entirely clear what exactly the medical benefits could be in acquiring all this information. However, with the price now being so low, deciphering one's genetic makeup could become a standard procedure for almost everybody in the population, similar to performing an x-ray, for example. In combination with AI, these sets of data could then be analyzed and compared with each other, thereby identifying patterns and irregularities that could aid in the discovery of new medications and more personalized approaches to treatment.

35. NIH, "June 2000 White House Event," §§9–10.
36. Topol, *Creative Destruction of Medicine*, 95.
37. Topol, *Deep Medicine*, 4. See, for example, the $249 for decoding 100 percent of the client's DNA offered by Nebula Genomics (however, the "Ultra Deep" option that provides the decoding "with ultra high accuracy" costs $899, down from $2,164). Nebula Genomics, "What Does Your DNA."

Further down in the future, genetics could also be used in order to repair or replace specific parts of the human DNA, so that certain hereditary diseases do not even develop in the first place.[38] Through gene-editing technologies like CRISPR (which stands for clustered regularly interspaced short palindromic repeats), genetic modification could also help in eliminating sicknesses like malaria, HIV, and some cancers. Scientists and ethicists recognize such powerful tools offer "both the greatest promise and, arguably, the greatest peril for the future of humanity."[39] As a reviewer of *A Crack in Creation: Gene Editing and the Unthinkable Power to Control Evolution* states so well,

> CRISPR heralds a new era of massively increased human control over life, one that will affect every person on Earth, directly or indirectly, and much of the rest of our planet's biosphere. If humans are to have any chance of harnessing its benefits, avoiding its risks, and using it in ways consistent with our values and cultures, then we all—not just the scientists, ethicists, and patent lawyers—need to understand something about CRISPR and its implications.[40]

Given these far-reaching developments, I argue Christians must engage in these conversations as well and begin to wrestle with these issues from a theological point of view.

A CHRISTIAN PERSPECTIVE ON HEALTHCARE

While much could be said about a theological perspective on healthcare, I here limit myself to the following three points. (1) Christians have a rich heritage in healthcare that goes back to Jesus himself. In our day and age, the church should therefore, whenever possible, embrace new technological advancements if these have the potential for greater well-being and a better level of care. (2) Theologically speaking, the *imago Dei* is a crucial concept affirming the unique worth and dignity of all human beings, including the unborn. (3) In view of the many innovations that may become available in the Fourth Industrial Revolution, we need to

---

38. Crucially, humans cannot only learn to read genes but also to write and edit them. Wünschiers, *Genetic Engineering*.

39. Doudna and Sternberg, *Crack in Creation*, xiv.

40. Greely, "CRISPR, Patents, and Nobel Prizes," §39.

remember and accept that humans are (and will remain) mortal beings. We therefore need to help people not only to get well, but also to die well.

Given the potential of new treatment methods, I argue the Christian church should embrace science and technology as never before. Christians have had a strong presence in healthcare for centuries, and across all continents. This commitment to care for the sick and dying goes back to the example of Jesus himself, who had an extensive healing ministry (Matt 4:23–24; 8:16; 9:35; 10:1–8; 12:15; 14:14; 15:30: 21:14; Mark 1:29–34; Luke 6:19; 8:49–56; John 4:46–53; 5:5–9; Acts 9:33–34). Jesus also changed the course of human history in this regard simply by telling one short but powerful story: the parable of the good Samaritan (Luke 10:25–37). In this parable, Jesus was primarily addressing the tensions between groups with racial and religious differences, but the example of the story's hero to care for a person in need has also inspired countless Christian initiatives, such as relief organizations, hospitals, and ambulance services that are named after the good Samaritan.[41]

Through the centuries, believers have often been at the frontlines of caring for the weak, the sick, and the dying. In fact, one of the reasons why early Christianity spread so rapidly throughout the Roman Empire was because followers of Jesus were known as people of high moral standards, who were displaying both chastity and charity in the midst of an increasingly corrupt culture.[42] The first Christians were highly missional in their impact on society because "a potent 'gospel of love and charity' was exercised toward the poor, orphans, widows, sick, miners, prisoners, slaves and travelers."[43] Such tangible care was also extended to the most vulnerable; in Roman society, abortion was common, as was the practice of infanticide, but believers saw these practices as murder, and therefore opposed them.[44]

While the roots of Western medicine go back to the Greco-Roman tradition, it was the Christian concept of philanthropy that led to the founding of hospitals offering both treatment and nursing of the sick,

---

41. Examples of Good Samaritan hospitals can be found throughout the US, including in West Islip, New York (https://www.catholichealthli.org/good-samaritan-university-hospital); San Jose, California (https://goodsamsanjose.com); and Cincinnati, Ohio (https://www.trihealth.com/locations/good-samaritan-hospital). In Germany, the *Arbeiter Samariter Bund* (ASB), a labor and aid organization that started in 1888, runs an ambulance network (https://www.asb.de/en).

42. Kane, *Concise History*, 24.

43. Goheen, *Introducing Christian Mission Today*, 125.

44. Kane, *Concise History*, 28.

as well as other innovations.[45] Nonetheless, there also can be tensions between medicine and religion, particularly in monolithic societies which discourage dissent and free scientific inquiry. For instance, in the Middle Ages, "numerous European writers interpreted the Great Plague as punishment for sin."[46] Back then, the Roman Catholic Church may not have outright banned the dissection of human bodies,[47] but neither did it encourage such evidence-based research. It was only during the Renaissance that "the strength of religious sanctions against dissection began to weaken and, by the sixteenth century, surgeons in Protestant countries such as England were officially given the authority to take the bodies of hanged criminals for use in their anatomical studies."[48]

Considering these historical lessons, it is important for Christians to embrace novel technologies that will propel healthcare to the next level. Granted, there can be excesses, and believers should be wary of any overreliance on technology. However, life expectancy has risen dramatically around the world in the past one hundred fifty years or so, and this achievement is mostly due to technological advances.[49] When Fleming discovered penicillin in 1928, this helped save millions of lives around the world, and one can expect the innovations of the Fourth Industrial Revolution will bring similar benefits. Specifically, I see potential in the following areas for Christians to play a proactive and pioneering role.

- Based on increasing amounts of data, health professionals and patients will be able to focus more on prevention.[50] Many of the most common chronic conditions in the United States (like heart diseases and type 2 diabetes) are lifestyle diseases, which could be avoided by observing a healthier diet and regular physical exercise.[51]

---

45. Ferngren, *Medicine and Health Care*; Schmidt, *How Christianity Changed the World*, 151–69; Aquilina, *Healing Imperative*.

46. Chapman, *Physicians, Plagues and Progress*, 114.

47. Shwayder, "Debunking a Myth." Compare Rankin, *Poison Trials*, 55–58.

48. Lambert and Walker, "Bioarcheological Ethics," 6.

49. Dattani, "Life Expectancy."

50. One way to collect more data would be by taking advantage of health-monitoring wearable devices, such as smart rings, that constantly measure a person's pulse, body temperature, blood oxygen levels, and bodily activity. Sawh, "Best Smart Rings 2024."

51. Obesity is a major factor in this context, and it is increasingly becoming a worldwide problem. Ahima, *Can the Obesity Crisis Be Reversed?*

- Christians should also be at the forefront of technological innovations that allow for less intrusive procedures, such as making use of nanorobots and microsensors.

- In addition, a whole new approach to healthcare is needed, one that radically removes the paternalistic attitude displayed by many medical doctors who practice what Topol refers to "as 'eminence-based' rather than 'evidence-based' medicine."[52] Instead, the patient should be at the center of all treatments, which means they not only need to have access to relevant data, but also own their entire medical record and then make informed decisions about what treatment they choose (or reject), based on transparent pricing.

But what about other novel methods like CRISPR? The tension inherent in such advances is acknowledged by the theologian Nathan A. Barczi in his article "In the Image of Our Choosing?" when he writes, "While CRISPR holds out tremendous potential to alleviate the suffering that follows from genetic diseases such as sickle cell anemia and Huntington's disease, it could eventually also make possible, to those with access to the technology, the selection of traits such as height, eye color, and greater strength and intelligence."[53] A Christian response to procedures like CRISPR must be rooted in careful reflections regarding what it means that humans are created in the image of God. Historically, the *imago Dei* has often been connected with the rational capabilities of humans, which far exceed those of any animal. However, more recently theologians have emphasized the relational and teleological dimension of the *imago Dei*. In this view, human beings have inherent value and dignity based on their very being, because they have been created by God to be in relationship with him, and to represent him on this Earth.[54]

The *imago Dei* is therefore part of every human being, even if they have limited rational capabilities (such as an embryo, or someone who suffered brain damage due to an accident). Through technologies like CRISPR people might be tempted to optimize human embryos in some way.[55] However, what a humanistic approach to these questions misses is that God is already at work in a person's life, even while they are still in

---

52. Topol, *Patient Will See You Now*, 33.
53. Barczi, "In the Image of Our Choosing?," 152.
54. Barczi, "In the Image of Our Choosing?," 158–68.
55. Having this conversation is even more urgent considering the Chinese scientist He Jiankui gene-edited two babies in 2018. Davies, *Editing Humanity*, 193–95.

their mother's womb. This is why David was able to pray, "Surely I was sinful at birth, sinful from the time my mother conceived me. Yet you desired faithfulness even in the womb; you taught me wisdom in that secret place" (Ps 51:5–6).[56]

Given these biblical and theological realities, an important involvement for Christians in healthcare has to do with protecting life from the moment of conception. Abortion is a critical issue for most believers, so much so that many have become single-issue voters regarding this matter, and rightly so. It is no coincidence the Declaration of Independence in its famous phrase about "life, liberty, and the pursuit of happiness" places "life" as the first and most fundamental human right, because without it all the other rights and privileges cannot be applied to any person.[57] In view of the primacy of life as a fundamental value and the most basic human right, it is a tragedy that more than sixty-two million abortions have been performed in the United States since the Roe v. Wade decision in 1973. Recently, some progress has been made in the legal realm, such as legislating so-called heartbeat bills in states like Texas, Georgia, and Florida. Determining the abortion issue at the state level became possible after Supreme Court Justice Ruth Bader Ginsburg (1933–2020) was replaced by the more conservative Amy Coney Barrett, thereby paving the way for the overturn of Roe v. Wade, a decision that was finally reached in 2022.[58]

However, America remains a country in which even late-term abortions are legally permitted in many states—in contrast to Norway, for example, where abortions are only allowed within the first three months of a pregnancy. Some countries have increased access to abortions as they have become more secular. Ireland, for instance, a traditionally Roman Catholic society, passed the Regulation of Termination of Pregnancy Act in 2018.[59] Both nationally and internationally it remains to be seen how much can be achieved through legal means in order to lower the number of abortions, as cultural, social, economic, and religious factors also play an important role.[60] In the context of the Fourth Industrial Revolution,

---

56. See also the biblical reflections by Hardin, "Fearfully and Wonderfully Made?," 177–84.

57. National Archives, "Declaration of Independence."

58. For the faith background of Amy Coney Barrett, see Graham and LaFraniere, "Inside the People of Praise." For the ongoing division in the country after the Supreme Court's decision, see Damante and Jones, "Year After the Supreme Court."

59. Calkin and Berny, "Legal and Non-Legal Barriers to Abortion."

60. Some of the highest abortion rates (measured in per one thousand women) are found in Vietnam, Madagascar, Cuba, and India. Immad, "25 Countries."

some of the biggest changes for the pro-life movement in the years ahead may be related to technology.

One way technology could help the pro-life cause is through preventing unwanted pregnancies by providing new forms of contraception. Of course, the pill is now widely available, but an increasing number of women feel skeptical toward taking it regularly, considering the potential side effects.[61] In addition, contraception can also be a hot issue for religious reasons, for those emphasizing there is a direct connection between sexual intercourse and procreation that should not be artificially interrupted. There is, however, a more natural way of birth control by paying close attention to a woman's monthly cycle, something that can be monitored through a smartphone app (such as Natural Cycles).[62] When a woman takes her temperature daily and records it in her app, she will know with a great degree of certainty on what days she can or cannot become pregnant.

Hopefully, these kinds of apps will create alternative forms of contraception with which many women (and men) are comfortable and feel safe, thereby avoiding unwanted pregnancies. However, even in the case of an undesired pregnancy, technology could help women toward taking a pro-life stand, such as by deciding to keep their baby or by giving up the child for adoption. Advances in genetics have now made it clear the unique DNA of a human being is arranged at conception, thereby strengthening the argument that life begins at conception. In addition, the high quality of ultrasound images available today has changed the perception of some pregnant women who were considering an abortion but then dismissed the idea after seeing the images. As newer imaging technologies with higher resolution become available, it may become even clearer that a new human being is growing inside a woman's womb, thereby further strengthening the pro-life cause.[63]

A third way technology could contribute to reducing the number of abortions is the creation of artificial wombs.[64] One of the strongest arguments of abortion activists (or the pro-choice movement) is that women should be able to be decide whether they want to see a pregnancy through or not. This argument carries special weight under particularly

61. In the United States, the usage of the pill peaked in 1973, when "more than a third of American women were on the pill." Holt, "Women Are Ditching the Pill," §2.
62. Burke, "Catholic Contraception? Get the App."
63. Beck, "Technology Changing Access and Outcomes."
64. Cohen, "Artificial Wombs Are Coming."

difficult circumstances, such as if a woman is pregnant because of rape (which causes only a relatively small percentage of unwanted pregnancies). From an ethical point of view, I believe even in an instance of a horrific crime like rape there is still a case to be made for the pro-life position. However, from a practical and political perspective, it seems very unlikely abortions can be fully banned in a liberal democracy, considering how divided people are on this complicated issue.

Given these realities, I think it is important pregnant women have a choice, while at the same time protecting the life of the baby. In the future, this could be accomplished by transferring the fetus to an artificial womb when the woman decides that she does not want to carry on with the pregnancy. The woman would be free from the burden of an unwanted pregnancy, and the baby would be kept alive (similar to the way premature babies are already being kept alive in an incubator), so that it could then later be released for adoption. Of course, such an artificial womb would first have to be developed, and besides the technical issues the question also must be raised what babies would be missing by not growing up in the womb of their mother. Still, considering the supreme importance of life and the challenge of declining birthrates in many developed countries, making use of artificial wombs could become one of the priorities in the era of the Fourth Industrial Revolution.[65]

As part of the quest to protect life, I strongly encourage Christian involvement in healthcare, including the pursuit of innovative technologies that will bring about new approaches to treating patients and eradicating diseases that currently cannot be cured. Nonetheless, believers also need to emphasize the limitations of technology (whether with regards to the medical field or any other form of practical application). Some of the limitations of technology are especially obvious when it comes to the treatment of older patients. Currently, a large portion of healthcare costs in the United States is directed toward end-of-life care.[66] In many cases, this means billions of dollars are spent—not to save lives, but to prolong a state of being in which the patients are often more dead than alive, frequently suffering from considerable pain and discomfort as they are hooked up to a plethora of machines and monitors. Of course, the value of any human life is priceless, which is why the church needs to continue

---

65. E.g., North, "You Can't Even Pay."

66. "Estimates of the percentage of Medicare costs that arise from patients in the last year of life differ, ranging from 13% to 25%, depending on methods and assumptions." Duncan et al., "Medicare Cost at End of Life," 705.

to take a stand against any form of active euthanasia. However, artificially prolonging life through purely technological means also creates its own set of problems. Within a system of limited resources, the question must be asked whether these vast sums of money could not be put to better use by channeling them toward younger people who, potentially, still have many years ahead of them.

In view of this ethical and economic conundrum, I suggest that we need to help people not only to live well but also to die well. Theologically speaking, death is the final enemy, and in this sense we are called to fight it tooth and nail, doing our best to save human life by combating deadly diseases. At the same time, it is crucial to recognize we live in a post-Gen 3 world in which sin and death will never be fully eliminated. That final victory does not belong to humankind, but to the God-man Jesus Christ. Only at Jesus's second coming will all of God's enemies, including death, be finally and completely defeated (1 Cor 15:20–58; 1 Thess 4:13–18; Rev 21:1–4). In the meantime, we live in an age of tension, in which we can experience healing to some degree, whether this healing is accomplished through prayer and the laying on of hands or through the advances of modern medicine.[67] However, sickness and disease will continue to be a reality, and even if somebody was miraculously raised from the dead, that person would nonetheless still die at some point (as was the case with Lazarus, for instance).

We must oppose any deification of medical doctors and modern medicine. Yes, technologies of the Fourth Industrial Revolution will bring about new and improved treatment opportunities, and we should embrace these whenever it is ethically responsible to do so. At the same time, we must realize the age-long problems of sin, sickness, and death will continue to haunt humanity. The Bible commands us to resist any kind of idolatry, and healthcare can easily become an idol. Idolatry is a sin that is especially addressed in the Hebrew Scriptures, and it would be wise to heed the warning of Harris Bor when he reminds us in *Staying Human: A Jewish Theology for the Age of Artificial Intelligence* "that every ideology is capable of leading to tyranny, every truth will be overturned, every tower of Babel falls, and every hero turns to dust."[68] Ultimate solutions can only be provided by the God of the Bible; all other gods and forces will fail us, no matter how powerful and promising they may seem at the time.

---

67. Ladd, *Theology of the New Testament*, 368, 568, 680.
68. Bor, *Staying Human*, 155.

Given these realities, Christians are called not only to heal the sick but also to accompany the dying. However, frantically hooking up a dying person to a set of machines, constantly sending a potent drug cocktail through their veins, and repeatedly bringing them back from the brink of death by resuscitating them through the electro shocks transmitted by a cardiac defibrillator may not be what this individual genuinely wants or needs. As an alternative path to end-of-life care we should think more about how such a person could die in peace, preferably at home, surrounded by friends and family, and what they would like to do with the little time they have left on Earth, before they undertake that final journey to go and meet their Creator.[69] Through a discerning usage of new technologies, Christians can help to make healthcare more humane, by enabling people to make their own decisions regarding treatment and care, including end-of-life care. One thing to keep in mind is that a person's medical data is highly sensitive and private, which is why it needs to be secure—accordingly, questions related to cybersecurity is one of the topics of the following chapter.

DISCUSSION QUESTIONS

1. What are some of the potential risks and opportunities associated with gene-editing technologies, such as CRISPR?
2. What kind of legal, socioeconomic, spiritual, and/or technological changes do you think need to take place in order to reduce the number of abortions in the United States?
3. What would your response be toward Christians who reject placing nanorobots and microsensors in the human body because they think these could be the mark of the beast described in Rev 13:16–18?
4. How might the church facilitate helpful conversations regarding mortality, and how could this topic deepen people's relationship with God?

---

69. "Meanwhile, of the Americans facing end-of-life care, 80 percent would prefer to die at home, but only a small fraction get to do so—60 percent die in the hospital." Topol, *Deep Medicine*, 187.

SUGGESTIONS FOR FURTHER READING

- Gary B. Ferngren, *Medicine and Health Care in Early Christianity* (2016). A historical description of how and why the early church got involved in healthcare, written by a professor of history.

- Michael R. Panicola et al., *Health Care Ethics: Theological Foundations, Contemporary Issues, and Controversial Cases* (2011). A comprehensive guide that includes case studies and discussion questions, suitable for both undergraduates and professionals.

- C. Ben Mitchell and D. Joy Riley, *Christian Bioethics: A Guide for Pastors, Health Care Professionals, and Families* (2014). An ethicist and a physician discuss issues like abortion, genetic engineering, and in vitro fertilization.

- Eric Topol, *Deep Medicine: How Artificial Intelligence Can Make Healthcare Human Again* (2019). One of America's best cardiologists explains where healthcare has gone wrong and how technology can help to fix it.

- Tina Stevens and Stuart Newman, *Biotech Juggernaut: Hope, Hype, and Hidden Agendas of Entrepreneurial BioScience* (2019). A critical analysis, warning of the dangers of genetic engineering as pursued by biotech companies.

- Jamie Metzl, *Hacking Darwin: Genetic Engineering and the Future of Humanity* (2019). Presents an optimistic view on the potential of genetic engineering, written by a futurist, science fiction author, and geopolitical expert.

6

Security

THE FEDERAL RESERVE BANK of New York on 33 Liberty Street is designed to be one of the most secure buildings in the world—and rightly so, bearing in mind this structure contains even more gold bars than are stored at Fort Knox, a US Army base in Kentucky with a daytime population of over twenty-six thousand people.[1] The gold in the former is kept in a vault eighty feet below street level, and the vault's only entry is guarded by a ninety-ton steel cylinder.[2] In addition, the vault is monitored 24–7 by security cameras and motion sensors, while also being protected by the armed Federal Reserve police force. Given these security measures, it comes as no surprise this building has never been breached by bank robbers, and probably never will. However, cyberattacks are a different matter; they are a phenomenon affecting all institutions, even the most secure ones.

As Federal Reserve Chair Jerome Powell acknowledged in an interview with CBS News in 2021, he is more worried about cyber risk than the prospect of another financial crash. Powell believes "'a cyber event' could have 'a broad part' to play in the financial system 'coming to a halt.'"[3] In contrast, "he dubs the risk of a 2008-style financial collapse 'very, very low.'"[4] Cyberattacks, however, are a "big part of the threat picture in today's world," which is why Powell affirms: "I would say that the

1. US Army, "Welcome to Fort Knox."
2. Philipps, "You're Planning a Heist."
3. Hinchliffe, "Federal Reserve More Worried," §1.
4. Hinchliffe, "Federal Reserve More Worried," §1.

risk that we keep our eyes on the most now is cyber risk."[5] Accordingly, he asserts "that the US central bank is therefore monitoring it very carefully and investing heavily in the prevention of major breaches."[6]

At the same time, security risks in the Fourth Industrial Revolution are also related to new kinds of weapons—risks including cyberwarfare, but also armed robots, laser weapons, and hypersonic missiles. Given these security risks in both cyberspace and physical spaces, governments will want to protect their citizens on various levels, of which I highlight three in the opening part of this chapter. First, even in times of peace, people are still subject to criminal activity in cyberspace, and governments must think about how they can protect the privacy and the data of their citizens. Second, war between nations increasingly may not be declared directly, but a country may still suffer from cyberattacks organized (or at least supported) by a foreign government. Third, national governments need to be able to defend their country against foreign intruders, and in the future this will have to include the ability to engage with autonomous weapon systems.

First, as data becomes more and more important for all social and economic interactions, it is essential that governments do more to protect sensitive data and the privacy of their citizens. In the past few years, there has been no shortage of cyberattacks affecting millions of individuals. Examples of enormous amounts of private data being breached in the commercial world include:

- In 2014, state-sponsored actors stole personal data from five hundred million Yahoo accounts.[7]
- The biggest ransomware attack hitherto took place in 2017, when around two hundred thousand computers were affected in more than one hundred fifty countries.[8] This outbreak had a considerable impact across several industries and had a global cost of billions of dollars.
- A massive data leak occurred in December of 2023 at Real Estate Wealth Network, at which 1.5 billion records were leaked.[9]

---

5. Hinchliffe, "Federal Reserve More Worried," §2.
6. Hinchliffe, "Federal Reserve More Worried," §3.
7. Hill and Swinhoe, "15 Biggest Data Breaches."
8. Dwoskin and Adam, "More Than 150 Countries."
9. Chin, "Biggest Data Breaches."

In the face of such common threats that can hit any kind of company and any consumer, protecting oneself in cyberspace becomes paramount. In the physical realm, people tend to be much more careful—for example, any reasonable person would think twice before showing a stranger on the street the details of their credit card or leaving the door of their home wide open in the middle of the night. However, people often do the equivalent of such actions when taking advantage of the many benefits the internet offers to them. Part of the challenge is that, within certain settings, people want others to see their online activity, such as when they post something on Facebook or upload a (modified) photo on Instagram.

Given these ambiguities, a threefold approach to personal protection in cyberspace might be useful. The first layer of protection applies to those social media platforms where people choose to have a public profile on purpose. Here it will be helpful to establish certain standards for oneself before one publishes any kind of information by asking question like: Would I want my spouse, my pastor, or a future employer to know about this text or picture I am about to upload? What kind of example do I want to set for my children regarding my online activity? Speaking of children—have I talked to them whether they are okay with me posting pictures of them on my social media platforms?[10]

The second layer of protection would be the equivalent of a person's wallet, where people keep important items they use regularly (like their driver's license or cash), but that they do not want others to see. The equivalent in cyberspace would be the use of passwords, whether these protect access to certain documents and folders on a person's computer or websites, such as their email account(s). Much could be said about this whole area, which would go far beyond the scope of this chapter, but here a few points about passwords. (1) Experts recommend using a long password that includes a mix of letters, numbers, and symbols.[11] (2) People should make sure they use different passwords for different applications. (3) Users should apply two-factor authentication for especially important accounts (which would require using a code sent to the person's mobile phone, besides the correct username and password on the website, for example).[12]

10. Steinberg, *Growing Up Shared*, 96–100.

11. Stouffer, "Password Security." However, since it is difficult to remember a long, complex word, it might be more realistic to use passphrases (consisting of several words) instead. Steinberg et al., *Cybersecurity All-in-One*, 134–35.

12. Nield, "How to Keep All."

A further level of cybersecurity can be reached by engaging third parties that can help individuals to create a more protected environment. In the physical world, many people buy a safe for their most important documents or pay a monthly fee to a private security service for their home. The equivalent in cyberspace could be to invest in certain areas, such as paying for a password manager or using a virtual private network (VPN), instead of regular internet access.[13] Beyond such measures that reflect the current IT-infrastructure, it may also be advantageous to invest in new, more secure products for the most important personal information (like one's investment portfolio or one's personal health history). This could be achieved by using new technologies like blockchain, which is currently best known for digital currencies like Bitcoin, but which may soon also offer other applications in areas like finance, law, and healthcare (for a more detailed discussion of blockchain technologies, see chapter 7).

Apart from targeting companies and their customers, cyberattacks can also be directed toward entire nations and their infrastructure. Here are some examples of such attacks that have occurred in the age of the internet we are living in:

- In April 2007, Estonia suffered a cyberattack that was most likely orchestrated by Russia and which affected the entire country, as dozens of important websites were shut down.[14]
- In 2009, Chinese hackers breached the Pentagon's Joint Strike Fighter project and stole data related to the F-35 fighter jet.[15]
- In 2018, India's database Aadhaar was attacked, "exposing information on more than 1.1 billion Indian citizens including names, addresses, photos, phone numbers, and emails, as well as biometric data like fingerprints and iris scans."[16]

As disruptive as these attacks are, they do not necessarily indicate a traditional war between two major powers (like the United States and China) lies ahead. Historically, the most devastating wars occurred when major geopolitical powers like Germany and France went to war, fighting directly against each other, which is what occurred in both the First and

13. Vigderman and Turner, "Best VPN Services of 2024."
14. Al Bawaba, " 10 Biggest Cyber Attacks."
15. Hjortdal, "China's Use of Cyber Warfare," 9.
16. Hill and Swinhoe, "15 Biggest Data Breaches," §7.

the Second World Wars. The second half of the twentieth century was characterized by the Cold War, in which the United States and the Soviet Union competed on many levels but did not clash directly in an armed conflict with each other (possibly because they both had a nuclear arsenal large enough to destroy the entire planet many times over). Instead, their rivalry led to several proxy wars, notably the Korean War (1950–53) and the war in Vietnam (1954–75).[17]

In the twenty-first century, major powers are often not only competitors but also important trading partners, which leads to economic interests that are more geared toward a mixed form of competition and cooperation, rather than open conflict on a traditional battlefield. Nonetheless, there can be considerable tension between two or several countries, which might intensify through non-traditional forms of warfare, including cyberattacks and information warfare. This kind of asymmetrical warfare has already begun, even if the exact extent of these activities may not be fully known.[18]

At times, criminal action is taken by a regional power toward a non-state actor, such as a corporation. A prominent example of this kind of illegal activity was a cyberattack conducted by North Korea against Sony in 2014, as retaliation for producing the satirical movie *The Interview*, which made fun of Kim Jong Un.[19] Dangerous and damaging activity in cyberspace can also come from non-state actors like terrorist or criminal organizations. An example of the latter would be the group of hackers that compromised the Colonial Pipeline, the largest fuel pipeline in the United States, on April 29, 2021. In response to the cyberthreat, the company shut down the entire pipeline, the first time such a drastic measure had been taken in its fifty-seven-year history.[20] This unprecedented action caused gas prices to rise, especially in the eastern part of the United States, thereby affecting a large portion of the population. In the end, "Colonial paid the hackers, who were an affiliate

---

17. Admittedly, I am doing these major conflicts no justice by just briefly mentioning them. For a more detailed study see, for instance, Martel, *Twentieth-Century War and Conflict*, which has 1959–75 for the dates of the Vietnam War. However, following the *Encyclopedia Britannica*, I chose 1954 as the start of this war, because that is when the United States began covert operations in Vietnam. Spector, "Vietnam War."

18. This combination of elements like irregular warfare, cyberattacks, and fake news is also called hybrid warfare. Weissmann et al., *Hybrid Warfare*.

19. Altman and Fitzpatrick, "Everything We Know."

20. Turton and Mehrotra, "Hackers Breached Colonial Pipeline."

of a Russia-linked cybercrime group known as DarkSide, a $4.4 million ransom shortly after the hack."[21]

It is likely Russia and China engage in, or at least encourage, a variety of activities designed to destabilize the United States, specifically by trying to influence election results or simply by exacerbating divisions in American society, whether along political or racial lines.[22] This threat became a major issue during the 2016 presidential election, with Russia becoming a prime suspect of having orchestrated such interference.[23] In addition, cyberwarfare could also become entangled in dangerous ways with traditional warfare, for instance if a hostile player were to cyberattack the command-and-control architecture of the United States, such as its early warning radars. These early warning systems are designed to inform the US and its allies about threats like incoming nuclear missiles—if the digital infrastructure of those systems were to be infiltrated, this could therefore easily escalate into a dangerous chain reaction.[24]

However, it is not only foreign governments who are interfering with the sensitive world of data; for many people, it is their own government, too. After 9/11, the US government expanded the role of the National Security Agency (NSA), thereby building up a surveillance infrastructure of unprecedented proportions. The intentions of this undertaking were certainly noble as the idea was to avoid another terrorist attack on American soil.[25] However, terrorist cells often operate undercover, pretending to be a regular part of the overall population, so in order to cover these cells the government began to spy on regular citizens as well. Phone calls, texts, emails—any kind of electronic communication was (and, to some extent, still is) scanned for suspicious keywords, creating a new paradox: Was America, in order to protect itself from outside enemies, becoming an unfree society through its own actions?[26]

---

21. Turton and Mehrotra, "Hackers Breached Colonial Pipeline," §15.

22. In terms of cyber capabilities, the globe is now divided into "two cyber centres of power. A developed world block spearheaded by the United States and are [sic] developing world block represented by Russia and China." Lenong, "State Cybersecurity Governance," 73.

23. However, election interference has been an issue at different times and in different countries, not just in 2016. Levin, *Meddling in the Ballot Box*; Shimer, *Rigged*.

24. DW News, "Future of Modern Warfare."

25. For a positive evaluation of the NSA in this regards, see Johnson, "Cyber Intelligence," 183–92.

26. Satter, "U.S. Court."

Obviously, in other countries the role of government in relation to the use (and abuse) of private data is much more heavy-handed. China, in particular, has become a nation that is often mentioned when privacy concerns are discussed, considering the government uses a large network of cameras for security purposes.[27] This includes facial recognition cameras, and the Chinese government has introduced a social credit score system through which every single citizen is monitored with a kind of stick and carrot approach. Within this scorecard system, citizens receive lower points for bad behavior (like jay walking, or endangering "the social harmony on the Internet") and positive points for the right kind of behavior, such as donating blood.[28] Once a person's credit score sinks too low, there will be consequences; for instance, these people will no longer be allowed to take a plane or send their children to a good school.[29]

Needless to say, this kind of approach would be unacceptable in a Western democracy, and in that sense, it seems right to point to China as a warning example of how things can go wrong. At the same time, it is also important to remember that different societies have different value systems and historical frameworks through which they distinguish between what is deemed to be attractive and what must be rejected. In the case of China, there is a long history of authoritarian rule, which is largely accepted by the population as long as there is a sense of economic well-being. So far, the Communist Party of China has been able to deliver economic growth and relative stability, which is why it is likely it will remain in power for many more years.

The relationship between Communist China and the United States as the leader of the free world will be one of the defining characteristics of the twenty-first century. Given their ideological differences, conflict may arise, particularly over the status of Taiwan, which is a key player in the global supply chain of microchips.[30] In the context of the Fourth Industrial Revolution, it looks like China and the United States are emerging as the two main players in technologies like autonomous vehicles and AI.[31] These technological capabilities will also be applied to the military sector, thereby creating new defense needs and security concerns.[32]

27. McGregor, "World's Largest Surveillance System."
28. Davies, "Facial Recognition and Beyond," §17.
29. Davies, "Facial Recognition and Beyond."
30. Minton Beddoes, "Rivalry between America and China"; Miller, *Chip War*.
31. Lee, *AI Superpowers*.
32. Johnson, *Artificial Intelligence*.

In the age of AI, war will be fought with new kinds of weapons. This should come as no surprise, considering the military has often been on the forefront of technological innovations that were later then also applied to civil life in various ways. Examples of this important dynamic include technologies as far-reaching as nuclear power (the Manhattan Project led to the invention of the atomic bomb in 1945, while the first nuclear power plant producing electricity was built in 1951). The Global Positioning System (GPS) was further developed by the Air Force in the 1970s, and in the 1980s President Ronald Reagan authorized it to be used by commercial airliners as well.[33] Even the internet has military origins: Although a variety of players contributed to this invention, the funding by the Department of Defense through the Advanced Research Projects Agency (ARPA) was essential.[34] In order to facilitate communication between a variety of entities, the agency put in place ARPANET in 1969, which over time developed into what today is known as the internet, with a crucial milestone being achieved in 1990 when the computer scientist Tim Berners-Lee invented the World Wide Web.[35]

This inter-mingling of military and civil inventions and applications is likely to continue. In fact, as described in chapter 1, autonomous cars and trucks are becoming more and more common, a development that was strongly encouraged through the DARPA challenge, beginning in 2004. Autonomous machines of all shapes and forms are going to be a major factor in designing the military of the future, affecting not only the army but the navy and the air force as well. For example, Dr. John Fossaceca, the program manager of the Artificial Intelligence of Maneuver and Mobility (AIMM) Essential Research Program, "said he seeks to develop the foundational capabilities that will enable autonomy in the next generation of combat vehicles. This include [sic] the construction of a robotic combat vehicle that operates independently of the main combat vehicle."[36]

With this kind of vision, it is only a matter of time before autonomous armored vehicles and specialized robots (e.g., to disarm explosives) will populate the battlefield. These will be supported by drones that can perform reconnaissance services, thereby increasing the situational

---

33. Aerospace, "Brief History of GPS."
34. Tarnoff, "How the Internet Was Invented."
35. Andrews, "Who Invented the Internet."
36. US Army, "Army Researchers Augment," §3.

awareness of troops on the ground.[37] Similarly, the navy is developing autonomous submarines and ships, and the air force is working on unmanned fighter jets.[38] The advantage of such unmanned vehicles is clear: If one of these machines fails or is shot down, there will be no human casualties. As indicated above, it is not only the United States that is pursuing this kind of innovation; China is heavily investing in military applications empowered by AI as well. As a senior executive at China's third largest defense company puts it, "In future battlegrounds, there will be no people fighting."[39]

It is precisely because countries like China take these novel technologies of the Fourth Industrial Revolution so seriously that a response is required from the United States, a response that considers the implications in the realm of national security. China has given itself the ambitious goal to become the leading nation in all matters AI by the year 2030.[40] This goal is highly significant, considering the Russian president Vladimir Putin declared in 2017, "Artificial intelligence is the future, not only for Russia, but for all humankind. It comes with colossal opportunities, but also threats that are difficult to predict. Whoever becomes the leader in this sphere will become the ruler of the world."[41]

Even so, AI and its many applications are not the only factor in a potential future arms race between various major geopolitical powers. Besides utilizing autonomous vehicles and swarms of drones (which could be used for both intelligence-gathering and targeted attacks) the militaries of the future will make use of other technologies as well, such as hypersonic aircrafts and missiles, electromagnetic railguns, high-energy laser weapons, and augmented reality systems for combat soldiers.[42] In addition, the weapons of the future will also operate in a new physical realm; while traditional wars have been fought on land, at sea, and in the air, the major powers of the world will want to be equipped to fight

---

37. "In 2016, the United States demonstrated 103 aerial drones flying together in a swarm.... Not to be outdone, a few months later China demonstrated a 119-drone swarm." Scharre, *Army of None*, 21.

38. Middendorf, "Meet the U.S. Navy's Unmanned Ships." For an example from the Air Force, see Losey, "New in 2024."

39. Gibson et al., "Autonomous Systems in the Combat Environment," §16.

40. O'Meara, "Will China Lead," 427–28.

41. Vincent, "Putin Says," §2.

42. Willings, "32 Interesting and Incredibly Futuristic Weapons."

in outer space as well.⁴³ Space is a critical realm already at this point, because satellite communications have become so essential; any weapon system that could damage satellites is therefore a major threat.⁴⁴ With so much at stake, what could be said about these topics from a theological point of view?

A CHRISTIAN PERSPECTIVE ON SECURITY

I begin this section with questions about warfare in the era of the Fourth Industrial Revolution, while issues related to cybersecurity and the protection of privacy will be addressed later. When it comes to deploying autonomous weapon systems, the gut reaction of many Christians might be that the development of such weapons should be avoided at all costs. They may tend to agree with the "Campaign to Stop Killer Robots," an initiative formed in 2013 that advocates for a ban on lethal autonomous weapons systems (LAWS).⁴⁵ This organization argues it is unethical for a machine to have the authority to make the fateful decision of killing a human, and that therefore the ultimate decision always must lie with another human being. While I think it is valuable organizations like these exist, I also believe a ban is ultimately the wrong approach, for several reasons.

First, the idea that only humans are allowed to kill other people is somewhat vague as an ethical principle, especially considering humans often make mistakes. Historically, humans have been much smarter than both animals and machines, and it is therefore natural that *Homo sapiens* feels she or he should be in the driver's seat when high-stake decisions are made. This is also why it was previously taken for granted that humans are the best drivers on planet Earth, that there would never be a computer which could master a complex situation, such as traffic, better than a human (see chapter 1). However, this perception could quickly begin to change. It is quite possible that within twenty years or so, AI-powered autonomous vehicles will be much safer than human drivers. Similarly, it

43. For that reason, initiating the Space Force as a new branch of the military might have been one of President Trump's most strategic decisions. Hartmann, "Let's Get to Know."

44. Dawson, *War in Space*, 1–32.

45. Other organizations like the International Committee for Robot Arms Control (https://www.icrac.net), Human Rights Watch (https://www.hrw.org), and the Future of Life Institute (https://autonomousweapons.org) make a similar case as the Campaign to Stop Killer Robots (https://www.stopkillerrobots.org). Compare Kallenborn, "Partial Ban on Autonomous Weapons."

is also conceivable that an autonomous weapon system would make fewer mistakes than a human soldier. Casualties of so-called friendly fire (or fratricide), in particular, could be reduced to a minimum, once all the weapon systems of one country are able to communicate with each other.[46]

In addition, going back to the analogy of autonomous vehicles, human drivers not only make honest mistakes, but also put others willingly at risk—through reckless behavior (e.g., drunk driving) and emotional outbursts like road rage. Similar dynamics could be at play in human soldiers; a soldier might be under tremendous stress after an intense combat situation, and then proceed to engage in unethical behavior that contradicts the Geneva Convention—such as looting, committing rape, murdering civilians, killing prisoners of war, or torturing people. By contrast, combat machines could be programed in such a way that they always adhere to the Geneva Convention, and since machines have neither emotions nor ambitions of their own, they would not be tempted to ever behave otherwise.[47]

However, heinous terrorists and dictators could develop killer robots with a focus on raping, torturing, and murdering civilians. For this reason, responsible state actors need to be technologically prepared to counter such a nightmare scenario. Furthermore, a liberal democracy and global leader like the United States will need to have an appropriate response as authoritarian regimes like China and Russia develop autonomous weapons.[48] If America's adversaries advance at machine speed, while the United States military still operates at human speed, this would create an unsustainable imbalance.[49] As Bradford Tousley, the director of DARPA's Tactical Technology Office (TTO), explained to the author of *Army of None: Autonomous Weapons and the Future of War*, "those machines are going to be challenged by machines on the adversary's side, and a human can't respond to that. It's got to be machines responding to machines."[50]

---

46. However, this would only be the case for highly sophisticated systems. The current systems, such as the Russian Platform-M, may cause considerable collateral damage, if not properly controlled. Scharre, *Army of None*, 113–14.

47. Scharre, *Army of None*, 279–84.

48. See also the evaluation of AI weapons by the ethicist and theologian Jason Thacker: "I fear the lack of development of these weapons will do more harm than good. These tools should be used as deterrents against rogue states and groups." Thacker, *Age of AI*, 136.

49. This argument was made by Bob Work, the deputy secretary of defense from 2014 to 2017. Scharre, *Army of None*, 99.

50. Scharre, *Army of None*, 82.

Apart from this pragmatic argument of having advanced autonomous weapon systems that can serve as a powerful deterrent, there may also be an ethical argument in favor of increasingly using machines in war. For instance, John Canning, a retired US Navy weapons designer, proposed in a paper "an autonomous weapon that would not target people directly, but rather would target their weapons. For example, the autonomous weapon would look for the profile of an AK-47 and would aim to destroy the AK-47, not the person."[51] Ideally, this would eventually lead to a type of warfare in which "machines target machines—not people."[52]

Within the tradition of the classical just war theory, the intention when going to war must be to "correct a grave injustice" and "to protect the innocent"; wars of aggression are not acceptable.[53] What America needs to do is to reorganize its defensive capabilities so it can protect its citizens from the threats that will characterize the twenty-first century. Traditionally, the United States has invested in large and expensive platforms, such as aircraft carriers, long-range bombers, and helicopters.[54] The problem is that these systems can increasingly fall victim to relatively inexpensive weapons like swarms of drones or hypersonic missiles. These kinds of missiles can also hit targets in the continental United States and will require new types of defenses like high-energy lasers that can quickly identify and destroy incoming threats. Instead of trying to project power in far-away places, the US military must make it a priority to protect its own assets. In other words, as Christian Brose convincingly argues in *The Kill Chain: Defending America in the Future of High-Tech Warfare*, the United States needs to switch from an offensive to a defensive mindset.[55]

However, even if there is no physical attack on the nation's assets, these still need to be protected in cyberspace. As mentioned in the beginning of this chapter, cyberattacks are a constant reality, and it is likely this will continue to be an ongoing challenge for decades to come. In the United States alone, there are over six million businesses.[56] All these companies need to be able to protect the data of their suppliers and

---

51. Scharre, *Army of None*, 261.
52. Scharre, *Army of None*, 261; compare 355.
53. LiVecche and Gabush, "Just War Tradition."
54. Brose, *Kill Chain*, xvii–xxix, 12–16, 181–82.
55. Brose, *Kill Chain*, 188–98.
56. Dudley, "How Many Businesses."

customers—this is especially critical for big corporations because they handle such large databases, making them an attractive target for hackers.

In addition, there are many other institutions and infrastructure items that need to be protected in order to ensure the safety and well-being of a nation's population. For instance, this includes the over six thousand hospitals that supply healthcare in the United States and around 1.9 million farms needed for food production.[57] Furthermore, there are almost five thousand two hundred public airports, over twelve thousand five hundred utility-scale electric power plants, and more than 2.6 million miles of pipeline for the transportation of natural gas and oil.[58] By looking at this list of high-value items in the United States, one begins to understand how massive the task is to protect all of them, be it from terrorist attacks or from hackers who are merely motivated by money.

Protecting these assets is a major task for the governing authorities charged with punishing those who do wrong (Rom 13:4). Traditionally, Americans have been intentional about honoring those who rise to the occasion when it comes to protecting these physical assets—such as firefighters, police officers, and soldiers. Going forward, I think we as Christians could add to this list those who are willing and able to protect our nation's most valuable and most vulnerable assets in cyberspace. We need to encourage our young people to dream of becoming cybersecurity experts and hackers who use their skills for the common good. In most circles, hackers have a bad reputation today—and appropriately so, if they engage in criminal activity. However, if hackers put their skills to use in order to protect the data of individuals and organizations by finding out about potential shortcomings in the security system, then this is a process that needs to be encouraged.

As David Brumley, a computer scientist at Carnegie Mellon University, affirms, a chief concern today "is a shortage of cybersecurity experts. We have weak cyber locks because we're not training enough people how to be better cyber locksmiths."[59] Believers should be at the forefront of such a much-needed shift toward prioritizing cybersecurity. We can do so by encouraging our little boys and girls to dream big, to see themselves as warriors of righteousness in cyberspace who will protect

---

57. American Hospital Association, "Fast Facts on U.S. Hospitals"; USDA, "Farming and Farm Income."

58. Statista, "Number of Public and Private Airports"; EIA, "How Many Power Plants"; PHMSA, "General Pipeline FAQs."

59. Scharre, *Army of None*, 227.

the Pentagon, our power plants, and our pipelines against powerful and sinister foes, both foreign and domestic. Besides the desire and vision to work professionally as a benevolent hacker, Christians also need to give young people the opportunity to be trained in this field, considering that "currently, there exists a huge deficit of personnel who are skilled and trained in data analytics."[60] Consequently, we should double our efforts in opening up boot camps and tech schools, as well as offering excellent undergraduate and graduate programs in fields like cybersecurity, computer science, and data analysis at Christian colleges and universities. In doing so, we would not only address one of the most pressing needs our society currently has but also offer a promising and rewarding career path to young people (see chapters 2 and 3).

However, even in times of peace and in the absence of cyberattacks, Christians are still called to stand up for the value of privacy. In an age and within a system in which "data is the new oil," it is more important than ever that citizens own their data, know what happens to their data, and can make informed decisions about whether and with whom they want to share their data.[61] In a democracy, there should at least be a public debate about what happens with the footage of security cameras and the data collected by agencies such as the NSA.

Crucially, the debate about privacy and the ownership of personal data needs to move beyond the realm of government and must be applied to private corporations as well. The business model of tech giants like Google and Meta is powerfully seductive: They offer a service for one of the things people crave the most—human connection—and then make it available, seemingly for free. However, using Gmail or setting up a Facebook profile is not free at all. Rather, consumers pay with something that is arguably more valuable, and certainly more sensitive, than money. They pay with their personal data, giving up privacy in exchange for some form of online service.[62]

The data economy of big tech is currently based on a business model which consists in making sure consumers stay as long as possible on a corporation's website(s). Consequently, people spend countless hours every day playing mindless games on their phones, being manipulated into buying things they do not need, and clicking on their newsfeed toward

60. Johnson, "Cybersecurity Threat Landscape," 317.
61. Richards, *Why Privacy Matters*, 4, 41.
62. As the saying goes, "If you are not paying for the product, *you* are the product." Adams, *Freedom Bible*, 177 (emphasis original).

links telling them what they want to hear (which tend to be news items that promote fear, outrage, and extreme views of one sort or another). Even more established news outlets such as the *New York Times* have recently been criticized for promoting news digitally in a way that is good for their bottom line, but bad for democracy.[63]

As John C. Lennox highlights in his book *2084: Artificial Intelligence and the Future of Humanity*, both "surveillance capitalism" (where consumers voluntarily give their personal data to a few dominant corporations) and "surveillance communism" (the social credit score system implemented in Communist China) are a danger to human freedom.[64] Regarding the latter, Lennox warns,

> It is not hard to see that these plans represent a massive hacking of human beings and are taking the world a rather scary step towards the perfection of a (potentially global) dictatorship, the setting up of an "authoritarian dream world" whose ideology could spread around the world like a virus and whose legitimacy is secured by the most comprehensive and powerful state surveillance apparatus in history.[65]

As history has demonstrated time and again, the concentration of power in a single entity or person is highly dangerous. Technology should be used to increase people's choices and their political liberties, not to undermine them.

Given these challenges, it would be beneficial for the church to be part of conversations that try to envision a different kind of reality in cyberspace. It must be possible to be grateful for the many benefits the internet and social media have brought about, to use these platforms for the glory of God, and at the same time to be critical of the addictive and predatory business practices that are currently often behind these platforms. As Christians, we should think about alternatives and discuss them in the public square. For instance, to stand up for our values, we could:

- Pay a small monthly fee for certain online services on a smaller platform, in exchange for a less intrusive environment.

---

63. Such is the argument in Ungar-Sargon, *Bad News*.
64. Lennox, *2084*, 67–74.
65. Lennox, *2084*, 70.

- Switch to services that emphasize privacy and safety, such as the search engine DuckDuckGo instead of Google, and Signal or Telegram instead of WhatsApp.
- Install ad-blockers on our devices and make it a matter of principle to never click on a personalized ad (considering these ads are a major factor why people's personal data is being traded between various tech giants).
- Use cash instead of debit cards or credit cards to reduce being monitored with regards to our financial transactions.
- Vote in secret and in person by using a paper ballot in a voting booth on election day, instead of using a voting machine or voting by mail.[66]

One of the voices thinking theologically about the way cyberspace currently works is Phil Chen, a graduate from Fuller Theological Seminary and a serial entrepreneur and investor in the realm of innovative technologies.[67] Chen is worth quoting here in full as he reflects on the exodus narrative in the Bible and explains,

> Internet users are being worked to generate and build modern treasure houses for their overlords, using their own data as bricks. Within the walls of these modern pyramids is all of our personal data, which empowers and wealthifies the modern-day Pharaohs: Facebook, Apple, Amazon, and Google (known, with the addition of Netflix, as the FAANGs), coupled with their Asian counterparts Baidu, Alibaba, and Tencent.
>
> The father of the world wide web himself, Tim Berners-Lee, has called for a new architecture that places security, privacy, and ownership of data back where it belongs: with the people. We are currently in a crisis of giving away our data and digital identity for cheap endorphins, and surrendering all of our attention and power to the Big Data monolithic cloud companies, which mine that data for artificial intelligent agents and advertising revenue. In some cases, our data has been used by bad actors to steal money or confidential information, but in the worst cases, it has gone as far as impacting and influencing democratic processes.[68]

66. See also Véliz, *Privacy Is Power*, 77, 198–207, 219.
67. Chen, "Journey to a New Internet."
68. Quoted in Callaway, "Yes (to Technology)," 48–49.

As we think biblically about social media and online news, we may come to the conclusion that we need to leave the comforts of Egypt, so that we can be liberated to worship God. This might lead to difficult times of transition in which we wander in the wilderness for a while, but such a courageous step will then enable us to one day enter the promised land. This kind of more promising future could include new technologies that will enable people to enjoy greater privacy and security, such as the blockchain, which is one of the technologies that will be highlighted in the following chapter.

DISCUSSION QUESTIONS

1. What are your thoughts on Phil Chen's metaphor when he says that, similar to the Israelites in Exodus, internet users today are using their data (instead of bricks) to build up the giant tech corporations of our time?
2. What steps should or could believers take to protect their personal data?
3. How can the church motivate more young Christians to become professionals in areas like cybersecurity?
4. Are you for a ban of autonomous weapons? Why or why not?

SUGGESTIONS FOR FURTHER READING

- Carissa Véliz, *Privacy Is Power: Why and How You Should Take Back Control of Your Data* (2021). A passionate and practical plea to fight back against the widespread surveillance being exercised by governments and corporations.
- Joseph Steinberg et al., *Cybersecurity All-in-One for Dummies* (2023). A helpful overview on the subject, which includes concrete suggestions and tips.
- Amy B. Zegart, *Spies, Lies, and Algorithms: The History and Future of American Intelligence* (2022). Highlights new threats caused by technology, written by a highly respected authority from Stanford University.

- Robert J. Marks, *The Case for Killer Robots: Why America's Military Needs to Continue Development of Lethal AI* (2020). Explains why these weapons are necessary to keep aggressors at bay, written by a professor of engineering at Baylor University.
- Dan Saxon, *Fighting Machines: Autonomous Weapons and Human Dignity* (2022). An expert in international law argues against the use of autonomous weapons.
- Deane Baker, *Should We Ban Killer Robots?* (2022). Presents the main arguments for such a ban and then refutes them.

7

Productivity

MANY CENTURIES AGO, THE inventor of the game of chess, so legend tells us, presented his invention to the king who was in power at that time. The king was so impressed with the game that he asked the inventor what his reward should be for such a magnificent invention. The inventor replied, "Oh, I am not asking for much. Just have your servants place one grain of rice on the first of the sixty-four squares of this chessboard. Then two grains of rice on the second square, four on the next one, and so on, doubling the amount of rice on every square, until the very last one!" The king thought this was indeed a modest request and ordered a servant to place down the rice grains, following the calculation they had just agreed on. However, toward the end of the chess board, this would have required the production of billions of tons of rice, and the king had to acknowledge the inventor had outsmarted him. Even in modern times, it would be impossible to fulfill this request, considering that, globally, the annual production of rice reaches around five hundred million tons.[1]

Whether in ancient or in modern times, exponential growth is a powerful (and often underestimated) dynamic, and this observation is also true when it comes to the development of computers. When IBM began to build the first modern computers in the 1960s, these were massive machines that cost millions of dollars and weighed thousands of pounds, occupying entire rooms.[2] What made the personal computer, and later

---

1. Maths Careers, "Rice and Chessboard Legend."
2. Perry, "Computer Prices and Speed." Earlier examples of computers include the German Z3 from 1941, the ERA 1101 (which was introduced in 1950), and the TX-0

the smartphone, possible is a principle called Moore's Law, which goes back to the businessman and engineer Gordon E. Moore (1929–2023), a cofounder of Intel.[3] According to Moore's Law, the number of transistors on a microchip doubles roughly every two years, while at the same time the production cost for these chips is cut in half. Consequently, computers have become both more powerful and affordable over the years.

Recently, some experts have raised the alarm, pointing out the era of Moore's Law may be coming to an end. After all, the transistors on microchips are already infinitely small; placing a larger number of them in such a tiny space may therefore soon challenge the limits of physics.[4] However, it is also likely that remarkable innovations will be brought forth in the context of the Fourth Industrial Revolution, leading to new levels of productivity in the years and decades ahead. In the realm of computers, this may include the development of an entire new category of machines, such as quantum computers. Whether with or without quantum machines, greater computing power will enable new products and services; for instance, manufacturing processes could be revolutionized through the internet of things (IoT), and new kinds of services may become available through blockchain technologies.

In the opening section of this chapter, I begin by describing quantum computers and then briefly discuss the IoT and blockchain technologies. With regards to a new generation of computers, these could be based on a variety of technological breakthroughs. There are certainly challenges when it comes to the development of quantum machines, but it is a possibility worth exploring. Technologically speaking, the basic idea behind a quantum computer is that it does not rely on bits but on qubits. Traditional computers function in a binary way as the billions of transistors that form the "brain" of today's laptops and smartphones are either *on* (which is then designated with the number 1) or *off* (represented by a 0). Computers based on this principle can manage powerful calculations, but they also have their limitations.[5]

---

built by MIT researchers in 1956. Computer History Museum, "Timeline of Computer History."

3. Tardi, "What Is Moore's Law."

4. Amit Katwala points out the following limitations: (1) energy: the more transistors are on a chip, the more power the computer will need to operate; (2) heat: transistors performing calculations become hot, which is why cooling systems are needed; (3) physics: once transistors are built on a very small scale, "the laws of physics change, and quantum mechanics takes over." Katwala, *Quantum Computing*, 21.

5. Sutor, *Dancing with Qubits*, 4–6.

One way to illustrate this is to think about a problem with many options, such as finding one's way through a maze. As the authors of the article "How Does a Quantum Computer Work?" explain, "If you think of a computer solving a problem as a mouse running through a maze [looking for cheese], a classical computer finds its way through by trying every path until it reaches the end."[6] By contrast, quantum computers are based on the principles of quantum physics, on how things work at the molecular and even submolecular level. In a way, a quantum computer behaves like "a programmable molecule," which is why quantum computers are better at dealing with complex systems characterized by uncertainties and probabilities.[7] The quantum mechanics at play in these machines include principles like superposition (the ability of quantum systems to exist in several states at the same time) and entanglement (the correlation between two or more quantum systems). To apply this to the example above of the mouse running through the maze: Contrary to traditional computers, "the superposition state would contain all the possible routes. And then you'd have to collapse the state of superposition to reveal the likeliest path to the cheese."[8]

To the non-scientific reader, all this talk about molecules and superposition (and cheese) probably sounds rather mysterious. This is because quantum computers are based on quantum physics, a scientific field of inquiry which is, in itself, somewhat of a mystery. Accordingly, building quantum computers that are of practical use comes with its unique set of challenges. In fact, these challenges are quite formidable, possibly so much so that quantum computers may not be the way forward when it comes to achieving new levels of productivity. However, there is reason for at least cautious optimism considering several breakthroughs have been achieved in recent years.

- In 2019, researchers at Google announced they had developed the chip Sycamore, which powers a quantum computer that performed a series of complex calculations within a few minutes—something a traditional supercomputer would have needed ten thousand years for.[9]

---

6. Tabb et al., "How Does a Quantum Computer Work?," §10.
7. Katwala, *Quantum Computing*, 101.
8. Tabb et al., "How Does a Quantum Computer Work?," §17.
9. Scientists speak of quantum supremacy as a point at which quantum computers can solve problems which would be practically unsolvable for traditional computers. However, whether quantum supremacy was achieved through this event is unclear, considering that competitors of Google (like IBM) have questioned the details of this

- Then, in the beginning of 2021, physicists at Google revealed they had made significant progress in reducing the likelihood of errors while operating a quantum computer.[10] (Due to the uncertainty associated with quantum physics, the calculations of quantum computers can be riddled with errors; consequently, these machines can only become precise enough to be useful in real-world scenarios if the problem of errors is successfully addressed).[11]

- In January 2022 it was reported that a team of Australian researchers had achieved an accuracy of over 99 percent while operating a quantum computer. As Professor Andrea Morello, who led the effort, explains, "When the errors are so rare, it becomes possible to detect them and correct them when they occur. This shows that it is possible to build quantum computers that have enough scale, and enough power, to handle meaningful computation."[12]

- In 2023, IBM created a 433-qubit machine called Osprey, which was then the world's largest quantum computer. However, at the end of the year, a California start-up called Atom Computing built a quantum computer with 1180 qubits, which, instead of superconducting wires used by Google and IBM, "uses neutral atoms trapped by lasers in a 2-dimensional grid."[13]

Once the technical issues are solved, quantum computers could be employed to master a variety of tasks that are currently unsolvable because there is simply not enough computing power accessible to analyze the available data in a reasonable amount of time. For instance, quantum computers could aid in the development of more accurate models for analyzing and predicting climate change. They could also be used

---

comparison between the Sycamore-chip powered engine and traditional supercomputers. Katwala, *Quantum Computing*, 1, 5–6. The Chinese have also been working on alternatives, and "in December 2020, a group of scientists at the University of Science and Technology in Hefei, China, claimed to have attained quantum supremacy on a photon-based quantum computer that they said was 10,000 times faster than Google's Sycamore chip." Katwala, *Quantum Computing*, 121.

10. Cho, "Physicists Move Closer."

11. Consequently, achieving greater accuracy (or fidelity) is a crucial step toward quantum supremacy, another field of the Fourth Industrial Revolution in which the United States and China are competing against each other. Chik, "Chinese Team's Classical Computing."

12. Madzik et al., "Major Breakthrough," §4.

13. Wilkins, "Record-Breaking Quantum Computer," §2.

to create new levels of encryption that are so complex they cannot be cracked with the current technologies available.[14] In addition, quantum computers may also lead to breakthroughs in the advancement of AI, the development of new drugs, the creation of new materials (for instance, with regards to battery technologies), and the in-depth analysis of highly complex systems, such as traffic.[15]

Another technology through which we could see new levels of efficiency and productivity is the IoT, particularly when applied to manufacturing.[16] In traditional manufacturing, efficiency was achieved through technologies like the conveyor belt, which led to the kind of standardization of processes that enabled the mass production of items that would otherwise have been prohibitively expensive. However, in the Fourth Industrial Revolution, customers may demand more and more personalized products, and for that the traditional factory is too static. This is where the IoT comes in; the vision is to design a smart factory, one in which every machine, every transportation unit, and every single product is equipped with sensors—thereby enabling all these items to communicate with each other at any time.

Due to the rapid development of new technologies, these kinds of sensors and digital interfaces now include a wide variety of products, such as accelerometers, audio and video monitors, barcode scanners, barometers, cameras, GPS devices, gyroscope sensors (which measure the angular motion of an object), humidity gauges, infrared sensors, level sensors, magnetometers, motion sensors, pressure sensors, sound sensors, thermometers, vibration sensors, and water quality sensors, as well as technologies like radar, sonar, and LiDAR (see also chapter 1 and the description of self-driving cars).[17]

---

14. On the other hand, this opportunity in terms of cybersecurity is also a threat to the currently existing system. This challenge is called "quantum surprise" or "Q-Day," which refers to a possible date in the future when "a quantum computer is developed that can break most modern cryptographic standards. If one country gets there first, it could cause problems." Katwala, *Quantum Computing*, 89.

15. Katwala, *Quantum Computing*, 2–3.

16. Alternative descriptions of this phenomenon include the industrial internet of things (IIoT), the "Factory of Things," and "Smart Factory Wave." In addition, "The Internet of Everything (IoE) (a term that Cisco helped to pioneer) takes this notion a step further by referring to not only the physical infrastructure of smart devices and services but also their impacts on people, businesses, and society." Shackelford, *Internet of Things*, xiii–xv.

17. Greengard, *Internet of Things*, 135; Shackelford, *Internet of Things*, 31.

These different types of sensors are able to detect "light, sound, temperature, magnetic fields, motion, moisture, tactile pressure, gravity, electrical fields, chemicals, and much more."[18] As such, these sensors are becoming "the eyes, ears, nose, and fingers of the IoT," and are therefore "dramatically redefining how machines interact with the world around us and how humans interact with each other."[19] Of course, it is not enough to simply collect massive amounts of data through myriads of devices; this data must then also be organized and interpreted. The amount of data available even today is already staggering, and through technologies like the IoT humanity will enter a new dimension when it comes to collecting and classifying data (Table 9).[20]

Table 9. Data Sizes from Byte to Quettabyte

Term	Number of Bytes	Example
Byte	1	A single text character (1 byte consists of 8 bits)
Kilobyte	10^3	A short email (1024 bytes)
Megabyte	10^6	A digital image
Gigabyte	10^9	Around 250 downloaded songs
Terabyte	10^{12}	Around 250 movies
Petabyte	10^{15}	500 billion pages of printed text
Exabyte	10^{18}	250 million DVDs
Zettabyte	10^{21}	Annual (estimated) internet traffic in 2016
Yottabyte	10^{24}	Largest term to measure magnitude, until 2022
Ronnabyte	10^{27}	Total storage in a large datacenter
Quettabyte	10^{30}	Measurement for future computers?

That is why, apart from sensors, other technologies like the cloud, machine learning, and computer vision analytics are also essential for the IoT to revolutionize entire business practices, such as production processes and supply chain management. Here are some examples of how specific companies and industries are benefiting from this new level of hyperconnectivity:

---

18. Greengard, *Internet of Things*, 65.
19. Greengard, *Internet of Things*, 53, 63.
20. Puiu, "How Big Is a Petabyte."

- The Italian luxury carmaker Lamborghini, for instance, "has built a smart factory specifically for its sport utility vehicle, Urus." In this facility, Lamborghini's highly skilled workers "control every aspect of production on site, as well as remotely, using tablets. The system has sped production and completely eliminated paper documents."[21]
- In the agricultural sector, "farmers use sensors embedded in machinery and fields to dispense fertilizers and pesticides at more precise—and environmentally friendly—levels."[22]
- Rolls Royce is not only a luxury car brand but also the world's second-largest manufacturer of jet engines (after General Electric). Rolls Royce collects data from both its jet engines and the flights and airplanes at which they are used, thereby enabling predictive maintenance schedules that help their customers, the airlines, optimize their operations.[23]
- Speaking of airlines, many large global airlines are already using IoT systems that enable them to save billions of dollars in fuel costs every year. They achieve this by "better understanding weather, mechanical conditions of equipment, and load factors," which enables them to "fly at the optimal altitude and take the optimal route."[24]

As these examples demonstrate, the IoT brings changes to sectors as diverse as farming, manufacturing, and transportation. It can be expected these technologies will be used more and more because, "when they are used effectively, these connected systems introduce massive productivity and efficiency gains, while lowering costs and improving safety," as Samuel Greengard explains in *The Internet of Things*.[25] Apart from a wide range of industries, the IoT will also become attractive in the nonprofit sector, for example among environmental organizations wanting to track the populations and movements of endangered species. Another area with exciting potential is the public sector, as cities will begin to monitor the patterns of energy consumption and traffic flows in order to reduce waste, congestion, and pollution levels.[26]

---

21. Greengard, *Internet of Things*, 154.
22. Greengard, *Internet of Things*, 151.
23. Olavsrud, "Rolls Royce."
24. Greengard, *Internet of Things*, 147.
25. Greengard, *Internet of Things*, 134.
26. Greengard, *Internet of Things*, 14, 47. The concept of smart cities could become

In addition to smart factories and smart cities, individuals might also embrace the concept of the smart home, and the IoT already plays a significant role in consumer electronics. Examples of such products include smart TVs, smart thermostats, smart lighting switches, surveillance cameras, smart security systems and monitoring devices, automated garden irrigation systems, cleaning robots, and interconnected appliances that can be managed via digital assistants and smart speakers.[27] Apart from a smart house, some consumers may also be attracted to wearable devices, such as smart watches, smart glasses, and smart clothing. Granted, some of these products may seem like expensive toys at this point, or maybe even something many people would find annoying or intrusive. However, once consumers perceive a tangible advantage (for instance, in terms of comfort, safety, or health benefits), it is likely that more and more people will start buying IoT products. For example, Linde, a manufacturer of forklift trucks, offers interactive warning vests that alert the "wearers of potential dangers using light signals, vibrations, and acoustic warnings, thereby maximizing safety in both inside and outside areas."[28]

Besides the manufacturing of various physical products, it is especially the realm of services that is essential for many advanced economies. One of the technologies that could bring new levels of productivity in the service sector is the blockchain, which, at its core is "a shared, trusted, distributed ledger that everyone can inspect, but which no single user controls."[29] Another definition puts it this way, "The blockchain, at its heart, is a method for disseminating knowledge. It is a public record of information, stored and maintained through a decentralized system of peers, and secured by sophisticated cryptographical algorithms."[30] In recent years, blockchain has become primarily known as the technology that powers cryptocurrencies, with Bitcoin being especially prominent.

However, besides cryptocurrencies, it is conceivable the blockchain could be applied to other sectors as well, such as banking, accounting, law, air travel, real estate, waste management, e-commerce, and publishing.[31]

---

particularly attractive in large cities in the developing world, such as in Mumbai, India, with its over twenty million inhabitants. Wilkins, *Internet of Things*, 30.

27. In addition, companies like Kohler offer smart toilets, smart showers, and smart mirrors (https://www.smarthome.kohler.com).

28. Linde, "Bodyguard 2.0."

29. Shackelford, *Internet of Things*, 118.

30. Magnuson, *Blockchain Democracy*, 60.

31. CB Insights, "Banking Is Only the Beginning."

As an article written by two experts from Indiana University affirms, "From making businesses more efficient to recording property deeds to engendering the growth of 'smart' contracts and even securing medical devices, blockchain technology is now being investigated by a huge range of organizations and is attracting billions of dollars in venture funding."[32] Blockchain is attractive whenever it is important to store or exchange confidential information, thereby potentially affecting every major segment of the economy. Still, we will begin by looking at Bitcoin, considering this application has been so prominent in the news over the past few years.[33]

Bitcoin was first introduced in 2008 through a white paper with the title "Bitcoin: A Peer-to-Peer Electronic Cash System," which was written by Satoshi Nakamoto, a person (or group) that has remained unidentified to this day.[34] Satoshi envisioned Bitcoin as a digital currency, through which people would be able to make financial transactions without the help of a third party (such as a bank, or an app like Venmo). Whether Bitcoin can live up to this promise remains to be seen considering this cryptocurrency also has its disadvantages. For example, one reason people want to circumvent a third party, such as a bank, is to avoid paying fees. However, Bitcoin has an indirect fee, because in order to calculate new transactions, these transactions need to be verified (or "mined"), and the reason these miners become engaged in this effort is because they are paid in bitcoin.[35]

However, for many ardent supporters, Bitcoin is much more than a currency; it is connected to the libertarian idea of being independent from traditional power brokers like governments, banks, and corporations. For instance, the renowned (and controversial) psychologist Jordan B. Peterson had a conversation with four advocates of Bitcoin named Gigi Der, John Vallis, Robert Breedlove, and Richard James. During this podcast event recorded on May 13, 2021, Peterson summarized what he had learned about Bitcoin as follows: "So [Bitcoin is] completely transparent. It's completely distributed. There's no centralized authority. It can't be cracked. It can't be stolen. It doesn't inflate. It can't be inflated. It isn't subject to—at least so far—to any form of overt administrative control."[36]

32. Shackelford and Myers, "Block-by-Block."
33. E.g., Sidel et al., "Almost Half a Billion"; Worrachate, "Bitcoin Could Pass $100,000"; Renteria et al., "El Salvador to Transfer."
34. Batey, "Brief History of Bitcoin."
35. Mehta et al., *Bubble or Revolution?*, 16–18.
36. McShane, "Jordan Peterson Releases," §8.

However, others are less enthusiastic, pointing out that Bitcoin has several weaknesses when it comes to using it as an alternative currency. For example, Bitcoin's security and privacy relies on the private key each owner holds—if this key is lost, there is no way to regain access to one's bitcoins (precisely because there is no third party, such as a bank, to turn to).[37] On the other hand, if anybody gets hold of a private key, "the money is theirs—and if they steal it, it's practically irreversible."[38] In addition, "while credit card transactions go through in seconds, Bitcoin transactions take an average of ten minutes to go through," and the fee for these transactions fluctuate, as they go up when demand is high.[39]

Although Bitcoin was the first digital currency, it has not remained the only one. Remarkably, there are now thousands of different cryptocurrencies, including Ethereum, Basic Attention Token (BAT), Tether, Binance Coin, and Monero.[40] In some cases, these cryptocurrencies aim to address some of the shortcomings of Bitcoin. Ethereum, for instance, was invented by the Russian-Canadian computer scientist Vitalik Buterin in 2013 and includes the option to run mini-apps and smart contracts.[41] Nonetheless, even without these additional features, Bitcoin can still be an attractive option, particularly as a form of investment that—similarly to investing in certain stocks—has the potential for high returns, for those who are willing to deal with the volatility.

Having said that, the main application for blockchain technologies may not be related to cryptocurrencies but using it to optimize processes in other sectors of the economy. One way to do that is through setting up public blockchains. For instance, "in 2016, a London-based group noticed that musicians were having trouble trademarking their band names, leading to identically-named bands bickering over who had the name first."[42] In response to this problem the group started a blockchain-based company called BandNameVault, "which would let any band register their name on a blockchain for $15."[43] Technically speaking, this is a great idea—because the blockchain is public, anyone can see which band

37. Mehta et al., *Bubble or Revolution?*, 46.
38. Mehta et al., *Bubble or Revolution?*, 78.
39. Mehta et al., *Bubble or Revolution?*, 68.
40. Daly, "How Many Cryptocurrencies Are There"; Mehta et al., *Bubble or Revolution?*, 104.
41. Mehta et al., *Bubble or Revolution?*, 108–14.
42. Mehta et al., *Bubble or Revolution?*, 147.
43. Mehta et al., *Bubble or Revolution?*, 147.

names were registered at exactly what point in time, thereby avoiding any fights over who came first. However, from a practical point of view, BandNameVault does not add much value for those who register, because such a registration cannot be defended in court.

For reasons like these, public blockchains have not had much impact so far. The greater potential probably lies in business blockchains, meaning in ledger systems that only a selected group of people has access to, such as those working for the company that owns the blockchain. As Ginni Rometty, the CEO of IBM, explains, "Anything that you can conceive of as a supply chain, blockchain can vastly improve its efficiency—it doesn't matter if it's people, numbers, data, money."[44] Walmart took this principle to heart when it was faced with a supply chain problem in 2018, when the United States had to deal with romaine lettuce that had been contaminated by *E. coli* bacteria. With the paper-based systems in place at the time, it was practically impossible to track each delivery back to the farmer who had grown a particular crop that turned out to be problematic. That is when Walmart, in cooperation with IBM, created a blockchain that made such tracking possible. With their entire supply chain digitized, the company "could now trace a given produce shipment to a Walmart all the way back to the original farm in 2.2 seconds, an over one hundred thousand-fold speedup."[45]

Another successful example comes from X-Box, which began to use a business blockchain to automatically pay royalties to its many external content creators. Video games require a large number of specialists to work together, such as character designers, musicians, and special effects studios. These artists often work on a freelance basis and are then paid according to how often the game they worked on is sold in the market. Managing all these details is usually a formidable undertaking, but through the smart contracts embedded in a blockchain created by Microsoft's cloud-computing arm (Azure), X-Box was able to automate this task and thereby save considerable amounts of time and money.[46]

Beyond the business world, blockchain could also be applied in the realm of government, for example in elections. The latter was tried in a very limited trial run (limited to two counties) in West Virginia. While this was a praiseworthy initiative aiming to make voting more accessible to people, it was also problematic because it involved insecure devices

44. Quoted in Buckenmaier et al., "Anything That You Can," §1.
45. Mehta et al., *Bubble or Revolution?*, 156.
46. Mehta et al., *Bubble or Revolution?*, 162.

and applications, such as people's mobile phones and apps. As Joseph Lorenzo Hall, the chief technologist at the Center for Democracy and Technology, critiqued: "Mobile voting is a horrific idea . . . . It's internet voting on people's horribly secured devices, over our horrible networks, to servers that are very difficult to secure without a physical paper record of the vote."[47]

However, in the big scheme of things, it is important to recognize blockchain is a technology which aims to decentralize power and therefore has a democratizing element to it. As William Magnusen affirms in *Blockchain Democracy: Technology, Law and the Rule of the Crowd*, "the blockchain is simply a technology that allows us to decentralize things that we have typically thought of as requiring centralization."[48] Consequently, Magnusen suggests, the blockchain might be similar to other technologies from the past that created new possibilities for people and gave individuals more freedom, such as the printing press, the motorized car, and the internet. In that sense, the blockchain is a technology that will most likely be widely used, because "it satisfies this deep desire for a 'say' in all our fundamental interactions."[49] Given the disruptive potential of the blockchain and other technologies of the Fourth Industrial Revolution, it is crucial for Christians to think about what these innovations might mean from a theological point of view.

A CHRISTIAN PERSPECTIVE ON PRODUCTIVITY

In the following, I highlight three aspects related to the technologies above: (1) the importance of personal ownership from a biblical perspective; (2) the value of productivity in God's economy; and (3) the idea of progress as found in a Christian worldview. First, from a biblical perspective, the concept of private property is of critical importance. After all, the Ten Commandments include the instruction not to steal (Exod 20:15; Deut 5:19; compare Matt 19:18; Mark 10:19; Luke 18:20; Rom 13:9), and stealing would not even be an issue if everything simply belonged to everybody (or nobody). Furthermore, the Tenth Commandment admonishes people to "not set your desire on your neighbor's house or land, his male or female servant, his ox or donkey, or anything that belongs to your

---

47. Quoted in O'Sullivan, "West Virginia to Introduce," §11.
48. Magnusen, *Blockchain Democracy*, 210.
49. Magnusen, *Blockchain Democracy*, 212.

neighbor" (Deut 5:21). In addition, private ownership is an important theme not only in the Ten Commandments, but in other parts of the Torah as well, such as when it regulates principles of restitution (Exod 21:33–22:15; Lev 6:1–5; Num 5:6–7), secure boundaries (Deut 19:14; 27:17), and inheritance (Num 27:1–11; Deut 21:15–17).

The inheritance of each tribe was carefully identified in Scripture (Num 34–36; Josh 13–19; Ezek 45:8; 47–48), and the piece of land allotted to a particular family was supposed to stay within that family (Lev 25:8–34; 1 Kgs 21; Ezek 46:16–18). That is why concepts like the kinsman-redeemer were so important because, according to this law, "land sold by a person could be bought back by a relative so as to keep the land in the family."[50] This is one reason why the prophets spoke out against economic injustice, criticizing the rich who bought one field and house after another, thereby taking away the inheritance of the weak and poor (Isa 5:8; Mic 2:1–2). The ideal, both during Solomon's historical reign and in the eschatological vision of the prophets, was that everyone would sit "under their own vine and under their own fig tree" (1 Kgs 4:25; Mic 4:4; compare Zech 3:10), thereby enjoying their personal property, their own piece of land.[51]

Granted, in the New Testament, there is a strong call toward contentment and radical generosity, a message beginning with John the Baptist that is then also found in both Jesus and Paul (e.g., Luke 3:11; 12:22–34; 1 Tim 6:6–10). However, even the call to give up material possessions for the sake of the kingdom of God presupposes private property, since one can only relinquish and share things that one possessed in the first place.[52] This call to give up one's possessions is always voluntary; the decision is up to the individual, not government, the church, or any other authority.

That is why the apostle Peter in the incident involving the land sale of Ananias and Saphira confronted them by saying, "How is it that Satan has so filled your heart that you have lied to the Holy Spirit and have kept for yourself some of the money you received for the land?" (Acts 5:3). However, then Peter also asked the two rhetorical questions, "Didn't it belong to you before it was sold? And after it was sold, wasn't

---

50. Hill and Walton, *Survey of the Old Testament*, 252.

51. The phrase was frequently used by George Washington, and can be seen as "creating an American metaphor for liberty in the nation." Dreisbach, *Reading the Bible*, 211.

52. Compare Trudolyubov, *Tragedy of Property*, 66–68.

the money at your disposal?" (v. 4a), thereby confirming the principle of private property both with regards to the land and the money they earned by selling their land. The problem was that Ananias and Saphira had been deceitful, which is why Peter ends by saying, "What made you think of doing such a thing? You have not lied just to human beings but to God" (v. 4b).

In the context of the Fourth Industrial Revolution, new technologies may enable people to affirm new forms of private ownership. Throughout the centuries, there have always been small minorities who felt called to a monastic lifestyle, but for most believers their personal belongings form an important part of their sense of identity and security. As discussed above, the blockchain may be a pathway for giving people a sense of privacy, ownership, and control, as this technology can provide a certain independence from powerful agents like corporations, banks, and the government. Decentralization could be a contribution to the common good by fostering the democratization of power structures and encouraging new forms of ownership. For example, as some art critics have argued, through the blockchain "there's finally a way to prove that you, and only you, own a piece of digital art."[53]

Of course, not everyone gets excited about owning a piece of digital art, but technologies like the IoT and 3D printing also have the potential of bringing a new quality to the physical items that people own. Ever since the First Industrial Revolution, consumers have gotten used to the idea of being able to buy standardized products at a low price. However, the downside of this system is that people must pay the price of conformity, in addition to the monetary amount the item costs. This economic model of massification is a significant departure from the previous economic system, in which craftsmen like potters and carpenters produced customized products, while women made their own blankets and clothes, thereby creating beautiful items with a personal touch.

Through technology, we might be able to return to a way of producing and buying things that are more personalized. Rather than going to giant stores like Walmart filled with cheap products that were made in China's massive factories and that are often soon thrown away again, people might then turn more toward local artisans and their handmade products. In doing so, Christians could choose to have fewer things, as they embrace uniquely made items that are of higher quality and last longer.

---

53. Mehta et al., *Bubble or Revolution?*, 117.

While private ownership and property laws are some of the foundation stones of economic development, productivity gains are essential for economic growth.[54] Theologically speaking, gains in productivity are important because they point to biblical concepts like fruitfulness and progression. When God created humans in the *imago Dei* (in God's image), being fruitful and taking dominion over the world around them was part of the creation mandate (Gen 1:26–28). Then, in Gen 2, Adam was entrusted with cultivating the garden, which—in a pre-fall world without thistles and thorns—would have led to great levels of fruitfulness, with all the different plants and trees that were available.

In the New Testament, Jesus often drew on analogies from nature to encourage fruitfulness in spiritual matters among his disciples, such as in the parable of the sower, where the seed falling on good soil produces an abundant harvest of a thirty-, sixty-, or hundred-fold return (Matt 13:1–23; Mark 4:1–20; Luke 8:4–15). Similarly, Jesus declared in the Gospel of John,

> I am the true vine, and my Father is the gardener. He cuts off every branch in me that bears no fruit, while every branch that does bear fruit he prunes so that it will be even more fruitful. You are already clean because of the word I have spoken to you. Remain in me, as I also remain in you. No branch can bear fruit by itself; it must remain in the vine. Neither can you bear fruit unless you remain in me. I am the vine; you are the branches. If you remain in me and I in you, you will bear much fruit; apart from me you can do nothing. . . . This is to my Father's glory, that you bear much fruit, showing yourselves to be my disciples. (15:1–8)

Much could be written about this well-known passage, which would go beyond the scope of this volume. Suffice it to say that Jesus here speaks of bearing fruit, and even much fruit, which points to a hopeful vision in which believers are on a pathway of growth.

Granted, the Bible does not use words like "productivity," but I think there is a connection to biblical themes like fruitfulness, multiplication, and growth. In *Ploductivity: A Practical Theology of Work and Wealth*, the Reformed theologian Douglas Wilson contributes to this discussion by explaining that tools that allow humans to be productive can be

---

54. See, for example, the third chapter ("Property") in Ferguson, *Civilization*, 96–140.

characterized as a form of wealth.[55] Wilson acknowledges the Bible does not talk much about tools and technology, so this is an area Christians might therefore easily overlook. In contrast, Scripture does have a lot to say about wealth, and so examining those Bible passages can help us to construct a biblical view of productivity. "Wealth," says Wilson, can be "monetary, technological, or otherwise," and as such it "is simply and solely a good thing, a gift of God."[56] However, because we live in a fallen world, wealth (and any technological tool) can seduce us into sinful behavior and attitudes, such as an arrogant self-sufficiency and the vanity of idolatry, as well as lack of concern for the poor and oppression. Consequently, "we should regard our tools the same way we regard our money—with grateful suspicion."[57]

Such grateful suspicion is necessary because technological tools can be both a blessing and a curse. As Ben Witherington explains in *Work: A Kingdom Perspective on Labor*, "The good news about labor-saving devices is that they take some of the Fall, some of the toilsomeness of our labor."[58] However, "the bad news is that by making labor easier they make labor more apt to be undertaken."[59] As is so often the case when it comes to matters of technology, such ambivalence leads to a paradox: The "oddity of technological advances in each generation (internal combustion engine, electrical appliances, computer, and email) has been that the very devices designed, at least in part, to reduce human labor have actually created more work!"[60]

Nonetheless, tools that lead to productivity gains are important on both the individual and societal level because they help people to save time and therefore become more productive. As suggested above when discussing the IoT, smart appliances and robots will take care of many daily chores, but this will then lead to the question: What could or should people do with their additional free time? In the technology-driven age we live in, there is a real danger people will become increasingly lonely. Much of the recent internet boom has been related to social media and the smartphone, technologies that facilitate connection with other

---

55. Wilson, *Ploductivity*, 99.
56. Wilson, *Ploductivity*, 21.
57. Wilson, *Ploductivity*, 32.
58. Witherington, *Work*, 134.
59. Witherington, *Work*, 134.
60. Witherington, *Work*, 134; compare 159.

people. However, the reality is these applications and devices also have the tendency to isolate us from each other.

This problem has been documented in a number of recent books, including *The Big Disconnect: The Story of Technology and Loneliness* (by Giles Slade), *Alone Together: Why We Expect More from Technology and Less from Each Other* (by Sherry Turkle), and *The Lonely Century: How to Restore Human Connection in a World That's Pulling Apart* (by Noreena Hertz). Given these concerning developments and trends, the church has a missional opportunity by pointing people to what is truly important in life: relationships. Yes, technologies of the Fourth Industrial Revolution will make life more convenient as new gadgets and services will help us to save time—but then people need to channel this additional free time in the right direction. The biblical priority we as Christians can offer to an increasingly isolated world is to focus on our relationship with God, which can include intentional times of solitude. In addition, Christ invites us to a life of community in which we love one another, bear one another's burdens, encourage one another, and show hospitality to one another (John 13:34; Gal 6:2; 1 Thess 5:11; 1 Pet 4:9).

Finally, growing degrees of productivity can lead to new levels of prosperity and overall progress in terms of personal and societal development. The latter is important when examining the worldview of the Bible, whose metanarrative begins in a garden (the Garden of Eden) but culminates in a city (the New Jerusalem). When God created Paradise, he had a natural environment in mind in which humans would be surrounded by plants, trees, and animals. However, this vision was not static. In the description of the Garden, precious metals, such as gold and onyx, are mentioned as well, thereby pointing to advanced production modes like mining and metallurgy (Gen 2:12). In addition, the Garden of Eden had "a prime geographic location for civilizational development" as it sat "at the intersection of four great rivers (Pishon, Tigris, Gihon, Euphrates)."[61]

Then, in the closing chapters of the Bible, in envisioning the eternal state, when God would dwell among humans once more, John saw a gigantic and sophisticated city (Rev 21:1–22:5). Therefore, one could conclude, human history is moving toward a more complex environment during this age of redemption in which we currently live—even if there will always be many shortcomings in all that humans create.

---

61. Ganski, "Sacrament and Technology," 81.

(Unfortunately, many of our cities today are certainly a testimony to the fallen nature of humanity).[62]

Nonetheless, this idea of progression, that history is moving toward a goal, has been one of the major contributions of the Judeo-Christian worldview to humanity.[63] All around the globe, the traditional worldviews of many cultures look back to the past, toward a golden age during which things were ideal. To some extent, this perspective is found in Scripture as well, such as in Chronicles where David is presented as an idealized king, and where the subsequent kings of Judah are then all compared to him. However, the Jews were not only looking back to David but also anticipating a future king in the line of David, a messianic king whose kingdom would be glorious and everlasting, thereby promising a future that would be far better than anything that had ever existed in the past (Pss 2; 72; Isa 9:6–7; 11; Dan 2:44; 7:13–14, 27).

This captivating vision of a coming kingdom became even more tangible through the kingdom of God that John the Baptist and Jesus announced. Jesus made clear his followers had something to look forward to—his future kingdom—but he also emphasized how this eschatological reality was already breaking into the present (Matt 4:23; 8:11; 9:35; 10:7–8; 12:28; 13:31–33; 25:34; 26:29; Luke 17:21; 18:29–30; 19:11–27; 22:29–30). Due to this framework, Christians are a people of hope. Inspired by the vision of a messianic kingdom and empowered by God's Spirit within them, they refuse to accept the status quo. They refuse to accept a world of hunger, disease, violence, injustice, and destruction. They also refuse to believe those who promise any kind of simple solution to the world's problems, knowing that the final triumph of redemption belongs to God, and to God alone.

However, in the meantime, Christians are called to get to work, driven by an unquenchable hope and the vision of a better future. Given the vast improvements in terms of life expectancy and other key indicators in

---

62. Given this tension and since the majority of the world's population now lives in urban areas, urban missions is an important topic in current missiologies. See, for instance, Greenway and Monsma, *Cities: Missions' New Frontier*; Van Engen and Tiersma, *God So Loves the City*.

63. As a Jesuit scholar affirms, "Among world religions, moreover, Christianity is the only one which has developed a close alliance with secular (and international) learning." Fudpucker, "Through Christian Technology," 36. This is one reason why "the Bible is unique in its account of a progressively unfolding salvation history, so much so that the modern idea of progress is unknown outside the Christian ambience." Fudpucker, "Through Christian Technology," 37.

the past two hundred years, it can be expected technology will continue to play a prominent role in improving people's lives. To what extent technologies like the IoT and the blockchain will contribute to such a hopeful vision remains to be seen. However, one thing is clear: All these devices will consume electricity, and lots of it. For this reason, energy is the topic we need to address in the following chapter.

DISCUSSION QUESTIONS

1. In your opinion, do blockchain technologies contribute to making society more democratic? Why or why not?
2. How is technology helping or hindering you to be productive in the kingdom of God?
3. Read Deut 8:10–20. How would you apply this passage to themes like tools, technology, and productivity?
4. What can the church do to help people who feel lonely in our technology-saturated world?

SUGGESTIONS FOR FURTHER READING

- Douglas Wilson, *Ploductivity: A Practical Theology of Work and Wealth* (2020). Presents a cautiously optimist worldview when it comes to tools and technology, including practical principles regarding one's personal productivity.
- Darrow L. Miller, *Discipling Nations: The Power of Truth to Transform Cultures* (2018). Argues that worldviews play a crucial role in bringing about positive change in entire societies.
- Daniel Hershberger, *Bitcoin Is Better: Natural Money That Works for the Working Class* (2023). Envisions Bitcoin as the future of money with the potential of battling inflation and creating a better world, written by a Christian family man and entrepreneur.
- Samuel Greengard, *The Internet of Things* (2021). A readable and informative introduction to the topic, written by a well-known business and technology writer.

- Michio Kaku, *Quantum Supremacy: How the Quantum Computer Revolution Will Change Everything* (2023). An easy-to read explanation of quantum technology and how it could help humanity to solve some of the major challenges that lie ahead.

- Noreena Hertz, *The Lonely Century: How to Restore Human Connection in a World That's Pulling Apart* (2021). Identifies a variety of factors, including technology, why loneliness is becoming a major crisis of our time.

8

Energy

THE PRECISE DATE HUMAN beings on this Earth first mastered the use of fire is unknown to us. However, what we do know is the course of human history changed that fateful day. By making use of a concentrated and controlled form of energy (such as fire), humans were able to stay warm in colder climates, keep predators at bay, and cook meals. The latter is an amazing cultural achievement and one of the many ways in which human beings are qualitatively different from any kind of animal.[1] In addition, there is also an immense biological advantage in boiling or roasting various kinds of food, whether that be meat or some form of produce: Through this procedure, the food becomes more easily digestible, thereby freeing valuable time and energy that humans can then use for more productive activities.[2]

One way to describe the story of human development is by identifying how much energy or power they were able to harness at different times in history. Initially, the only energy available for any kind of production was muscle power, whether supplied by humans or by domesticated animals, such as oxen, horses, and elephants. Renewable energies like water and wind were used at times (for instance, by building windmills) but, overall, these played a limited role. Notable breakthroughs in

---

1. Wrangham, *Catching Fire*.
2. Herrera and Garcia-Bertrand, *Ancestral DNA*, 54–57, 93.

productivity were achieved once greater amounts of energy could be produced by taking advantage of coal, oil, natural gas, and nuclear power.[3]

As this brief overview demonstrates, energy is essential for economic advancement and human development. However, not all energy forms are the same, and different sources of energy may be more suitable than others during certain periods of development. For example, during much of human history, people have taken advantage of fire by burning wood. These fires were a great blessing for people, but the Industrial Revolution of the eighteenth century would not have been possible by merely relying on wood. Rather, the first major industrial centers (not only in England, but also in other countries like France and Germany) developed near areas where coal could be mined, which was then used to develop the steel industry.[4]

Compared to wood, coal has major advantages, but it has its downsides as well, notably high degrees of air pollution. It also cannot be used to power cars, for which a more compressed energy form like gasoline is needed. Oil was essential for the Second Industrial Revolution, but a finite resource like oil cannot be the final word in terms of finding sustainable energy sources.[5] Nuclear power (fission), the energy form of the Third Industrial Revolution, may seem practically inexhaustible, but it also has its drawbacks, particularly when it comes to safety concerns. To move forward into the Fourth Industrial Revolution, societies will therefore have to embrace new energy sources on an unprecedented scale.[6] Environmental concerns certainly need to be taken into consideration, but the answer cannot be to produce less energy. On the contrary, humanity will need more energy than ever before—for several reasons.

First, worldwide, more energy will be needed due to the demographic developments in coming decades. At the time of writing, the

---

3. Penna, *History of Energy Flows*.

4. Murphy et al., *European Culture Area*, 240–48.

5. In principle, coal, oil, and gas are also renewable resources in that the energy stored in them ultimately comes from the sun. However, since it takes millions of years for these carbon-based forms of energy to be produced, these resources are generally classified as non-renewable. Aldinger, "What Are Fossil Fuels." It is difficult to predict when humanity will run out of oil; one prognosis says by the year 2063, but there are many factors that could change that. In any case, it looks like global demand for oil will peak already around 2040, an indication that we are entering a new era as far as energy is concerned. McFadden, "Don't Worry"; Ellyatt, "Global Oil Demand to Peak."

6. Rhodes, *Energy*, xiii, 338–43.

world population already stands at over eight billion people.[7] In 1960, there were three billion people. According to projections of the United Nations, humanity will reach nine billion in 2037 and ten billion people sometime in the 2050s. That is to say, compared to large parts of the twentieth century, population growth has slowed down, but the number of people is still increasing. There is no necessity to raise the alarm about *The Limits to Growth* as the Club of Rome famously did in the 1970s.[8] Nonetheless, the world population continues to grow, and each person born will have a certain amount of energy needs that must be added to the calculation.

However, even if the world's population was stagnating, there would still be a growing demand for energy. The reason is that, in countries like India, millions of people are climbing out of poverty. As people in India experience the benefits of economic growth, they become first-time buyers of goods like fans, televisions, and refrigerators—all products that consume electricity. While it is fully understandable people in other parts of the world want to acquire these kinds of goods, such a development comes at a price. In China, where hundreds of millions of people have climbed out of poverty since economic reforms were implemented in the 1980s and 1990s, a large number of coal power plants were built to foster this kind of economic growth and to bring electricity to the entire country, including its rural areas.[9] As of January 2022, there were already over one thousand coal power plants in mainland China.[10]

Throughout Asia, national governments have plans to build six hundred new coal power plants in the years to come.[11] India, for instance, has also turned to coal as a relatively cheap and reliable form of energy. And it is not only China and India; other countries are experiencing economic growth as well, with some portions of their population escaping from poverty, and others climbing up toward the middle class, which allows them to buy cars, go on vacations, and cool their houses using air conditioning. The fastest-growing middle class can now be found on the African continent, where Nigeria, in particular, is becoming a major economic player.[12] In countries like these, shopping malls, five-star hotels,

---

7. Worldometers, "World Population."
8. Meadows et al., *Limits to Growth*.
9. Gates, *How to Avoid a Climate Disaster*, 72–74, 103–4, 150.
10. Statista, "Countries and Territories."
11. Braun, "Why Build 600."
12. Heeralall and Abdelkrim, "World's Fastest-Growing Middle Class."

and industry parks are being set up—and building and maintaining all this infrastructure takes energy.

However, growing energy demands are not only a phenomenon in developing countries. Even though developed countries are experiencing less population growth and less economic growth, there are still growing energy demands due to new technologies and processes that require substantial amounts of energy. One example that has caused quite a stir in recent years in this regard is Bitcoin, a cryptocurrency that can not only be bought but can also be acquired through crypto mining (see chapter 7). Bitcoin is valuable because its supply is limited, and in order to add new bitcoins, complex calculations need to be performed. To perform these calculations, massive server farms are needed, and all those computers operating around the clock consume considerable amounts of electricity. In fact, it has been calculated that Bitcoin already consumes as much electricity every year as entire countries, such as Finland or Austria.[13]

And it is not only Bitcoin—all those servers that power the data for AI applications, e-commerce, social media, etc. need electricity. As more and more people around the world acquire smartphones and other devices, the demand for energy will only increase on a global scale. In addition, in the context of the Fourth Industrial Revolution, we may soon see new technologies that will also need electricity or other forms of energy in order to function. One example would be the military as it develops high-energy weapons (such as laser weapons), as well as space technologies—building rockets and spaceships that will enable humans to mine asteroids or to colonize other planets will consume vast amounts of energy (see chapter 9). Another major reason the energy situation is going to change in the years and decades ahead is because many major players have decided to become carbon-neutral (or climate-neutral) relatively soon. This move would not necessarily increase the overall demand for energy, but it will require developing alternative energy sources. Besides corporations and entire countries planning for a different future, cities are making similar decisions, too.[14] The Carbon Neutral Cities Alliance (CNCA), for instance, is a collaboration of leading global cities working to achieve carbon neutrality in the next decades, an initiative

13. Mehta et al., *Bubble or Revolution?*, 82. "And while some commentators have criticized these studies for adopting unrealistic assumptions, even the most conservative estimates of blockchain's energy use are still massive." Magnuson, *Blockchain Democracy*, 127.

14. Wallach, "Race to Net Zero"; Olya, "16 Companies."

that includes both American cities like New York, Boulder, and Portland, as well as international cities, such as Amsterdam, Melbourne, Rio de Janeiro, and Yokohama.[15]

As the world is moving away from fossil fuels, while at the same time creating the demand for more energy, the question must be asked: Where is all this energy going to come from? One option is various forms of renewable energy. In fact, when people think about the energy forms of the future, they often think of wind and solar. And rightly so, considering both wind and sunshine exist in abundance and create (relatively) clean energy. However, critiques point out some of these energy forms are quite expensive and, especially in the case of wind, not sufficiently reliable. In addition, they can create their own environmental problems—wind turbines, for instance, take up a lot of space, might ruin the landscape, and can cause the death of migrating birds.[16]

The first challenge, the economics of renewables, deserves particular consideration. After all, it is difficult and problematic to change the energy landscape by regulations alone, but if a particular form of energy is more affordable, then market forces will encourage people to switch to that energy form in droves. On the other hand, if renewable energies are more expensive than other energy forms, then taking care of the climate and avoiding emissions becomes a luxury that regular people simply cannot afford. In fact, caring for the environment could then become an endeavor that creates unacceptable hardships for the poorer segments of society (for example, people for whom energy costs are a large portion of their household budget, or employees who need to commute to their workplace every day).

It is vital to remember solar energy was prohibitively expensive not that long ago. In 2005, the price for photovoltaic solar modules was four dollars per watt, but it dropped rapidly in recent years, to just twenty cents in 2020.[17] Nonetheless, in 2021, only 3 percent of the world's energy came from solar. Part of the problem is solar energy only works when the sun shines, but in many parts of the world energy is especially needed on cloudy and rainy days. Energy storage systems, such as advanced batteries, therefore have to be part of the solution. Much progress has been made on a variety of fronts, which is why the author and entrepreneur Tony Seba is convinced solar, wind, and batteries (SWB) "is both physically

---

15. CNCA, "Our Cities."
16. Mulvaney, *Sustainable Energy Transitions*, 114–16.
17. DW Planet A, "How Solar Energy."

possible and economically affordable across the entire continental United States as well as the overwhelming majority of other populated regions of the world by 2030."[18] Consequently, he says, "Coal, gas, and nuclear power assets will become stranded during the 2020s, and no new investment in these technologies is rational from this point forward."[19]

Others believe nuclear power needs to be part of the future energy mix as well, so they may find this evaluation by Seba surprising. Proponents of nuclear power argue it is an abundant source of energy that avoids carbon emissions. The counterargument is that nuclear energy produces radioactive waste, which is difficult to deal with, and that nuclear power stations are not completely safe. Granted, Chernobyl, which melted down in 1986, was a particular case, considering this accident happened during the time of the Soviet Union, a Communist dictatorship which did not have the same control mechanisms in place as a Western democracy would. However, there is also the more recent incident in Fukushima, Japan, which occurred in 2011, after which Germany decided to not only abandon coal but to step away from nuclear energy as well. Other countries have made different decisions; France, for instance, receives around 70 percent of its energy from nuclear reactors.[20]

The marketplace of ideas will have room for different approaches to energy. Nobody died directly from the accident in Fukushima; the many deaths were caused by a tsunami that occurred several days later, not by radioactivity. In fact, scientists at the NASA Goddard Institute for Space Studies and the Columbia University Earth Institute have estimated that, worldwide, nuclear power led to the prevention of "1.84 million air pollution-related deaths," compared to if the burning of fossil-fuel had been used instead to produce the equivalent amount of energy.[21] Still, the problem of hazardous waste remains. In addition, even if, from a technical point of view, any kind of malfunctioning could be avoided consistently, nuclear reactors could still become targets of terrorist attacks, or during war—with potentially devastating consequences for the people living nearby for years to come.[22] With all these considerations

18. Dorr and Seba, "Rethinking Energy 2020–2030," 7, 60.
19. Dorr and Seba, "Rethinking Energy 2020–2030," 7, 60.
20. As of 2021, there are four countries that obtain more than half of their energy from nuclear: France (69 percent), Ukraine (55 percent), Slovakia (52.3 percent), and Belgium (50.8 percent). NEI, "Top 15 Nuclear Generating Countries."
21. Quoted in Rhodes, *Energy*, 324.
22. Cravens, "Terrorism and Nuclear Energy"; Sohn, "Opinion."

in mind, it looks like humanity will need a new kind of source of energy, and fusion is an attractive candidate for the age of the Fourth Industrial Revolution in this regard.

In contrast to nuclear reactors, fusion reactors cannot melt down. While nuclear energy as we know it today relies on the splitting of atoms, fusion requires the combining of atoms, which is the process that powers the sun. One of the great advantages of fusion energy is that it is relatively safe, for, as Bill Gates explains, "there's no chain reaction to run out of control, because the fusion ceases as soon as you stop supplying fuel or switch off the device."[23] It is also abundant, because all it takes is the fusion of hydrogen, which is a widely available element (in other words, fusion does not rely on rare elements like uranium, as fission energy does). Furthermore, fusion produces clean energy, at least for the most part—the only leftovers in the process are "about as dangerous as radioactive hospital waste," and these "waste products would be radioactive for hundreds of years, versus hundreds of thousands of years for waste plutonium and other elements from fission."[24]

To produce fusion energy, three basic elements are needed: high temperatures, density, and confinement. For those hydrogen atoms to collide, a temperature of one hundred fifty million degrees Celsius is needed.[25] That is much hotter than the sun, which reaches around fifteen million degrees Celsius at its core. Given these parameters, the main problem with fusion energy is the technical difficulties associated with this process.[26] There is hope these difficulties can be overcome, but as a well-known saying goes: "Fusion is 40 years away, and it always will be."[27] Considering fusion energy was already perceived as a promising pathway several decades ago, there seems to be some truth to this statement. However, this time, things might be different. Both public and private initiatives have recently intensified their quest to provide energy through fusion, and important milestones have been reached.

---

23. Gates, *How to Avoid a Climate Disaster*, 88.

24. Gates, *How to Avoid a Climate Disaster*, 88.

25. So the physicist Henderson, "Dawn of the Fusion Age."

26. According to Nick Walden, the six major technological challenges with regards to fusion are: (1) burning plasmas, in order to generate extreme heat; (2) resilient materials that can handle such extreme heat; (3) removing excess heat; (4) fuel self-sufficiency; (5) robotics (for instance, to do repairs); and (6) integrated engineering. Walden, "Delivering Fusion Energy."

27. Gates, *How to Avoid a Climate Disaster*, 88.

- To begin with, there is the global cooperation project called the International Thermonuclear Experimental Reactor (ITER), which is located in the south of France. With billions of dollars in investment, the ITER "is likely to be the most expensive scientific facility on Earth," and it has frequently been criticized for going over budget and not being able to meet its deadlines.[28]
- Rather than using powerful magnets to contain the extremely hot plasma (like ITER does), the National Ignition Facility (NIF) at Lawrence Livermore National Laboratory in California is pursuing a different approach, which "involves confining the fusion fuel and compressing it in a tiny space with the aid of lasers."[29]
- In the United Kingdom, the Joint European Torus (JET) achieved an important breakthrough on February 9, 2022, when scientists reported "they had generated the highest sustained energy pulse ever created by fusing together atoms, more than doubling their own record from experiments performed in 1997."[30] This suggests "that a follow-up fusion-reactor project that uses the same technology and fuel mixture—the ambitious US$22-billion ITER, scheduled to begin fusion experiments in 2025—should eventually be able to reach this goal."[31]
- In South Korea, the Korea Superconducting Tokamak Advanced Research (KSTAR) reactor "set a new fusion record after superheating a plasma loop to 180 million degrees Fahrenheit" for forty-eight seconds, as scientists reported in early 2024.[32]

With national governments around the world investing in a variety of different approaches, there is a reasonable chance fusion energy will become a possibility within the next few decades. In addition to these public projects, there are now dozens of private firms that are researching ways to make fusion energy technologically feasible and commercially viable. These companies include Commonwealth Fusion Systems in Cambridge, Massachusetts (a spin-off of MIT's Plasma Science and Fusion Center), TAE Technologies (a Californian company that has received

28. Claessens, *ITER: The Giant Fusion Reactor*, 115.
29. Irfan, "Fusion Energy," §18.
30. Gibney, "Nuclear-Fusion Reactor," 371.
31. Gibney, "Nuclear-Fusion Reactor," 371.
32. Turner, "Nuclear Fusion Reactor," §1.

investments from Google and Goldman Sachs), Helion Energy (in Everett, Washington), General Fusion (which, based in Burnaby, Canada, is backed by Jeff Bezos), and Tokamak Energy (in Oxfordshire, England).[33]

For a long time, fusion energy was perceived as an area of foundational research, the kind of only governments would get involved in. However, now that private entrepreneurs and investors are getting interested as well, there is increased competition, which could lead to better solutions at more affordable prices. "In this respect," reports Philip Ball, writing for *Nature*, "advocates of fusion technology say it has many parallels with the space industry. That, too, was once confined to government agencies but is now benefiting from the drive and imagination of nimble (albeit often state-assisted) private enterprise."[34] Consequently, "as with space exploration, one of the benefits of a private fusion sector is greater diversity of approaches than monolithic state enterprises can muster."[35] Whether the breakthrough in fusion energy will come about through a government-based program, the investment of a private firm, or some form of public-private partnership, one thing seems certain: When it comes to the future of energy, humanity is entering into a new era. For this reason, it is essential the church is part of these conversations as well.

A CHRISTIAN PERSPECTIVE ON ENERGY

In the following, I address three areas of concern related to energy, evaluating them from my perspective as a Christian. First, the supply of energy needs to be decentralized, thereby enabling people to exercise more direct control over one of the most important economic resources. Second, believers can offer a hopeful narrative when it comes to the challenge of climate change, rather than giving in to fear created by doomsday scenarios. Third, energy independence on the national level is a moral and strategic priority, so that consumers are not indirectly financing corrupt and authoritarian regimes in oil-exporting countries like Venezuela, Saudi Arabia, and Russia.

As for the first point, the energy supply of nations is currently a highly centralized matter.[36] However, with the advent of alternative en-

---

33. Roston, "Investors Get Serious"; EnergyStartups, "Top 10 Fusion Energy Startups."
34. Ball, "Chase for Fusion Energy," §5.
35. Ball, "Chase for Fusion Energy," §21.
36. As in most countries, electricity in the United States is produced in centralized

ergy sources and more advanced storage solutions, we could experience a democratization of energy, where every household (and possibly also most office buildings, manufacturing facilities, etc.) produce their own energy.[37] Such a shift would create great economic potential, as well as have implications for the stability of energy supply and matters related to national security. From an economic point of view, energy at this point is simply a cost factor, something people need to pay for based on their utility bill that is issued to them every month (or every two months). Under this arrangement, customers have limited say with regards to choosing the energy source that is providing electricity for their home. But once homeowners place solar panels on their roof, things begin to shift dramatically: They know their energy comes from a renewable source and they are now not only consumers but producers of electricity as well. If their home generates more energy than it consumes, they can feed the surplus back into the grid, thereby creating an additional source of income for their household.[38]

In addition to economic advantages, this kind of independent energy supply can also provide greater security: In case of a blackout, the lights would stay on for those homes that have solar panels and battery storage. Such an arrangement would not only provide greater convenience but could literally save lives. While it is annoying each time electricity is not available, even if only for a few hours, things can get really serious when energy supply is disrupted over several days, especially when this occurs during a chilly winter. One example is the power outages in Texas that took place in February of 2021, which caused over two hundred deaths.[39]

Even if nothing goes wrong, there is still a tangible benefit to quite literally living off the grid: a sense of greater independence and freedom. As highlighted in chapter 7, the Hebrew prophets had a vision of peace

---

power plants and then distributed through the electric grid, which has three interconnections: "the Eastern, Western, and Texas interconnections." McBride and Siripurapu, "How Does the U.S." While Texas has its own grid, this is not enough to create healthy competition; it is still a functional monopoly within that large geographical area, which creates vulnerabilities (as became obvious during the winter storm that hit Texas in February 2021).

37. One company promoting this vision is Tesla. Although Tesla is currently primarily seen as a car manufacturer, it may turn into an energy company, considering the expertise it has with batteries (https://www.tesla.com/energy). Barhat, "Tesla's Musk Says Solar."

38. See, for example, Peak Substation Services, "Centralized vs. Decentralized Energy."

39. Weber and Buchele, "Texas Has an Official Death Count."

and prosperity where everyone would "sit under their own vine and under their own fig tree, and no one will make them afraid" (Mic 4:4). When individuals and families depend less on megastructures (whether provided by the government or by multinationals) and more on themselves, they become stronger citizens and more self-confident consumers who can challenge the abusive power dynamics monopolies tend to create.

Another area where Christians living in the Fourth Industrial Revolution can make a difference is by resisting an overly pessimistic narrative when it comes to the effects of climate change by telling the story of a hopeful future instead. Doomsday scenarios have a long history, and they continue to be successful because they appeal to one of the most basic human instincts: fear. Whether expressed through documentaries like *An Inconvenient Truth* (released in 2006) or movies such as the apocalyptic film *2012*, predicting the end of the world can be a profitable endeavor.

From a theological point of view, it is worth noting how religious some of the more extreme forms of environmentalism have become. As Western societies have become more secularized in the past two hundred years or so, it seems some people are turning to environmentalism to fill the spiritual void that is in their hearts. In environmentalism, religious or even sectarian sentiments can be fully satisfied; after all, it offers an apocalyptic vision, an insider group (those "who get it"), purity standards (such as abstaining from meat), feelings of guilt and shame (when choosing to fly, for example), a priestly caste (a mix of experts and prominent activists), and a pathway to redemption based on a form of indulgences (the wealthy can buy carbon credits and in this way live with a good conscience, without having to change their lifestyle).[40]

In some cases, apocalyptic environmentalism can also lead to a deification of nature, to the degree that the role of humans in the earth's ecosystem is severely criticized.[41] In such a vision, humans are seen as a danger to the planet, and it is claimed the earth would be better off if there were no people living on it, considering how much damage humans cause to the environment.[42] Such misguided thinking reveals a radical departure from the Judeo-Christian worldview that affirms the unique dignity and role of humans as image bearers of God.[43]

---

40. Garreau, "Environmentalism as Religion." This perspective is also acknowledged by some secularists, such as Davis, "Environmentalism: A New Religion."

41. Glover, "Environmentalism: The New Religion."

42. May, "Opinion"; Shead, "Climate Change."

43. This kind of secular view can lead to extreme statements like: "In *The Challenge*

Instead of leaning toward despair, Christians see humans as moral agents who are capable of change and of innovation. When God created Adam and Eve, he placed them in the Garden of Eden, while the eschatological vision of Scripture ends with a city, the New Jerusalem. Accordingly, the metanarrative of the Bible encompasses the idea of development and hope. The end of human history will not be a climate catastrophe that ends all life; rather, history as we know it will come to an end when Jesus returns in glory and ushers in a new age. In the meantime, we have work to do: preaching the gospel to every nation and demonstrating God's redemptive purposes here on Earth as an expression of God's inbreaking kingdom (Matt 10:7–8; 13:31–33; 24:14; 28:18–20).[44]

One concept that could help in addressing future energy needs would be making human flourishing the overall framework. Theologically speaking, human flourishing is about making a contribution toward people living in shalomic relationships.[45] To be sure, shalom in this holistic vision includes God's creation, but also restored relationships with others and, most importantly, with the Creator. In that sense, human flourishing goes beyond the concerns secular environmentalists typically address. In pursuing a holistic vision of shalom by emphasizing human flourishing, it is particularly crucial to pay special attention to the "least of these," a group Jesus emphasized in the parable of the sheep and the goats (Matt 25:31–46). In this parable, Jesus talked about his brothers and sisters, particularly those who were hungry, naked, sick, and in prison. In today's age of global Christianity, most believers are now living in the Majority World (in Asia, Africa, and Latin America).[46] While there is certainly relative poverty in Western countries like the United States, the most extreme realities of absolute poverty, as well as of persecution of Christians, are found in the global South. From a global perspective, the "least of these" are especially found in various parts of Asia, Africa, and Latin America.

---

of Man's Future, Brown wrote that much of humanity was behaving as if it 'would not rest content until the earth is covered completely and to a considerable depth with a writhing mass of human beings, much as a dead cow is covered with a pulsating mass of maggots.'" Rhodes, *Energy*, 309.

44. For signs of healing as one expression of the inbreaking kingdom of God, see Thelen, *Biblical Foundations*, 7–13, 84–85.

45. E.g., DeVine, *Shalom Yesterday, Today, and Forever*; Suh, *Empowering God*, 5–70.

46. Several theologians, historians, and missiologists have highlighted how the center of global Christianity has moved to the South; for instance, Jenkins, *Next Christendom*; Horsfjord, *Global Christianity*, 2, 252–53.

In these geographical contexts, both energy poverty and issues of climate justice need to be addressed. First of all, people in the global South need energy in order to climb out of poverty. Historically, Western nations were able to industrialize and move beyond sustenance farming by making use of fossil fuels, such as coal, oil, and gas. It would be unfair to now put pressure on developing countries to the point of not allowing them to use such energy sources in order to better the lives of their people.[47] At the same time, developed countries are responsible for much of the greenhouse gases found in the atmosphere today. Tragically, to the extent these lead to extreme heat and the flooding of coastal areas, it is those countries that have contributed the least to these climate imbalances that will be affected the most. As people in the Majority World suffer from droughts, or small island nations are endangered by rising sea levels, it is the "least of these" from Matt 25 who are suffering, and the body of Christ worldwide has a moral obligation to do something about it.[48]

Developed nations consuming large amounts of energy have an additional moral obligation, namely, to become energy independent for strategic reasons.[49] Given the foreign policy implications of energy sourcing decisions, this needs to be a priority, especially for those countries that want to maintain their freedom and democracy. For too long, Western countries have enriched oil and gas producers from problematic regions of the world, whether that be the Middle East with all its volatility, or a country like Russia with its authoritarian power structures (see Table 10).[50] Europe has been especially dependent on Russia, and although America has become energy-independent in recent years, in 2022 Saudi Arabia was still its third-largest source for imported oil, after Canada and Mexico.[51]

---

47. Friedman, *Hot, Flat, and Crowded*, 154–69, 186–87.

48. Compare the moving messages delivered during the twenty-sixth United Nations Climate Change Conference of the Parties (COP26) in Glasgow, Scotland, especially the appeals coming from small island nations (such as the Maldives, Tuvalu, and Barbados). See, for example, this speech by an activist from Samoa: TheCoconetTV, "Pacific Climate Change Leader." It is also worth mentioning that, like many Pacific islands, Samoa is deeply Christian—with a population where 96.6 percent are Christians and 18 percent are evangelical believers (https://operationworld.org/locations/samoa).

49. Energy independence has been a topic in American politics for some time: Homans, "Energy Independence," 1–5; Dall, "National Energy Security," 38–50. Compare Topf, "America's New Independence Day," 123–44.

50. Workman, "Crude Oil Exports."

51. EIA, "Oil and Petroleum Products Explained."

Table 10. The Largest Exporters of Crude Oil in 2022

	Country	Revenue	Percentage of Global Exports
1	Saudi Arabia	$224.8 billion	16.7 percent
2	Canada	$120.5 billion	8.9 percent
3	Russia	$119.5 billion	8.9 percent
4	United States	$117 billion	8.7 percent
5	United Arab Emirates	$112.7 billion	8.4 percent
6	Iraq	$82.3 billion	6.1 percent
7	Norway	$57.8 billion	4.3 percent
8	Kuwait	$54.3 billion	4 percent
9	Nigeria	$49.9 billion	3.7 percent
10	Brazil	$42.7 billion	3.2 percent

The States has been described as a nation addicted to oil, and this is especially problematic when the oil came from countries like Iran, Nigeria, Venezuela, Iraq, and Saudi Arabia.[52] Since Iran became hostile toward America in 1979, no trade is conducted with this nation anymore, and imports from Venezuela (which has the world's largest oil reserves) came to a halt as well, after it became a socialist dictatorship.[53] As for Saudi Arabia, the United States considers it an ally in the Middle East, and certainly good relationships with this nation are needed in order to provide a counterbalance in the region to Iran, which is the largest state sponsor of terrorism worldwide.[54] However, the human-rights record of Saudi Arabia is so abysmal that trade with it should be reduced to a bare minimum. Instead, Americans have been financing this regime each time they have filled up their gas tank for decades.[55] A nation that champions democracy and human rights and is considered the leader of the free world should keep a different kind of company.

Unfortunately, other Western powers, such as Germany, are not doing much better. For years, the German government promoted the building of Nord Stream 2, in order to further increase their gas imports from Russia. Warnings that this would lead to an even greater dependency

---

52. President George W. Bush spoke about America's addiction to oil in his 2006 State of the Union Address. Herbstreuth, *Oil and American Identity*, 67, 73.

53. Mamchii, "Top 10 Countries."

54. McInerney et al., *America's End Game*, 152.

55. Schaer and Knipp, "Is Saudi Arabia Winning."

on Vladimir Putin were not heeded. Then the whole situation exploded when Putin invaded Ukraine in February 2022.[56] It was a wake-up call for Western nations, who quickly agreed on economic sanctions. Ironically, even after imposing these sanctions, the European Union continued to pay hundreds of millions of dollars to Russia every day.[57] The reason? Many parts of Europe depend on Russia for their energy needs; Germany, for instance, used to get more than 50 percent of its gas from Putin's Russia. Obviously, it is impossible to conduct a sound foreign policy when one is entangled in this kind of dependency, be it in times of peace or in times of war.

What needs to be done? The short-term goal needs to be to become energy independent as quickly as possible, meaning no free nation should depend on energy imports from countries that do not share its values.[58] In order to achieve this goal, it will be necessary to tap into a wide range of energy sources, including fossil fuels. This could mean finishing a certain pipeline in order to import more oil from Canada, or to expand fracking in the United States. Currently, fossil fuels still supply around 70 percent of the world's energy needs, which is why this will continue to be the case for some time to come.[59] It is because of these realities that even somebody like Elon Musk, who is deeply committed to the transition toward renewable energy, highlighted in the context of Russia's invasion of Ukraine "the need for greater oil and gas output and urged Europe to turn toward nuclear power for its energy needs."[60]

To power the Fourth Industrial Revolution in the long term, all sustainable energy forms need to be considered, from biogas to nuclear energy.[61] While energy independence is a priority right now, the world also needs a strategy for a greener future, and Christians can be at the forefront of developing such a hopeful vision. In this vision for the future,

---

56. This should have come as no surprise, considering that Putin already used the threat of withholding gas as a political weapon back in 2006. Friedman, *Hot, Flat, and Crowded*, 42–43.

57. Chestney, "Putin Wants."

58. Fortunately, the US is now mostly an exporter of oil; even so, it continued to import oil from Russia. Roberts, "Percent of U.S. Oil Imports."

59. Rapier, "World Energy Outlook 2023."

60. Keane, "Elon Musk," §1.

61. Additional energy forms include hydropower, bioenergy (biofuels, biomass, biogas), geothermal energy, wave power, and tidal power. Mulvaney, *Sustainable Energy Transitions*, 129–41. Considering the earth is basically a gigantic fireball with a relatively thin crust, geothermal energy has great potential. Cuthbertson, "World's Deepest."

a new era of energy superabundance may become reality, powered by wind and solar, as well as new technologies, such as fusion reactors.[62] Granted, energy superabundance sounds like a wild dream, considering all the problems and shortages that currently exist in this sector. However, it is worth remembering that not too long ago the transition from scarcity to abundance was already accomplished in other areas, in sectors where this previously seemed impossible, too. One such example is communications. Just two hundred years ago, any king or general could only dream of having a quick and reliable way to exchange information over long distances, such as by using a telephone. And even after the telephone was invented, calls were still quite expensive, especially long-distance calls.[63] Fast-forward to our time, and today people can have not only phone calls but even video conferences over the internet, which are basically free.

A similar development could take place around energy. Just like we take it for granted that we have free Wi-Fi when we go to a Starbucks, for example, so it could also be common in the future that people can charge their electric vehicle for free in the parking lot of a store or supermarket while they go shopping. When that person returns home, their energy is basically free as well, because the solar panels on the roof of their house produce enough electricity for their daily consumption. Office towers, factories, and government buildings may similarly become energy-independent and have minimal energy costs once the initial investment in solar panels has been amortized. In addition, solar panels could be installed in so many places—for instance, as roofs over freeways and canals, alongside noise protection walls, and even on the streets within cities.[64] In this way, green, reliable, and cheap energy would literally become available anywhere, anytime.[65] However, abundant energy is not only needed to make life on Earth more comfortable; it is also a necessity for humanity to start reaching into space, which will be the topic of the next (and final) chapter of this book.

---

62. Vernon and Dourado, "Energy Superabundance."

63. In 1927, a three minute call from New York to London cost seventy-five dollars. *New York Times*, "Rates on Overseas Phone Calls."

64. Granted, solar roadways are a challenging concept, so Chester, "Revisiting Solar Roadways." However, solar panels could be installed in many other areas, such as in deserts, over landfills, and other unused lands. Laughlin, *Powering the Future*, 98–102; Fox-Penner, *Power after Carbon*, 41–44.

65. Seba and Dorr, "100% Solar, Wind and Batteries."

DISCUSSION QUESTIONS

1. What limitations and opportunities do you see when it comes to various energy sources, such as solar, oil, and nuclear energy?
2. Do you think becoming and remaining fully energy-independent is an important goal for the United States? If so, how could this goal be achieved long term?
3. How should Christians respond to the challenge of climate change?
4. How would people's lives change in an age of energy abundance in which energy would be green, reliable, and inexpensive?

SUGGESTIONS FOR FURTHER READING

- Vaclav Smil, *Energy and Civilization: A History* (2018). A historical overview on energy usage, written by a distinguished academic and bestselling author.
- Darren Dochuk, *Anointed with Oil: How Christianity and Crude Made Modern America* (2019). Highlights how big oil and American evangelicalism supported each other, written by an associate professor of history at Notre Dame.
- John Armstrong, *The Future of Energy: The 2023 Guide to the Energy Transition* (2023). A comprehensive overview of different energy forms and their implications, written by an engineer from the UK.
- Harold Hamm, *Game-Changer: Our Fifty-Year Mission to Secure America's Energy Independence* (2023). A personal and political reflection on the importance of oil, written by one of America's greatest entrepreneurs in the industry.
- Bill Gates, *How to Avoid a Climate Disaster: The Solutions We Have and the Breakthroughs We Need* (2022). Explains why tackling climate change is essential and how carbon-neutrality can be achieved.
- Alex Epstein, *Fossil Future: Why Global Human Flourishing Requires More Oil, Coal, and Natural Gas—Not Less* (2022). Argues that the benefits of fossil fuels outweigh their negative side effects.

9

Space

UNTIL RECENTLY, GOING TO space was an adventure reserved for a very tiny group of professionals called astronauts. That changed on September 16, 2021, when four civilians boarded a SpaceX rocket to embark on a mission to space that, for the first time in history, had only private citizens on board.[1] It was an extraordinary event because, ever since that day, it is now conceivable leaving the earth's orbit will be a form of traveling available to ordinary people. Initially, this might be mostly about traveling from one city to another by taking advantage of the speed of rockets. However, going forward, people may be able to vacation in space stations, enjoying the magnificent views of the only planet humans have hitherto called home. In addition, people might also be able to explore the moon, Mars, and other planets, and maybe one day to even work and live there. If and when the latter vision will become a reality is uncertain, but one thing seems to be clear: Space has become an attractive place for entrepreneurs, and it can therefore be expected a number of groundbreaking innovations related to space travel will be part of the new realities characterizing the Fourth Industrial Revolution.[2]

Launching rockets into orbit used to be something only governments do, and only a few nations have been able to do. So far, only the

---

[1]. This event made it to the cover of *Time* magazine on August 23, 2021, and was summarized as follows: "Four Civilian Astronauts. Three Days in Orbit. One Giant Leap. Meet the Inspiration4 Crew." Kluger, "Four Civilian Astronauts."

[2]. See chapter 16 ("Space Technologies") in Schwab and Davis, *Shaping the Fourth Industrial Revolution*, 211–19.

United States has sent astronauts to the moon, while a few other major powers are active in space as well, such as China, various European countries, Russia, and India.[3] However, when it comes to operating satellites in orbit, the number of players involved is much larger. There are now thousands of satellites circling the earth and, according to one count, there are over seventy nations operating at least one satellite.[4] The new and noteworthy development in our time is that private companies are becoming involved as well. This increased competition is accelerating innovation and leading to more affordable space solutions. In particular, it is billionaires like Jeff Bezos (who founded Blue Operations, the precursor to Blue Origins, in 2000), Richard Branson (the founder of Virgin Galactic), and Elon Musk (the CEO of SpaceX) who have ambitious plans with regards to offering commercial solutions related to space travel.[5]

Companies like SpaceX provide alternatives when it comes to bringing satellites into orbit, removing the monopoly that the National Aeronautics and Space Administration (NASA) exercised for so many years in this area. In fact, Musk even has his own network of satellites, which form the backbone of the internet service called Starlink. The vision of Starlink is to make highspeed and low-latency internet available anywhere in the world as SpaceX builds a satellite network in space consisting of thousands of satellites. Starlink already has over five thousand satellites in place, a number that eventually may go up to ten thousand or even forty-two thousand satellites.[6] As satellites become more commonplace, this will not only bring advances in communications, but other sectors will benefit from it as well. Through a wide network of satellites, every single detail on Earth will be documented in real time, thereby creating immense amounts of data, which can be used, for instance, to improve traffic flows and make more precise weather forecasts. Another practical application is smart agriculture, which enables farmers to be more efficient, such as by taking advantage of water management systems that dispense the right amount of water exactly when a particular crop needs it.[7]

---

3. The website World Population Review also lists Japan, Australia, Brazil, Kenya, South Korea, North Korea, Iran, Israel, and Ukraine under "Countries with Space Programs 2024."

4. Kizer Whitt, "Who Owns All the Satellites?"

5. Christian Davenport also mentions Paul Allen (1953–2018), "the cofounder of Microsoft, who had backed the first commercial spacecraft to reach space" and who at one point was "building the largest airplane the world had ever seen." Davenport, *Space Barons*, 4.

6. Wall, "SpaceX Launches"; Anders et al., "Starlink Internet Review."

7. Jacobson, *Space Is Open for Business*, 71–76.

Furthermore, there is the exciting opportunity to use rockets to travel—initially, not to get to the moon or other planets (more about that later), but to cut down travel times here on Earth. Of course, airplanes have already revolutionized international travel, which looks dramatically different today compared to the time when people had to board a ship in order to cross an ocean. However, air travel is still time consuming; a flight from Singapore to New York, for example, takes around twenty hours. By contrast, with a rocket, such as envisioned by SpaceX, one could reach any major destination on Earth in less than an hour.[8]

The crucial breakthrough making these flights affordable is reusability.[9] Traditionally, rockets were only used once, thereby making space travel prohibitively expensive. Imagine how much a plane ticket would cost if the airplane would have to be discarded after its first and only flight (a Boeing 747, for instance, costs over four hundred million USD).[10] However, with the innovative breakthrough of reusing rockets, space travel could become relatively affordable. The key to this approach is to not only have a successful launch, but to also navigate the rocket in such a way that it can perform a vertical landing on a platform, be refueled, and then take off again.[11]

Besides intercontinental transportation, these reusable rockets would also open the door to other commercial applications in space like mining asteroids. Going beyond the earth's orbit, such as to explore asteroids, would be a major step forward in the history of space travel. It was a tremendous achievement when Neil Armstrong (1930–2012) first stepped onto the moon on July 20, 1969. However, for all that was achieved, going to the moon brought no direct economic benefits. In the context of the Cold War, it was an important triumph demonstrating the US was superior to the Soviet Union.[12] Once this had been demonstrated, there was not much of a motivation to return to the moon on a regular basis. In fact, the last manned mission to the moon was carried out onboard Apollo 17, in 1972. By contrast, things could be different when it

8. Davenport, *Space Barons*, 273.
9. Jacobson, *Space Is Open for Business*, 57–62.
10. Boon and Pande, "How Much Is."
11. For a successful landing of a SpaceX rocket on a platform in the ocean, see Verge, "SpaceX Lands Rocket at Sea."
12. This was especially critical considering that, in 1957, the Soviets had surprised the Americans by launching the first satellite (called Sputnik). Williams, "Essay 92."

comes to asteroids, because they are not only of scientific but of commercial interest as well.

Asteroids are giant rocks that orbit the sun, with many of them being around one hundred million to two hundred million miles away from Earth (as a point of comparison, the moon is, on average, 238,855 miles away; see Table 11).[13] Reaching an asteroid would mean advancing to a new frontier in space exploration, but it might also bring tangible economic benefits. For instance, *USA Today* reported in 2020 that "the asteroid 16 Psyche, one of the most massive objects in the main asteroid belt orbiting between Mars and Jupiter, could be made entirely of metal, according to a study published this week. Even more intriguing, the asteroid's metal is worth an estimated $10,000 quadrillion (that's 15 more zeroes), more than the entire economy of Earth."[14] The valuables that could be harvested from asteroids like this include nickel, cobalt, platinum, and other precious metals.[15]

Table 11. Distances in Our Solar System

Object	Average Distance from Earth	Travel Time
The Moon	283,855 miles	3 days
Venus	67 million miles	4 months
The Sun	93 million miles	7 months
Mars	140 million miles	9 months
The Asteroid Belt	250 million miles	15 months
Jupiter	444 million miles	20 months
Saturn	887 million miles	3 years
Uranus	1.7 billion miles	6 years
Neptune	2.8 billion miles	10 years

Granted, at this point it is unclear whether mining asteroids will be technically possible or financially feasible. However, if there is a pathway toward tapping into these vast resources, then the economic consequences would be substantial. As Texas senator Ted Cruz said in 2018, in the context of signing a bill to increase NASA's budget, "The first trillionaire

---

13. Williams, "How Far Is."
14. Rice, "This Isn't Your Typical Space Rock," §§2–3.
15. Zubrin, *Case for Space*, 136–38.

will be made in space."[16] Naturally, there is also a cost side to these kinds of endeavors—but it is not as high as one may at first think. According to estimates calculated by Caltech, mining an asteroid would cost around 2.6 billion USD.[17] That is a respectable amount, to be sure, but it becomes less overwhelming once one compares it with the one billion dollars it can cost to set up a rare-earth-metal mine here on Earth. Of course, once one has a product, there is also the challenge of bringing it to market (in this case, bringing it back to Earth) and of finding a buyer. Few buyers may be willing to pay for the vast quantities a space company might have mined on an asteroid; in addition, if supply suddenly increases by so much, this would likely have an inflationary effect, causing prices for these products to fall.

As briefly outlined here, there are uncertainties when it comes to the economics of mining asteroids for profit. Nonetheless, several companies have already been established for this or related purposes, including Planetary Resources (now defunct), iSpace (a Japanese company), Asteroid Mining Corporation from the UK, and OffWorld, which is based out of Pasadena, California.[18] Besides offering financial opportunities, asteroids also pose an existential threat. If an artifact the size of a mountain crashed into Earth at high speed, the consequences would be catastrophic. Importantly, such a scenario is not entirely hypothetical; it is quite possible the dinosaurs were wiped out after an asteroid hit the earth with such an impact that it caused dramatic changes in the earth's climate.[19] More recently, a massive explosion took place in Tunguska, Russia, in 1908.[20] It remains unclear what caused this explosion, which had a force equivalent to thirty Hiroshima bombs, but an asteroid seems to be the best explanation. Since such impactful events have occurred before, it is possible they

---

16. Glester, "Asteroid Trillionaires," §1. However, the first trillionaire could also become someone with a current business model, or someone achieving a breakthrough in an area like AI or finding a cure for cancer. Klawans, "Rise of the World's First Trillionaire."

17. Glester, "Asteroid Trillionaires."

18. Britt, "Companies Are Preparing for Space Mining."

19. Physical evidence for this event could be the impact site "known as the Chicxulub crater," which is "centred on the Yucatán Peninsula in Mexico." Osterloff, "How an Asteroid Ended." As this article featured by the Natural History Museum in London continues to explain, "The asteroid is thought to have been between 10 and 15 kilometres wide, but the velocity of its collision caused the creation of a much larger crater, 150 kilometres in diameter. It's the second-largest crater on the planet." Osterloff, "How an Asteroid Ended."

20. Zubrin, *Case for Space*, 288.

will happen again in the future.[21] It therefore seems wise humans prepare for such a catastrophe by learning more about how an incoming asteroid could be destroyed or diverted, so that it does not hit the earth.

The danger from asteroids is one reason why some are advocating to promote space travel that would enable humans to live on other planets one day. However, an apocalyptic vision of asteroids destroying much of human existence is not the only reason to venture out. Another reason is the concern that humans might destroy themselves, whether through an environmental catastrophe or nuclear war. Now, the vision to becoming a multiplanetary species is not all doom and gloom; it is also about defining a new frontier for humanity and envisioning a bold and exciting future.[22] Even if life on Earth continues to be wonderful, venturing out toward other planets could enable the human species to grow by many billions of individuals more, since the constraints of Earth would not be an issue anymore. In addition, colonizing new planets is also an exciting vision because it creates opportunities to start new societies from scratch, enabling the participants to experiment with different political and economic models.[23]

Whatever the motivation for going beyond planet Earth may be, the natural starting point for such endeavors would be the moon. The moon could serve as a crucial base for longer trips, considering gravity on the moon is only one sixth compared to Earth's, thereby making it easier for spacecrafts and rockets to depart from there.[24] The natural resources found on the moon could also help in these endeavors; helium-3, for instance, could be used as fuel for a fusion reactor. The latter might be somewhat speculative, but there is also evidence that the moon contains ice; as this ice is turned into water, it "can be electrolyzed into hydrogen and oxygen, an excellent rocket propellant combination."[25] With the current technology available, it takes a spacecraft around three days to get to the moon.[26] In the process of getting back to the moon on a more regular basis, humans would also be inspired to reach the next major milestone

---

21. Zubrin, *Case for Space*, 289–92.

22. Becoming a multiplanetary species is part of Musk's vision for the future. Sivolella, *Space Mining and Manufacturing*, 8–9.

23. Zubrin, *Case for Space*, 271–84.

24. Davenport, *Space Barons*, 274.

25. Zubrin, *Case for Space*, 73.

26. Urbain, "How Long Does It Take."

in space travel by reaching Mars, which would necessitate a journey of around nine months.[27]

Establishing a colony on Mars will not be easy, considering how hostile its environment is. Mars does not have an atmosphere, so the initial living space there would have to be all indoors. Over time, it may be possible to terraform Mars, by melting the ice and thereby creating liquid water. Through producing fluorocarbon greenhouse gases, the temperature on Mars could then be raised over a period of several decades, to the point that the permafrost would start to melt.[28] Beyond Mars, other places in the solar system might be of interest as well. Most likely, this would not so much relate to other planets (it is all but impossible to land on Jupiter, for example, due to its massive gravity and storms, and Venus is boiling hot). However, the moons of the large planets could become an interesting option.

Titan, for instance, one of Saturn's many moons, is larger than the planet Mercury and "possesses an abundance of all the elements necessary to support life."[29] Still, rather than trying to live in such a place, colonizing Titan could turn into a mostly industrial project, similar to mining asteroids. This task would then largely be accomplished by robots, which points to a crucial reality: The technologies of the Fourth Industrial Revolution will make expanded space travel possible in the first place, especially through advances in AI, new forms of energy, and material sciences. At the same time, space travel will also push forward many of the inventions and applications of this new era. Space has always served as a platform for innovation, and this trend is likely to accelerate in the coming decades.[30] Whatever happens in outer space will profoundly impact life on Earth, which is why it is crucial Christians start thinking about this dimension of the Fourth Industrial Revolution as well.

A CHRISTIAN PERSPECTIVE ON SPACE

Theologically speaking, I want to highlight three aspects why it could be important for humanity to venture into space at this point in history. First, through space exploration people will make new discoveries and

---

27. Taylor Tillman and Dobrijevic, "How Long Does It Take."
28. Zubrin, *Case for Space*, 117–18.
29. Zubrin, *Case for Space*, 162.
30. Pappas, *One Giant Leap*.

learn more about the amazing universe God created. Second, space technologies may enable us to protect and enhance human life, such as by diverting or destroying asteroids that otherwise would be on collision course with Earth. Third, given the vastness of the universe, it may be part of God's plan for humans to expand beyond Earth, embracing the opportunities that various planets may have to offer for human flourishing.

Regarding the first point, there are certainly still many discoveries to be made on Earth, especially when it comes to exploring the depths of its oceans. However, in the grand scheme of things, many more mysteries wait to be solved in space. In fact, as Robert Zubrin argues in *The Case for Space*, several of the major scientific discoveries in modernity in the recent past have been related to space, considering that "the laws of gravity, electromagnetism, relativity, and nuclear fusion were all discovered through astronomical observation."[31] When we gaze into space, we realize how much we do not (yet) know, and I believe by discovering more and more about God's creation we can bring joy to the Creator's heart. After all, Scripture tells us, "The heavens declare the glory of God; the skies proclaim the work of his hands" (Ps 19:1). There is a whole solar system waiting for us to be explored by launching space probes, and one day possibly also by sending explorers and scientists.

In addition, by placing telescopes in outer space and on the moon, we could also discover more about distant solar systems and galaxies. Similar to the Hubble Telescope that was able to give us much more accurate pictures because it was placed in orbit, a telescope placed on the moon could provide us with additional insights, because the moon has no atmosphere that would hinder the view. Even so, a single telescope placed on the moon would not be sufficient to explore the depths of the universe. What would be needed would be a whole system of optical telescopes, "in which groups of telescopes all focus on a single object and coordinate the signals they receive via computer."[32] With such an arrangement, explains Zubrin, humans would be able to observe not only stars but even planets belonging to other solar systems in considerable detail.

However, venturing into space would not only satisfy the curiosity of scientists, but it would also be an opportunity to address some of the most pressing problems humanity currently faces. One of these pressing issues is to produce enough energy for people to enjoy a high standard

---

31. Zubrin, *Case for Space*, 254.
32. Zubrin, *Case for Space*, 252.

of living, particularly by providing electricity that is both green and reliable. Great Britain is addressing this challenge by planning a massive system of solar panels that would be placed in outer space. By placing the panels in space, they have a tremendous advantage compared to any system installed on Earth: They can now produce electricity around the clock, since the sun is constantly shining on them. The energy is then transferred to Earth through high-frequency waves, where they are collected by an antenna placed on the ground, which then transfers them back into electricity.[33]

Not surprisingly, the dimensions for this project are gigantic. The antenna to collect the energy would occupy a space of almost seven by thirteen kilometers (around 4.5 by eight miles), and therefore cover a surface similar to a small town. In space the solar satellite structure would have a diameter of over a mile and weigh around two thousand tons. Transporting a structure of this size into space and assembling it there would be a massive undertaking, and the British government has allocated sixteen billion pounds for this project. Clearly, both financial and technical challenges will have to be overcome before this project can become a reality, but the vision is to start with small trial runs in 2040, so that by the year 2050 Great Britain would be able to achieve its goal of becoming a carbon neutral nation.[34]

Besides acquiring sustainable energy, space could help us address other challenges as well, environmental pollution and limited resources being foremost among them. Through the mining of asteroids and the usage of gigantic solar panels in space, we might be able to outsource the heavy industries that currently pollute our planet and burry waste far away (rather than shipping it to poor countries, burning it, or letting it rot in landfills). Through such a fundamental shift in our production cycles, the earth would then primarily become a place for humans to enjoy each other and a pristine environment, and nobody would have to live near a large factory or garbage dump.[35] In this way, the earth would once again become more similar to what God envisioned in the Garden of Eden, and we as Christians should advocate for such a restorative process.

33. Schwichtenberg, "Solar aus dem Weltraum."
34. Schwichtenberg, "Solar aus dem Weltraum."
35. Such a vision has been formulated by Jeff Bezos, who advocates moving all heavy industry into space. That way, Earth would be turned into a kind of national park, something he envisioned already when he was still in high school. Stone, "Jeff Bezos in San Diego."

Aside from environmental calamities, our beautiful planet may also be in danger from asteroids. How should believers respond to this challenge? Some might be tempted to think this would never happen, since God would not allow for such a catastrophe to occur. There is some merit to this argument, considering that the stability and durability of Earth is affirmed at various points in Scripture (1 Chr 16:30; Pss 104:5; 119:89–90; Eccl 1:4). However, there is also the question of human agency since, beginning with Adam and Eve, God has entrusted Earth to humanity. As part of the assignment to rule over creation, does this not also include to exercise dominion over the asteroids that might put our planet in danger? I would suggest studying the threat of asteroids and proposing solutions to this problem is a worthy endeavor for believers. Unlike people who are without hope, we do not have to respond to this challenge with a sense of despair (see also my reflections on the climate change crisis in chapter 8).[36] Rather, we can give ourselves to this task with a great degree of confidence, trusting God will enable us to find the right kind of solutions at the right time.

But what about venturing beyond the asteroid belt, toward other planets, and maybe even toward new solar systems one day? Is that not a waste of resources, considering there are so many pressing problems here on Earth that should be solved first? After all, to give just one example, "Over its 20+ years in orbit, the international space station costs over $150 billion to develop, making it the most expensive thing ever built."[37] As a point of comparison, the World Food Programme (WFP), the world's largest humanitarian agency, raised 8.3 billion USD in 2023, while its total budgetary need is 22.8 billion USD.[38] Compared to going to space, investing in essentials like providing enough food for everyone or making sure all children receive a quality education certainly seem to be more of a priority when it comes to allocating financial resources, whether these are part of public funds or come in through private donations.

The counterargument to this line of thinking would be that the solution to some of humanity's greatest challenges may lie in space and that important scientific breakthroughs and groundbreaking inventions could be made in the context of an emerging space industry. However, space enthusiasts must be careful not to overpromise what such endeavors

---

36. As an example of an apocalyptic scenario, see the Netflix movie *Don't Look Up* (2021). Sherman, "It's the Ultimate Disaster Scenario."
37. Martin, "Is the International Space Station," §2.
38. World Food Programme, "WFP at a Glance."

could achieve. An example of this kind of hubris is provided by Princeton physicist and professor Gerard K. O'Neill (1927–92)when he states in *The High Frontier: Human Colonies in Space* that the goal is nothing short of

> ending hunger and poverty for all human beings; finding high-quality living space for a world population; achieving population control without war, famine, dictatorship or coercion; increasing individual freedom and the range of options available to every human being; unlimited low-cost energy available to everyone; unlimited new material sources, available without stealing or killing or polluting.[39]

As highlighted in previous chapters, it is unrealistic to expect this much from any kind of technological innovation—or any other expression of human progress, be it social or political. Nonetheless, there is a real possibility that space will be a vital component going forward in terms of reaching new milestones in areas like the preservation of the environment, economic development, and national defense.

But even if it turns out that it would be technologically and financially feasible to mine asteroids and maybe even colonize Mars, should we? Some may argue humans have already done enough damage to Earth, and therefore should leave other parts of the universe alone.[40] Christians believe humans are the crown of creation who are equipped with a dominion mandate—but how far does this mandate go? In other words, what about theologically defined boundaries—since God has entrusted this Earth to us humans, would we not overstep our realm of authority by venturing into outer space? To answer this question, I am going to speculate a bit, inviting a conversation I think is important for us to have, for those of us who, by God's providence, are living in the opening decades of the era of the Fourth Industrial Revolution.

Scripture affirms a fundamental distinction between "heaven and earth" (Gen 1:1; Ps 146:6; Matt 11:25; 24:35; Acts 17:24; Rev 21:1).[41] Gen-

---

39. Quoted in Sivolella, *Space Mining and Manufacturing*, 154.

40. Billings, "Colonizing Other Planets," 44–46. The following article highlights the technological challenges, but his tenth point is about leaving space untouched: Malikyte, "10 Reasons Colonizing Mars."

41. The words *earth* and *world* are sometimes used interchangeably (Gen 11:9; Job 34:13; Ps 97:4; Rom 10:18). The well-known verse in John 3:16 affirms God so loved the world that he sent his only Son, and the Greek word used for *world* here is *kósmos*. However, the Fourth Gospel's focus is not on cosmology but on humanity. In John, the word *world* refers to "the totality of creation and especially of humanity as the object of God's love," but it is also used "to designate mankind in so far as it rejects Christ, lives in

erally speaking, Earth is the realm where human beings live (Gen 6:1; Pss 8:6–8; 115:16b), while heaven is the realm of God and the angels (Pss 33:13–14; 115:3, 16a; John 3:13). In the Bible, the word *heaven* sometimes also refers to the sky and its clouds, or to the planets and stars that God created (e.g., Gen 8:2; Deut 4:19).[42] However, Scripture also indicates that God's house, his heavenly temple, is in a different dimension, outside the physical world known to humans (Gen 28:17; 1 Kgs 8:30; 2 Chr 18:18; Ps 11:4; Isa 57:15; 66:1; John 14:2; Heb 9:24; 12:22; Rev 5:13–14). Clearly, this heavenly temple does not exist anywhere in the sky, which people regularly traverse with airplanes nowadays. Similarly, it seems unlikely God's throne would be located somewhere in the Milky Way or in another galaxy. Rather, God's throne is beyond the sky and the universe, in a realm humans cannot access, and which one might therefore call the third heaven (2 Cor 12:2).

Accordingly, it is conceivable that the space God has arranged for us as humans is not only this Earth, but the entirety of the physical universe.[43] Of course, the universe is so large there is no way we could ever fully explore it in this present age.[44] Maybe this is something that will only occur in a comprehensive manner in the eschaton, after Jesus returns in glory. Still, this would mean that, in the meantime, we as humans could take small steps toward this goal. Operating in the tension of the "already" but "not yet" could then become a theological basis for becoming a multiplanetary species.

Stepping out to explore Mars and other planets will be a risky endeavor. There are many unknowns, and the trips will take a long time. However, when the first humans decided to sail over the Atlantic or cross the Pacific Ocean, there were also many unknowns, and these journeys took a long time as well. Colonizing Mars or other planets will mean forsaking comfort and being willing to risk one's life in order to start a new chapter in the history of humanity, and conceivably this is an area

---

darkness, does evil works, is ignorant of the Father, rejoices over the death of the Son." Niebuhr, *Christ and Culture*, 198.

42. Fowler, "Dwelling Place of God."

43. An interesting source of inspiration in this regard could be the space trilogy written by C. S. Lewis (1898–1963), which includes the titles *Out of the Silent Planet*, *Perelandra*, and *That Hideous Strength*. See Lewis, *Space Trilogy*.

44. According to one estimate, it would take trillions of years to travel to the edge of the universe: Rice, "How Long Does It Take." For a description of the size of the universe by a Christian theologian, see Amaral, *Story in the Stars*, 6–8.

where Christians can shine by being at the forefront of these endeavors.[45] Wherever people may move to in the future, this will create an opportunity and responsibility for believers to be a witness for the gospel in this new context. Reflecting on the future of evangelical missiology, Sam George mentions megatrends like urbanization and migration but then also affirms, "The access and cost of travel will plummet drastically, and more earthlings will become extra-terrestrial as we set up factories and homes in neighboring planets."[46]

This kind of sacrificial commitment inspired by a long-term vision will be especially necessary when attempting to travel to a different solar system. Reaching Alpha Centauri (the next star, which is 4.3 lightyears away) would take eighteen thousand years, traveling at a speed of two hundred fifty thousand kilometers per hour.[47] It is unclear what kind of technologies might be available in the future to propel a spaceship capable of reaching this destination within a human's lifespan, but assuming a speed of 10 percent of the speed of light, it would take around forty years.[48] What seems to be clear is such a journey and vision would require great sacrifices, and that is where, potentially, followers of Jesus come in.

As Neal Stephenson shared in a conversation with Lex Fridman, a computer scientist and host of a popular podcast, he likes the science fiction drama *The Expanse* (first released in 2015) because there the people building a starship to go to another solar system "are doing it for religious reasons. And I think that's the only reason that you would do it."[49] Fridman then asked whether everything is not, ultimately, done for religious reasons, meaning that an endeavor such as exploration is fueled by a quest for meaning. It is interesting how Fridman here points to the necessity of spirituality in the context of long-range space travel, and maybe this perspective could become a conversation starter for Christians to share about their faith and the hope that propels them.

Granted, some of these topics discussed here point to a more distant future. Most of what I have described in this volume has to do with technological developments that might become a reality in the next ten or twenty years. For all we know, traveling to a different solar system is not

---

45. See also Musk recognizing that a number of people will probably die on the way to Mars. Gohd, "Elon Musk Reminds Us."
46. George, "Past, Present, and Future," 12.
47. Clery, "U.S. Lawmaker Orders NASA."
48. Byrd, "New Solar Sail."
49. Fridman, "Neal Stephenson."

going to happen within that time frame. However, there are important milestones that will probably be reached in the 2030s and 2040s, such as sending the first humans to Mars.[50] In addition, the challenges and opportunities of space will invite progress with regards to various technologies, including AI, robotics, and new materials. In this sense, space travel is a characteristic element of the era of the Fourth Industrial Revolution: As technological change creates new ways of doing things in different fields, these developments then also have important socioeconomic, political, and ethical implications. With this general principle in mind, we have come full circle, and it is now time to turn to this book's conclusion.

DISCUSSION QUESTIONS

1. What is the significance of space when it comes to new opportunities in terms of tourism, business, and national defense?
2. Given that large meteorites may have crushed into Earth in the distant past, do you believe God would allow this to happen again sometime in the future? Why or why not?
3. What are some of the arguments against further engagement in outer space?
4. Why do you think God created such a large universe that includes not only billions of stars, but many planets as well?

SUGGESTIONS FOR FURTHER READING

- Rod Pyle, *Space 2.0: How Private Spaceflight, a Resurgent NASA, and International Partners Are Creating a New Space Age* (2019). Describes current developments and future opportunities with regards to space, enhanced by a large number of illustrations in color.
- Daniel Deudney, *Dark Skies: Space Expansionism, Planetary Geopolitics, and the Ends of Humanity* (2020). Highlights the negative consequences of expanding into space, written by a professor of political science and international relations.

---

50. WION Web Team, "NASA Is Recruiting"; Oakes, "Will Humans Ever Go."

- Robert Zubrin, *The Case for Space: How the Revolution in Spaceflight Opens Up a Future of Limitless Possibility* (2019). A fascinating and passionate plaidoyer for why expanding into space is essential and how it can be achieved.
- Kelly Weinersmith and Zach Weinersmith, *A City on Mars: Can We Settle Space, Should We Settle Space, and Have We Really Thought This Through?* (2023). Discusses the many challenges and problems associated with venturing into space, using down-to-earth language.
- C. S. Lewis, *The Space Trilogy* (2014). Three novels (*Out of the Silent Planet*, *Perelandra*, and *That Hideous Strength*) that explore profound theological themes—like so many works by Lewis, a classic.
- Mary Doria Russell, *The Sparrow* (2016). A science fiction novel of philosophical and moral depth; the sequel is called *Children of God*.

Conclusion

My goal with this book was to introduce followers of Jesus to the concept and reality of the Fourth Industrial Revolution, and to outline some of the implications for Christian witness in the complex world of the twenty-first century. Whether we approve of these developments or not, a new era is upon us—an era that is increasingly being shaped by novel and powerful technologies. Some of these technologies that we as believers should be aware of are autonomous vehicles, artificial intelligence (AI), augmented reality (AR) and virtual reality (VR), nanotechnologies, gene editing, quantum computers, the internet of things (IoT), blockchain-based innovations like cryptocurrencies, new approaches to generating energy like fusion reactors, and various innovations related to space technologies that could propel humans toward becoming a multi-planetary species.

These technologies are already impacting people's daily lives, and they have the potential to substantially disrupt major sectors of society and the economy, including transportation, industry and commerce, education, healthcare, entertainment, national security, the service sector, and energy. As this volume demonstrates, technology is a potent force that profoundly influences the socioeconomic and political dynamics of the world we live in. This, in turn, means these shifts lead to a host of challenges and opportunities, inviting the church to reflect on the ethical and spiritual dimensions of such transformative changes. Some of these questions we need to ponder are quite fundamental, such as: What is the role of paid work? How should we spend our free time? What does it mean to be human?

I have mostly focused on raising these kinds of questions, but it was not necessarily my intention to provide any ultimate answers, at least not in a comprehensive manner. As indicated in the headings introducing the theological sections of my chapters, my intention was to offer "*a* Christian perspective" on these issues (emphasis added). I wanted to provide my perspective to encourage discussion and debate, being fully aware that other followers of Jesus may see things quite differently. In particular, I can imagine some readers of this book anticipated more critical reflections regarding the many downsides of technology.

I agree we need warning voices in this regard. One helpful conversation partner for such an undertaking might be the French philosopher Jacques Ellul (1912–94), who spoke about *technique* as "a creature of the scientific revolution, a force beyond us which seeks to exercise ever greater control over our lives in its striving for absolute power."[1] In a more recent essay, a similar idea is proposed by George A. Blair, who believes that "technology as such is not anti-Christian."[2] However, Blair differentiates between technology and technique. The former "implicitly recognizes a finality in things, and makes predictions based on that finality."[3] By contrast, "technique is anti-Christian" because "it uses the world as if it has no other reality than do to my will—as if it were a pure vehicle for me to achieve my goals."[4] For this reason, technique is an idolatrous undertaking, because it is "trying to pretend that it is God, who can create out of nothing, which is anti-Christian."[5]

Given these realities and dangers, it is crucial for Christians to formulate a critical distance toward technology. A helpful theological framework to do so can be the biblical Sabbath, which was already mentioned in the context of education (chapter 3) and entertainment (chapter 4). Work is a reality of our human existence, and the Bible instructs us to work six days a week—but, at the same time, it also tells us to rest on the seventh day, and to sanctify it. By keeping the Sabbath in mind, Christians could develop a rhythm in which they accept that technology is constantly present during six days a week, but then decide to live in a screen-free environment on the seventh day. This would mean enjoying a day of rest without emails, without social media, and without television

---

1. This is a summary by Bor, *Staying Human*, 1. For the original work, see Ellul, *Technological Society*. For a theological perspective on Ellul's contribution, see Prior, *Confronting Technology*.
2. Blair, "Faith outside Technique," 19.
3. Blair, "Faith outside Technique," 18.
4. Blair, "Faith outside Technique," 19.
5. Blair, "Faith outside Technique," 19.

or movies.[6] Similarly, believers might benefit from taking a break from technology every day (for instance, by turning off their devices an hour before going to sleep) and also during a longer period each year, such as by going on a weeklong retreat.[7] These breaks are important because technology provides us with constant distraction, which is problematic because they "can keep a Christian from contemplating God or the things of God."[8]

I think it is vital that we as the body of Christ are intentional in how we relate to technology, instead of becoming simply "stuck in the middle."[9] This term is used in the business world to describe a situation in which a company will likely not be competitive in the market because it does not have a clear strategy in terms of pricing. One successful pricing strategy would be offering a product at a low price—the profit margins per unit sold will then be relatively small, but since the price is low, many customers will buy this product, thereby producing an attractive revenue for the seller. On the other side of the spectrum, a business may see itself as catering to the luxury segment—here only a small number of units are sold, but since the price is so high, this company enjoys high profit margins. Then there are those companies that are stuck in the middle; meaning they have neither a low-price nor a high-value strategy, making it difficult for them to compete.

As the church, we are competing in the marketplace of ideas when it comes to presenting the gospel in the pluralistic context of the twenty-first century.[10] With regards to technology, I am suggesting the church must be proactive rather than reactive; the body of Christ needs to take the lead, instead of just following the general flow of society in a passive manner. For some believers, this could mean to be innovative and to exercise leadership regarding the development of new technologies. For others, it might mean to operate at the opposite end of the spectrum, intentionally choosing a lifestyle of simplicity.

---

6. Brooks, *Creating a Tech Sabbath Habit*; Scarlata, *Sabbath Rest*; Swoboda, *Subversive Sabbath*. For a Jewish perspective on the Sabbath as a day that encourages tangible things such as good food and physical intimacy, while staying away from technology, see Bor, *Staying Human*, 214–29.

7. See also Wu Song, "Digital Life and Social Media," 208, 216.

8. Huggins, "Proceed with Caution," 98.

9. Hill and Jones, *Essentials of Strategic Management*, 128–29.

10. Muck and Adeney, *Christianity Encountering World Religions*; Copan and Litwak, *Gospel in the Marketplace of Ideas*.

The key will be to avoid a vacuous lukewarmness, and to be either hot or cold instead (see Rev 3:15–16).

Accordingly, one promising strategy would be to present an alternative lifestyle, one which intentionally limits the use of gadgets and other technological innovations. An inspiration in this regard could be the Amish communities, who live in certain parts of the United States, such as rural Ohio and Pennsylvania.[11] The Amish are not technophobic; they are willing to take advantage of useful tools. Nonetheless, before adopting a new technology, they ask themselves: Will this facilitate or hinder our communal life and the close relationships we enjoy with each other and with God?[12] With this kind of perspective, Christians could embrace an alternative lifestyle that is radically countercultural, for example by living together in remote parts of the country, growing organic food, and offering retreats to churches and individuals who want to undergo a digital detox.[13]

However, Christians who make this kind of choice will always be the exception. The majority of believers will live in a world dominated by various technologies, which is why it is so important that we as followers of Jesus learn how to be proactive and intentional in relating to the numerous innovations of the Fourth Industrial Revolution. As Deut 28:13 states, God invites his people to be the head and not the tail if they live a life of obedience to God's commandments. For this reason, I have focused on an optimistic tone in the present book, highlighting the opportunities associated with many of the novel technologies that are already reshaping the way people think, live, and work.

As the Christian technologist Ben Elmore said during an event about "The Future of Missional Engagement," in today's society, "technology is taking over everything that we do."[14] Consequently, "technology is the new front door for the church," and in this kind of environment, "standing still is not an option."[15] Rather, faith communities will have to adapt to constantly changing circumstances, and this may include getting

---

11. Recently, the Amish have also been expanding into other parts of the United States. Berg, "Why the Amish Population."

12. Wetmore, "Amish Technology"; Reinke, *God, Technology, and the Christian Life*, 269–72.

13. If Christians do not offer such opportunities to unplug, others will. Bunch, "12 Unplugged Destinations."

14. Elmore, "Future of Missional Engagement."

15. Elmore, "Future of Missional Engagement."

ready for an era of total integration, in which innovations like AR and VR will lead to a "screenless revolution."[16]

The disruptive technologies of the Fourth Industrial Revolution will impact not only local churches but global missions and outreach as well. SIL International, for instance, is already using AI in their Bible translation efforts, and they anticipate Natural Language Processing (NLP) will play a significant role in making Scripture available in both text and audio formats.[17] Jon Hirst, the chief innovation officer at SIL International, sees also great potential in using chatbots, personalized tutors, and AI coaches in evangelism and discipleship, making relevant messages available to seekers and believers in hundreds of languages.[18]

Two of the major forces shaped by technology are transportation and communication. These two forces have always been crucial in the history of missions, as they enabled missionaries to travel where Christ had not yet been preached and to proclaim the good news using a variety of avenues. In order to be missional in our time, I believe it is essential for the church to take advantage of today's tools and to become familiar with future possibilities that might assist believers in communicating the gospel in the twenty-first century.[19] It is also important Christians are knowledgeable about the disruptions the Fourth Industrial Revolution is bringing about, so they will have a seat at the table when the challenges, opportunities, and implications of these new technologies are discussed. It is my hope and prayer this volume will serve as such a conversation starter for many Christians in this regard, which is why I end here with one last set of discussion questions.

DISCUSSION QUESTIONS

1. What are your thoughts on what Jacques Ellul calls *technique*? Do you agree with him that technology threatens to overpower every aspect of our lives? Why or why not?

---

16. Elmore, "Future of Missional Engagement." Elmore is the executive chairman of Intevity (https://www.intevity.com), a digital consultancy, and he is passionate about helping churches to manage innovative technologies.

17. SIL International, "SIL AI and NLP Projects."

18. Hirst, "Webinar: AI and Its Impact."

19. Using social media as a strategic tool, for instance, is not only something that churches in the West do; it is also a common practice among many of the growing megachurches in the Majority World. Gitau, *Megachurch Christianity Reconsidered*, 49.

2. What kind of practices or habits, if any, do you currently have in place allowing you to take a break from technology? In view of the biblical concept of the Sabbath, what kind of boundaries would you like to establish going forward?

3. To what extent is your church using technology as a new kind of front door, inviting people to come in? In what ways can believers use technology to step out into this world and become a blessing to others?

4. In your opinion, what topics that were not covered in this book are going to be important when it comes to describing what the world might look like in the 2030s and 2040s?

SUGGESTIONS FOR FURTHER READING

- Jacques Ellul, *The Technological Society* (1964). Warns that technology and efficiency are increasingly becoming an end in itself, creating a monoculture that destroys traditional values.

- Abraham Joshua Heschel, *The Sabbath: Its Meaning for Modern Man* (2005). A classic of Jewish spirituality, this book highlights the sanctity of time.

- Jeff Smith, *Becoming Amish: A Family's Search for Faith, Community, and Purpose* (2016). Tells the true story of an American family that converted to the Amish faith and lifestyle.

- Kevin Kelly, *The Inevitable: Understanding the 12 Technological Forces That Will Shape Our Future* (2016). Envisions life in the year 2046 by highlighting several key trends in technology, written by the founding executive director of *Wired* magazine.

- Jay Y. Kim, *Analog Church: Why We Need Real People, Places, and Things in the Digital Age* (2020). Argues for the importance of incarnational living, written by the lead pastor of a church in Silicon Valley, California.

- Dave Adamson, *MetaChurch: How to Use Digital Ministry to Reach People and Make Disciples* (2022). Encourages churches to embrace online tools and strategies in order to reach people with the gospel.

Bibliography

Adamson, Dave. *MetaChurch: How to Use Digital Ministry to Reach People and Make Disciples.* Cumming, GA: Orange, 2022.

Adams, Ted. *The Freedom Bible: An A-to-Z Guide to Exercising Your Individual Rights, Protecting Your Privacy, Liberating Yourself from Corporate and Government Overreach.* New York: Skyhorse, 2023.

Adkins, Jonathan. "Small Decrease in 2022 Traffic Deaths Sustains Pandemic-Fueled Surge in Roadway Fatalities as NHTSA Still Lacks a Confirmed Administrator." Governors Highway Safety Association, Apr 20, 2023. https://www.ghsa.org/resources/news-releases/NHTSA-2022-Traffic-Deaths23#:~:text=WASHINGTON%2C%20 D.C.%20%E2%80%93%20The%20National%20Highway,0.3%25%20from%20 the%20year%20before.

Aerospace. "A Brief History of GPS." https://aerospace.org/article/brief-history-gps.

Agrawal, A. J. "Competition for Online Eyeballs: Here's How to Break through the Noise." *Forbes*, Feb 22, 2016. https://www.forbes.com/sites/ajagrawal/2016/02/22/competition-for-online-eyeballs-heres-how-to-break-through-the-noise.

Ahima, Rexford S. *Can the Obesity Crisis Be Reversed?* Baltimore, MD: Johns Hopkins University Press, 2021.

Alaniz, Katie, and Dawn Wilson. *Naturalizing Digital Immigrants: The Power of Collegial Coaching for Technology Integration.* Lanham, MD: Rowman & Littlefield, 2015.

Al Bawaba. "The 10 Biggest Cyber Attacks in History." Oct 23, 2023. https://www.albawaba.com/business/10-biggest-cyber-attacks-history.

Aldinger, Carl. "What Are Fossil Fuels and When Will They Run Out?" *My Twin Tiers*, Nov 11, 2021. https://www.mytwintiers.com/news-cat/international/what-are-fossil-fuels-and-when-will-they-run-out/.

Ali, Javed. "Opinion: Collaboration Key to Preventing Autonomous Vehicle Terror." *Detroit News*, Jul 21, 2019. https://www.detroitnews.com/story/opinion/2019/07/22/opinion-collaboration-key-preventing-autonomous-vehicle-terror/1778204001/.

Altman, Alex, and Alex Fitzpatrick. "Everything We Know about Sony, *The Interview* and North Korea." *Time*, Dec 17, 2014. https://time.com/3639275/the-interview-sony-hack-north-korea/.

Amaral, Joe. *Story in the Stars: Discovering God's Design and Plan for Our Universe.* New York: FaithWords, 2018.

Amazon. "Oculus Quest 2—Advanced All-in-One Virtual Reality Headset—64 GB (UK Model)." https://www.amazon.com/Oculus-Quest-Advanced-All-One-Virtual/dp/

B08HK24JSD/ref=sr_1_13?dchild=1&keywords=virtual+reality&qid=1630282195&sr=8-13.

American Hospital Association. "Fast Facts on U.S. Hospitals, 2024." https://www.aha.org/statistics/fast-facts-us-hospitals.

American Trucking Associations. "ATA American Trucking Trends 2023." Jul 19, 2023. https://www.trucking.org/news-insights/ata-american-trucking-trends-2023.

Anders, David, et al. "Starlink Internet Review: A Top Choice Where Options Are Limited." *CNET*, last updated May 2, 2024. https://www.cnet.com/home/internet/starlink-internet-review/.

Anderson, Ange. *Virtual Reality, Augmented Reality and Artificial Intelligence in Special Education: A Practical Guide to Supporting Students with Learning Differences.* London: Routledge, 2019.

Andrews, Evan. "Who Invented the Internet?" *History*, last updated Oct 28, 2019. https://www.history.com/news/who-invented-the-internet.

Androne, Mihai. *Martin Luther: Father of the Reformation and Educational Reformer.* Cham, Switzerland: Springer, 2020.

Aquilina, Mike. *The Healing Imperative: The Early Church and the Invention of Medicine as We Know It.* Steubenville, OH: Emmaus Road, 2017.

ARK Invest. "Big Ideas 2024." https://ark-invest.com/big-ideas-2024.

Armstrong, John. *The Future of Energy: The 2023 Guide to the Energy Transition.* Energy Technology, 2023.

Atala, Anthony. "Growing New Organs." TEDEd. https://ed.ted.com/lessons/printing-a-human-kidney-anthony-atala.

Atkinson, Robert D. "Shaping Structural Change in an Era of New Technology." In *Work in the Digital Age: Challenges of the Fourth Industrial Revolution*, edited by Max Neufeind et al., 103–16. London: Rowman & Littlefield, 2018.

Autor, David H., et al. *The Work of the Future: Building Better Jobs in an Age of Intelligent Machines.* Cambridge, MA: MIT, 2022.

Awari, G. K., et al. *Additive Manufacturing and 3D Printing Technology: Principles and Applications.* Boca Raton, FL: CRC, 2021.

Bachelors Degree Center. "30 Best College Majors for the Future." https://www.bachelorsdegreecenter.org/highest-paying-bachelors-degrees-future/.

Baker, Deane. *Should We Ban Killer Robots?* Cambridge, UK: Polity, 2022.

Baldwin, Roberto. "K.I.T.T., David Hasselhoff's Personal Knight Rider Car, Is for Sale." *Car and Driver*, Jan 5, 2021. https://www.caranddriver.com/news/a35131520/david-hasselhoff-knight-rider-kitt-auction/.

Ball, Philip. "The Chase for Fusion Energy." *Nature*, Nov 17, 2021. https://www.nature.com/immersive/d41586-021-03401-w/index.html.

Barber, Courtney. "Drug and Alcohol Rehab for Doctors Near Me." American Addiction Centers, last updated Apr 26, 2024. https://americanaddictioncenters.org/medical-professionals/substance-abuse-among-doctors-key-statistics.

Barczi, Nathan A. "In the Image of Our Choosing? Personhood, the Image of God, and the Ethics of Gene Editing." In *Technē: Christian Visions of Technology*, edited by Gerald Hiestand and Todd A. Wilson, 151–71. Eugene, OR: Cascade, 2022.

Barhat, Vikram. "Tesla's Musk Says Solar, Energy Storage Will Grow Faster Than Electric Cars, and There's Some Truth to It." CNBC, Dec 14, 2019. https://www.cnbc.com/2019/12/14/teslas-musk-says-solar-energy-storage-to-grow-faster-than-cars.html.

Barker, Graeme. *The Agricultural Revolution in Prehistory: Why Did Foragers Become Farmers?* New York: Oxford University Press, 2009.
Batey, Nadia. "A Brief History of Bitcoin." James Moore, last updated Feb 6, 2024. https://www.jmco.com/brief-history-bitcoin/.
Beck, Madelyn. "Technology Changing Access and Outcomes in Abortion Debate." *Illinois Public Media*, Sep 13, 2018. https://will.illinois.edu/news/story/technology-changing-access-and-outcomes-in-abortion-debate.
Berg, Janine, and Valerio De Stefano. "Employment and Regulation for Clickworkers." In *Work in the Digital Age: Challenges of the Fourth Industrial Revolution*, edited by Max Neufeind et al., 175–84. London: Rowman & Littlefield, 2018.
Bergmann, Jonathan, and Aaron Sams. *Flip Your Classroom: Reach Every Student in Every Class Every Day*. Rev. ed. Eugene, OR: International Society for Technology in Education, 2012.
Berg, Nate. "Why the Amish Population Is Exploding." *Bloomberg*, Aug 1, 2012. https://www.bloomberg.com/news/articles/2012-08-01/why-the-amish-population-is-exploding.
Bethel College. "Catalog: 2023–2024 Academic Year." https://betheltech.net/pdfs/bethel-tech-catalog-2023-2024.pdf.
Billings, Linda. "Colonizing Other Planets Is a Bad Idea." *Futures* 110 (Jun 2019) 44–46.
Bishop, Richard. "Big Dawgs in Automated Trucking Make Big Moves Towards Commercialization." *Forbes*, Aug 21, 2023. https://www.forbes.com/sites/richardbishop1/2023/08/21/big-dawgs-in-automated-trucking-make-big-moves-towards-commercialization/?sh=29f2700a3fbb.
———. "U.S. States Are Allowing Automated Follower Truck Platooning While the Swedes May Lead in Europe." *Forbes*, May 2, 2020. https://www.forbes.com/sites/richardbishop1/2020/05/02/us-states-are-allowing-automated-follower-truck-platooning-while-the-swedes-may-lead-in-europe.
Bittencourt, Ig Ibert, et al. *Artificial Intelligence in Education: 21st International Conference, AIED 2020, Ifrane, Morocco, July 6–10, 2020, Proceedings, Part II*. Cham, Switzerland: Springer Nature, 2020.
Blair, George A. "Faith outside Technique." In *Theology and Technology: Essays in Christian Analysis*, edited by Carl Mitcham et al., 1:18–24. Eugene, OR: Wipf & Stock, 2022.
Bloom, Jonathan, and Sheila Blair. *Islam: A Thousand Years of Faith and Power*. New Haven, CT: Yale University Press, 2002.
Bock, Darrell, and Jonathan Armstrong. *Virtual Reality Church: Pitfalls and Possibilities*. Chicago: Moody, 2021.
Bock, Kenneth, and Cameron Stauth. *Healing the New Childhood Epidemics: Autism, ADHD, Asthma, and Allergies: The Groundbreaking Program for the 4-A Disorders*. New York: Ballantine, 2008.
Boon, Tom, and Pranjal Pande. "How Much Is a Boeing 747-8 Worth in 2023?" Simple Flying, last updated Oct 11, 2023. https://simpleflying.com/boeing-747-8-value/#:~:text=It%27s%20time%20to%20answer%20the,Air%2C%20ending%20the%20type%27s%20history.
Bor, Harris. *Staying Human: A Jewish Theology for the Age of Artificial Intelligence*. Eugene, OR: Cascade, 2021.

Bos, Chanan. "Tesla's New HW3 Self-Driving Computer—It's a Beast (CleanTechnica Deep Dive)." *Clean Technica*, Jun 15, 2019. https://cleantechnica.com/2019/06/15/teslas-new-hw3-self-driving-computer-its-a-beast-cleantechnica-deep-dive.

Bosch, David J. *Transforming Mission: Paradigm Shifts in Theology of Mission*. 20th anniversary ed. Maryknoll, NY: Orbis, 2011.

Bostrom, Nick. *Superintelligence: Paths, Dangers, Strategies*. Oxford: Oxford University Press, 2014.

Boyle, Mark. *Human Geography: An Essential Introduction*. 2nd ed. Hoboken, NJ: Wiley-Blackwell, 2021.

Brahambhatt, Rupendra. "Settling the Debate: Does Tesla's Autopilot Save Lives or Risk Them?" *Interesting Engineering*, Sep 8, 2021. https://interestingengineering.com/does-teslas-autopilot-save-lives-or-risk-them.

Braun, Stuart. "Why Build Unprofitable New Coal Plants?" DW, Jun 30, 2021. https://www.dw.com/en/why-build-600-new-unprofitable-coal-plants/a-58095657.

Britt, Hugo. "Companies Are Preparing for Space Mining." *Thomas*, Aug 19, 2021. https://www.thomasnet.com/insights/companies-are-preparing-for-space-mining/.

Brooks, Bryan. *Creating a Tech Sabbath Habit: Unplug Your Mind, Restore Your Spirit, and Transform Your Technology Lifestyle*. Mustang, OK: Tate, 2011.

Brooks, Michael. "The Porn Pioneers." *Guardian*, Sep 30, 1999. https://www.theguardian.com/technology/1999/sep/30/onlinesupplement.

Brose, Christian. *The Kill Chain: Defending America in the Future of High-Tech Warfare*. New York: Hachette, 2020.

Broussard, Meredith. *Artificial Unintelligence: How Computers Misunderstand the World*. Cambridge, MA: MIT Press, 2018.

Brynjolfsson, Erik, and Andrew McAfee. *The Second Machine Age: Work, Progress, and Prosperity in a Time of Brilliant Technologies*. New York: Norton, 2014.

Buckenmaier, Chester, III, et al. "Anything That You Can Conceive of as a Supply Chain, Blockchain Can Vastly Improve Its Efficiency." *U.S. Medicine*, Feb 10, 2021. https://www.usmedicine.com/editor-in-chief/anything-that-can-conceive-of-as-a-supply-chain-blockchain-can-vastly-improve-its-efficiency/.

Bullock, Dave. "Sir, Your Liver Is Ready: Behind the Scenes of Bioprinting." *Wired*, Jul 11, 2010. https://www.wired.com/2010/07/gallery-bio-printing.

Bunch, Erin. "12 Unplugged Destinations for an Epic, Digital-Detox Vacay." *Well and Good*, Jan 23, 2018. https://www.wellandgood.com/tech-free-unplugged-vacation-ideas-for-2018/.

Burke, Lilah. "Catholic Contraception? Get the App." *Inside Higher Ed*, Jan 24, 2020. https://www.insidehighered.com/news/2020/01/24/catholic-colleges-develop-apps-natural-family-planning.

Burns, Lawrence D. *Autonomy: The Quest to Build the Driverless Car—And How It Will Reshape Our World*. New York: Ecco, 2018.

Burtchaell, James Tunstead. *The Dying of the Light: The Disengagement of Colleges and Universities from Their Christian Churches*. Grand Rapids, MI: Eerdmans, 1998.

Byrd, Deborah. "New Solar Sail May Travel to Alpha Centauri." *EarthSky*, Mar 12, 2022. https://earthsky.org/space/alpha-centauri-travel-time/.

Byrd DeRegibus, Missy. "On Human Transcendence, Artificial Intelligence, and the Gathering Gnostic Storm." In *Technē: Christian Visions of Technology*, edited by Gerald Hiestand and Todd A. Wilson, 139–50. Eugene, OR: Cascade, 2022.

Cairns, Earle E. *Christianity through the Centuries: A History of the Christian Church.* 3rd ed. Grand Rapids, MI: Zondervan Academic, 2009.

Calkin, Sydney, and Ella Berny. "Legal and Non-Legal Barriers to Abortion in Ireland and the United Kingdom." *Med Access Point Care* (Aug 2021). https://www.ncbi.nlm.nih.gov/pmc/articles/PMC9413599/.

Callaway, Kutter. "The Yes (to Technology) in Our No (to Social Media)." *Fuller Magazine* 15 (2019) 48–49. https://fullerstudio.fuller.edu/the-yes-to-technology-in-our-no-to-social-media/.

Carpenter, Joel et al., eds. *Christian Higher Education: A Global Reconnaissance.* Grand Rapids, MI: Eerdmans, 2014.

Carr, Nicholas. *The Shallows: What the Internet Is Doing to Our Brains.* Rev. ed. New York: Norton, 2020.

Castellano, Jaime A., and Andrea Dawn Frazier, eds. *Special Populations in Gifted Education: Understanding Our Most Able Students from Diverse Backgrounds.* New York: Routledge, 2011.

CB Insights. "Banking Is Only the Beginning: 65 Big Industries Blockchain Could Transform." Mar 9, 2022. https://www.cbinsights.com/research/industries-disrupted-blockchain/.

CDC. "Global Road Safety." Mar 4, 2024. https://www.cdc.gov/transportation-safety/global/?CDC_AAref_Val=https://www.cdc.gov/injury/features/global-road-safety/index.html.

Center for Global Policy Solutions. *Stick Shift: Autonomous Vehicles, Driving Jobs, and the Future of Work.* Washington, DC: Center for Global Policy Solutions, 2017.

Chapman, Allan. *Physicians, Plagues and Progress: The History of Western Medicine from Antiquity to Antibiotics.* Oxford, UK: Lion, 2016.

Chaves, Mark. *American Religion: Contemporary Trends.* 2nd ed. Princeton, NJ: Princeton University Press, 2017.

Chen, Connie. "11 Photos of Amazon's New Prime Air Drone That Can Fly in Light Rain and Deliver Packages Up to 5 Pounds in under an Hour." About Amazon, Oct 18, 2023. https://www.aboutamazon.com/news/transportation/amazon-prime-air-drone-delivery-mk30-photos.

Chen, Phil. "The Journey to a New Internet: A Reading from the Book of Exodus." *Quartz*, Mar 29, 2019. https://qz.com/1582078/the-bible-holds-lessons-on-data-ownership-and-internet-privacy.

Chester, Matt. "Revisiting Solar Roadways: Is the Concept Still Too Good to Be True?" *EcoWatch*, Sep 14, 2021. https://www.ecowatch.com/solar-roadways-too-good-to-be-true-2655025285.html.

Chestney, Nina. "Putin Wants 'Unfriendly' Countries to Pay for Russian Gas in Roubles." Reuters, Mar 23, 2022. https://www.reuters.com/business/energy/putin-says-russia-will-start-selling-gas-unfriendly-countries-roubles-2022-03-23/.

Chik, Holly. "Chinese Team's Classical Computing Tackles the 'Impossible' to Challenge Google's 'Quantum Supremacy.'" *SCMP*, Nov 13, 2021. https://www.scmp.com/news/china/science/article/3155902/chinese-teams-classical-computing-tackles-impossible-challenge.

Childs, Dan. "Tiger Woods May Be Role Model for Battling Sex Addiction." ABC, Jan 24, 2010. https://abcnews.go.com/Health/Wellness/tiger-woods-sex-addict/story?id=9649709.

Chin, Kyle. "Biggest Data Breaches in US History (Updates 2024)." *UpGuard*, last updated Feb 20, 2024. https://www.upguard.com/blog/biggest-data-breaches-us.

Cho, Adrian. "Physicists Move Closer to Defeating Errors in Quantum Computation." *Science*, Jul 14, 2021. https://www.science.org/content/article/physicists-move-closer-defeating-errors-quantum-computation.

The Church.digital. "Episode 188: The Future Church in the Metaverse." YouTube video, Nov 21, 2021. https://www.youtube.com/watch?v=vT4xsAWuVuk.

Cipolla, Carlo M. *Before the Industrial Revolution: European Society and Economy, 1000–1700*. 3rd ed. New York: Norton, 1994.

Claessens, Michel. *ITER: The Giant Fusion Reactor: Bringing a Sun to Earth*. Cham, Switzerland: Springer, 2020.

Clarke, Steve, et al., eds. *The Ethics of Human Enhancement: Understanding the Debate*. Oxford: Oxford University Press, 2016.

Clery, Daniel. "U.S. Lawmaker Orders NASA to Plan for Trip to Alpha Centauri by 100th Anniversary of Moon Landing." *Science*, May 23, 2016. https://www.science.org/content/article/us-lawmaker-orders-nasa-plan-trip-alpha-centauri-100th-anniversary-moon-landing.

Clevenger, Seth. "Who's Still in Autonomous Trucking? Several Developers Drop Out While Others Prepare to Go Driverless." *Transport Topics*, Feb 23, 2024. https://www.ttnews.com/articles/autonomous-trucking-development.

CNCA. "Our Cities." https://carbonneutralcities.org/our-cities/.

Cohen, I. Glenn. "Artificial Wombs Are Coming. They Could Completely Change the Debate over Abortion." *Vox*, Aug 23, 2017. https://www.vox.com/the-big-idea/2017/8/23/16186468/artificial-wombs-radically-transform-abortion-debate.

Collart-Dutilleul, Simon, et al., eds. *Reliability, Safety, and Security of Railway Systems. Modelling, Analysis, Verification, and Certification: Third International Conference, RSSRail 2019, Lille, France, June 4–6, 2019, Proceedings*. Cham, Switzerland: Springer, 2019.

Collender, Michael, and Jonathan Shaw. *Wiser Than the Machine: The Value of Classical Christian Education in an Age of Artificial Intelligence*. Kalispell, MT: Theorian International, 2024.

Collis, William. *The Book of Esports: The Definitive Guide to Competitive Video Games*. New York: RosettaBooks, 2020.

Companies Market Cap. "Largest Automakers by Market Capitalization." https://companiesmarketcap.com/automakers/largest-automakers-by-market-cap/.

———. "Market Capitalization of Apple." https://companiesmarketcap.com/apple/marketcap/.

Computer History Museum. "Timeline of Computer History." https://www.computerhistory.org/timeline/.

Copan, Paul, and Kenneth D. Litwak. *The Gospel in the Marketplace of Ideas: Paul's Mars Hill Experience for Our Pluralistic World*. Downers Grove, IL: InterVarsity, 2014.

Cox, Harvey. *Fire from Heaven: The Rise of Pentecostal Spirituality and the Reshaping of Religion in the Twenty-First Century*. Cambridge, MA: Da Capo, 2001.

Cravens, Gwyneth. "Terrorism and Nuclear Energy: Understanding the Risks." Brookings, Mar 1, 2002. https://www.brookings.edu/articles/terrorism-and-nuclear-energy-understanding-the-risks/.

Crawford, Matthew B. *Why We Drive: Toward a Philosophy of the Open Road*. New York: Custom, 2021.

Cressler, John D. *Silicon Earth: Introduction to Microelectronics and Nanotechnology.* 2nd ed. Boca Raton, FL: CRC, 2018.

Cronin, Irena, and Robert Scoble. *The Infinite Retina: Spatial Computing, Augmented Reality, and How a Collision of New Technologies Are Bringing about the Next Tech Revolution.* Birmingham, UK: Packt, 2020.

Crouch, Andy. "The Alchemists' Dream: Three Judgments about Technology." In *Technē: Christian Visions of Technology*, edited by Gerald Hiestand and Todd A. Wilson, 36–60. Eugene, OR: Cascade, 2022.

——. *The Tech-Wise Family: Everyday Steps for Putting Technology in Its Proper Place.* Grand Rapids, MI: Baker, 2017.

Crowl, Jonathan. "Esports Olympics—Could Esports Be an Olympic Event?" *Ting*, Jul 28, 2021. https://blog.ting.com/internet/esports-olympics.

Cuthbertson, Anthony. "World's Deepest Hole Offers 'Inexhaustible Clean Energy.'" *Independent*, Mar 16, 2022. https://www.independent.co.uk/tech/geothermal-energy-renewables-quaise-hole-b2036201.html.

Dall, Henry D. "National Energy Security and Reliance on Foreign Oil." *Air Force Journal of Logistics* 33.3/4 (Fall 2009) 38–50.

Daly, Lyle. "How Many Cryptocurrencies Are There?" Motley Fool, Nov 20, 2023. https://www.fool.com/investing/stock-market/market-sectors/financials/cryptocurrency-stocks/how-many-cryptocurrencies-are-there/.

Damante, Becca, and Kierra B. Jones. "A Year after the Supreme Court Overturned *Roe v. Wade*, Trends in State Abortion Laws Have Emerged." Center for American Progress, Jun 15, 2023. https://www.americanprogress.org/article/a-year-after-the-supreme-court-overturned-roe-v-wade-trends-in-state-abortion-laws-have-emerged/.

Danaher, John. "The Symbolic-Consequences Argument in the Sex Robot Debate." In *Robot Sex: Social and Ethical Implications*, edited by John Danaher and Neil McArthur, 103–31. Cambridge, MA: MIT Press, 2018.

Danaher, John, and Neil McArthur, eds. *Robot Sex: Social and Ethical Implications.* Cambridge, MA: MIT Press, 2018.

Danaher, John, et al. "Should We Campaign against Sex Robots?" In *Robot Sex: Social and Ethical Implications*, edited by John Danaher and Neil McArthur, 47–72. Cambridge, MA: MIT Press, 2018.

Danielian, Jeff, et al., eds. *Teaching Gifted Children: Success Strategies for Teaching High-Ability Learners.* New York: Routledge, 2021.

Dattani, Saloni, et al. "Life Expectancy." Our World in Data, 2023. https://ourworldindata.org/life-expectancy.

Davenport, Christian. *The Space Barons: Elon Musk, Jeff Bezos, and the Quest to Colonize the Cosmos.* New York: PublicAffairs, 2019.

Davidson, Cathy N. *The New Education: How to Revolutionize the University to Prepare Students for a World in Flux.* Rev. ed. New York: Basic, 2022.

Davies, Alex. *Driven: The Race to Create the Autonomous Car.* New York: Simon & Schuster, 2021.

Davies, Dave. "Facial Recognition and Beyond: Journalist Ventures inside China's 'Surveillance State.'" NPR, Jan 5, 2021. https://www.npr.org/2021/01/05/953515627/facial-recognition-and-beyond-journalist-ventures-inside-chinas-surveillance-sta.

Davies, Kevin. *Editing Humanity: The CRISPR Revolution and the New Era of Genome Editing*. New York: Pegasus, 2020.

Davis, Rowenna. "Environmentalism: A New Religion." *Guardian*, Jun 25, 2009. https://www.theguardian.com/commentisfree/belief/2009/jun/25/environmentalism-religion.

Dawson, Linda. *War in Space: The Science and Technology behind Our Next Theater of Conflict*. Cham, Switzerland: Springer, 2018.

De La Bastide, Danielle. "A Chinese Robot Just Performed the First Fully Automated Dental Surgery Ever." *Interesting Engineering*, Sep 23, 2017. https://interestingengineering.com/a-chinese-robot-just-performed-the-first-fully-automated-dental-surgery-ever.

DePillis, Lydia, et al. "Most Americans Still Have to Commute Every Day. Here's How That Experience Has Changed." *New York Times*, Nov 6, 2023. https://www.nytimes.com/interactive/2023/11/06/business/economy/commuting-change-covid.html.

De Propris, Lisa, and David Bailey. *Industry 4.0 and Regional Transformations*. New York: Routledge, 2020.

Detweiler, Craig. *iGods: How Technology Shapes Our Spiritual and Social Lives*. Grand Rapids, MI: Brazos, 2013.

Deudney, Daniel. *Dark Skies: Space Expansionism, Planetary Geopolitics, and the Ends of Humanity*. New York: Oxford University Press, 2020.

DeVine, Mark. *Shalom Yesterday, Today, and Forever: Embracing All Three Dimensions of Creation and Redemption*. Eugene, OR: Wipf & Stock, 2019.

Devlin, Kate. *Turned On: Science, Sex and Robots*. New York: Bloomsbury Sigma, 2018.

Dhawan, Chander. *Autonomous Vehicles Plus: A Critical Analysis of Challenges Delaying AV Nirvana*. Victoria, BC: FriesenPress, 2019.

Dizikes, Peter. "Study Finds Stronger Links between Automation and Inequality." *MIT News*, May 5, 2020. https://news.mit.edu/2020/study-inks-automation-inequality-0506.

Dochuk, Darren. *Anointed with Oil: How Christianity and Crude Made Modern America*. New York: Basic, 2019.

Donally, Jaime. *The Immersive Classroom: Create Customized Learning Experiences with AR/VR*. Portland, OR: International Society for Technology in Education, 2021.

Donovan, Paul. *Profit and Prejudice: The Luddites of the Fourth Industrial Revolution*. London: Routledge, 2021.

Door International. "Reaching the Largest Unreached People Group You Never Considered: White Paper on Reaching the Deaf Worldwide with the Gospel." 2018. https://doorinternational.org/wp-content/uploads/2018/08/White-Paper-on-Reaching-the-Deaf-upload-2018.pdf.

Doriani, Dan. "Should Churches Have Christian Schools? A Test Case Regarding Church and Society." Place for Truth, Sep 12, 2019. https://www.placefortruth.org/blog/should-churches-have-christian-schools-a-test-case-regarding-church-and-society.

Doria Russell, Mary. *The Sparrow*. 20th anniversary ed. New York: Ballantine, 2016.

Dorr, Adam, and Tony Seba. "Rethinking Energy 2020–2030: 100% Solar, Wind, and Batteries Is Just the Beginning." Oct 2020. https://tonyseba.com/wp-content/uploads/2020/11/RethinkingEnergy2020-2030-LRR.pdf.

Doudna, Jennifer A., and Samuel H. Sternberg. *A Crack in Creation: Gene Editing and the Unthinkable Power to Control Evolution.* Houghton, MI: Mariner, 2018.

Doyle, Alison. "Is Your Job at Risk of Automation?" *The Balance,* Feb 24, 2021. https://www.thebalancecareers.com/robot-takeover-is-your-job-at-risk-of-automation-4169632.

Dreisbach, Daniel L. *Reading the Bible with the Founding Fathers.* New York: Oxford University Press, 2017.

Dudley, Thomas. "How Many Businesses Are There in America and What Does It Mean for Employee Ownership?" Certified EO, Jul 14, 2022. https://www.certifiedeo.com/blog-posts/how-many-businesses-are-there-in-america-and-what-does-it-mean-for-employee-ownership.

Duncan, Ian, et al. "Medicare Cost at End of Life." *American Journal of Hospice and Palliative Care* 36.8 (Aug 2019) 705–10. https://doi.org/10.1177/1049909119836204.

DW News. "The Future of Modern Warfare: How Technology Is Transforming Conflict: DW Analysis." YouTube video, Jun 4, 2021. https://www.youtube.com/watch?app=desktop&v=TmlBkW6ANsQ.

Dwoskin, Elizabeth, and Karla Adam. "More Than 150 Countries Affected by Massive Cyberattack, Europol Says." *Washington Post,* May 14, 2017. https://www.washingtonpost.com/business/economy/more-than-150-countries-affected-by-massive-cyberattack-europol-says/2017/05/14/5091465e-3899-11e7-9e48-c4f199710b69_story.html.

DW Planet A. "How Solar Energy Got So Cheap, and Why It's Not Everywhere (Yet)." YouTube video, Jan 15, 2021. https://www.youtube.com/watch?v=sUvaYycoWqI.

Dyer, John. *From the Garden to the City: The Place of Technology in the Story of God.* 2nd ed. Grand Rapids, MI: Kregel, 2022.

Dzhanova, Yelena, and Mike Calia. "Democrat Andrew Yang Drops Out of the 2020 Presidential Race." CNBC, Feb 11, 2020. https://www.cnbc.com/2020/02/11/andrew-yang-drops-out-of-the-2020-presidential-race.html.

Edgar, Brian. *The God Who Plays: A Playful Approach to Theology and Spirituality.* Eugene, OR: Cascade, 2017.

EIA. "How Many Power Plants Are in the United States?" https://www.eia.gov/tools/faqs/faq.php?id=65&t=2.

———. "Oil and Petroleum Exports Explained: Oil Imports and Exports." Last updated Jan 19, 2024. https://www.eia.gov/energyexplained/oil-and-petroleum-products/imports-and-exports.php.

Ellul, Jacques. *The Technological Society.* Translated by John Wilkinson. New York: Vintage, 1964.

Ellyatt, Holly. "Global Oil Demand to Peak around 2040 or 'Much Sooner,' IMF Says." CNBC, Feb 6, 2020. https://www.cnbc.com/2020/02/06/global-oil-demand-to-peak-around-2040-imf-says.html.

Elmore, Ben. "The Future of Missional Engagement." Presentation at the Church United South Florida Gathering in Boca Raton, Florida, May 24, 2022.

EnergyStartups. "Top 10 Fusion Energy Startups." Energy Startups, Apr 21, 2024. https://www.energystartups.org/top/fusion-energy/.

Entinger, Chad. "The Deaf: An Unreached People Unlike Any Other." *Mission Frontiers,* Jan 1, 2014. https://www.missionfrontiers.org/issue/article/the-deaf.

Epstein, Alex. *Fossil Future: Why Global Human Flourishing Requires More Oil, Coal, and Natural Gas—Not Less.* New York: Portfolio, 2022.

Espindola, David, and Michael W. Wright. *The Exponential Era: Strategies to Stay Ahead of the Curve in an Era of Chaotic Changes and Disruptive Forces.* Hoboken, NJ: Wiley, 2021.

Fan, Jialu, et al. "The Four Great Inventions." In *A History of Chinese Science and Technology: Volume 2,* edited by Yongxiang Lu, 161–300. Berlin: Springer, 2014.

Ferguson, Niall. *Civilization: The West and the Rest.* New York: Penguin, 2011.

Ferngren, Gary B. *Medicine and Health Care in Early Christianity.* Baltimore, MD: Johns Hopkins University Press, 2016.

———. *Medicine and Religion: A Historical Introduction.* Baltimore, MD: Johns Hopkins University Press, 2014.

Fischer, Peer. "How Nanorobots Are Used in Medicine?" *Serious Science,* Feb 3, 2020. http://serious-science.org/nanorobots-in-medicine-9686.

Fisher, Tim. "5G Speed: How to Understand the Numbers." *Lifewire,* Sep 21, 2023. https://www.lifewire.com/5g-speed-4180992.

Fleming, Sean. "How Can We Prepare Students for the Fourth Industrial Revolution? 5 Lessons from Innovative Schools around the World." *European Sting,* Feb 3, 2020. https://europeansting.com/2020/02/03/how-can-we-prepare-students-for-the-fourth-industrial-revolution-5-lessons-from-innovative-schools-around-the-world/.

Ford, Martin. *Rise of the Robots: Technology and the Threat of a Jobless Future.* New York: Basic, 2015.

Formlabs. "Introduction to Medical 3D Printing and 3D Printers for Healthcare." https://formlabs.com/blog/3d-printing-in-medicine-healthcare.

Fowler, Ray. "The Dwelling Place of God." http://www.rayfowler.org/sermons/real-answers-about-heaven/the-dwelling-place-of-god/.

Fox-Penner, Peter. *Power after Carbon: Building a Clean, Resilient Grid.* Cambridge, MA: Harvard University Press, 2020.

Freeberg, Ernest. *The Age of Edison: Electric Light and the Invention of Modern America.* New York: Penguin, 2014.

Freitas, Robert A., Jr. "Welcome to the Future of Medicine." In *The Transhumanist Reader: Classical and Contemporary Essays on the Science, Technology, and Philosophy of the Human Future,* edited by Max More and Natasha Via-More, 67–72. Chichester, UK: Wiley-Blackwell, 2013.

Fridman, Lex. "Neal Stephenson: Sci-Fi, Space, Aliens, AI, VR and the Future of Humanity: Lex Fridman Podcast #240." YouTube video, Nov 11, 2021. https://www.youtube.com/watch?v=xAfdSak2fs8.

Friedman, Thomas L. *Hot, Flat, and Crowded: Why We Need a Green Revolution—and How It Can Renew America.* Rev. ed. New York: Picador, 2009.

Fudpucker, Wilhelm E. "Through Christian Technology to Technological Christianity." In *Theology and Technology: Essays in Christian Analysis,* edited by Carl Mitcham et al., 1:25–41. Eugene, OR: Wipf & Stock, 2022.

Galazzo, Richard. "Timeline from 1G to 5G: A Brief History on Cell Phones." CENGN, Sep 21, 2020. https://www.cengn.ca/information-centre/innovation/timeline-from-1g-to-5g-a-brief-history-on-cell-phones/.

Ganski, Christopher J. "Sacrament and Technology." In *Technē: Christian Visions of Technology,* edited by Gerald Hiestand and Todd A. Wilson, 77–91. Eugene, OR: Cascade, 2022.

Garcia, David R. *School Choice.* Cambridge, MA: MIT Press, 2018.

Garreau, Joel. "Environmentalism as Religion." *The New Atlantis* 28 (Summer 2010), 61–74. https://www.thenewatlantis.com/publications/environmentalism-as-religion.

Gates, Bill. *How to Avoid a Climate Disaster: The Solutions We Have and the Breakthroughs We Need*. New York: Vintage, 2022.

Gay, Craig M. *Modern Technology and the Human Future: A Christian Appraisal*. Downers Grove, IL: IVP Academic, 2018.

George, Sam. "The Past, Present, and Future of Evangelical Missiology." In *The Present and Future of Evangelical Mission: Academy, Agency, Assembly, and Agora Perspectives from Canada*, edited by Narry F. Santos and Xenia Ling-Yee Cham, 3–14. Eugene, OR: Wipf & Stock, 2022.

Gibney, Elizabeth. "Nuclear-Fusion Reactor Smashes Energy Record." *Nature* 602.7897 (Feb 9, 2022) 371. https://doi.org/10.1038/d41586-022-00391-1.

Gibson, Adriana, et al. "Autonomous Systems in the Combat Environment: The Key or the Curse to the U.S." *Strategy Bridge*, Oct 8, 2020. https://thestrategybridge.org/the-bridge/2020/10/8/autonomous-systems-in-the-combat-environment-the-key-or-the-curse-to-the-us.

Gitau, Wanjiru M. *Megachurch Christianity Reconsidered: Millennials and Social Change in African Perspective*. Downers Grove, IL: IVP Academic, 2018.

Glanzer, Perry L., and Joel Carpenter. "Conclusion: Evaluating the Health of Christian Higher Education around the Globe." In *Christian Higher Education: A Global Reconnaissance*, edited by Joel Carpenter et al., 277–305. Grand Rapids, MI: Eerdmans, 2014.

Glester, Andrew. "The Asteroid Trillionaires." *Physics World*, Jun 11, 2018. https://physicsworld.com/a/the-asteroid-trillionaires/.

Glover, Peter. "Environmentalism: The New Religion." *Evangelical Times*, Sep 1, 2007. https://www.evangelical-times.org/articles/scientific-including-creation/environmentalism-the-new-religion/.

Gnanadurai, Jasmine Beulah, et al. "Exploring Immersive Technology in Education for Smart Cities." In *Immersive Technology in Smart Cities: Augmented and Virtual Reality in IoT*, edited by Sagaya Aurelia and Sara Paiva, 1–26. Cham, Switzerland: Springer, 2022.

Gohd, Chelsea. "Elon Musk Reminds Us All That 'a Bunch of People Will Probably Die' Going to Mars." *Space*, Apr 28, 2021. https://www.space.com/elon-musk-mars-spacex-risks-astronauts-die.

Goheen, Michael W. *Introducing Christian Mission Today: Scripture, History and Issues*. Downers Grove, IL: InterVarsity, 2014.

Goodwin, John. "Learning through Play: How Schools Can Educate Students through Technology." World Economic Forum, Jan 24, 2020. https://www.weforum.org/agenda/2020/01/technology-education-edtech-play-learning/.

Goshay, Charita. "'Difficult Days Are Ahead' for America's Churches, Faith Institutions." *Akron Beacon Journal*, Aug 22, 2020. https://www.beaconjournal.com/story/news/local/2020/08/22/lsquodifficult-days-are-aheadrsquo-for-americarsquos-churches-faith-institutions/42282593/.

Graesser, Arthur C., et al. "Instruction Based on Tutoring." In *Handbook of Research on Learning and Instruction*, edited by Richard E. Mayer and Patricia A. Alexander, 408–26. New York: Routledge, 2011.

Graham, Ruth. "Christian Schools Boom in a Revolt against Curriculum and Pandemic Rules." *New York Times*, Oct 19, 2021. https://www.nytimes.com/2021/10/19/us/christian-schools-growth.html.

Graham, Ruth, and Sharon LaFraniere. "Inside the People of Praise, the Tight-Knit Faith Community of Amy Coney Barrett." *New York Times*, Oct 8, 2020. https://www.nytimes.com/2020/10/08/us/people-of-praise-amy-coney-barrett.html.

Greely, Henry T. "CRISPR, Patents, and Nobel Prizes." *Los Angeles Review of Books*, Aug 23, 2017. https://lareviewofbooks.org/article/crispr-patents-and-nobel-prizes.

Greengard, Samuel. *The Internet of Things*. Rev. ed. Cambridge, MA: MIT Press, 2021.

Greenway, Roger S., and Timothy M. Monsma. *Cities: Missions' New Frontier*. Grand Rapids, MI: Baker Academic, 2000.

Grifantini, Kristina. "The State of Nanorobotics in Medicine." IEEE Pulse, Oct 7, 2019. https://www.embs.org/pulse/articles/the-state-of-nanorobotics-in-medicine.

Gringer, Bonnie. "History of the Autonomous Car." https://www.titlemax.com/resources/history-of-the-autonomous-car.

Grush, Bern, and John Niles. *The End of Driving: Transportation Systems and Public Policy Planning for Autonomous Vehicles*. Amsterdam: Elsevier, 2018.

Guiness, Os. *The Call: Finding and Fulfilling the Central Purpose of Your Life*. Nashville: Thomas Nelson, 2003.

Hahn, Barbara. *Technology in the Industrial Revolution*. Cambridge, UK: Cambridge University Press, 2020.

Hamm, Harold. *Game-Changer: Our Fifty-Year Mission to Secure America's Energy Independence*. Brentwood, TN: Forefront, 2023.

Hannam, James. *God's Philosophers: How the Medieval World Laid the Foundations of Modern Science*. London: Icon, 2009.

Harari, Yuval Noah. *21 Lessons for the 21st Century*. New York: Random, 2019.

———. *Homo Deus: A Brief History of Tomorrow*. New York: Harper Perennial, 2018.

———. *Sapiens: A Brief History of Humankind*. New York: Harper Perennial, 2018.

Hard, Andrew. "The Most Incredible James Bond Cars of All-Time." *Digital Trends*, May 23, 2017. https://www.digitaltrends.com/cars/all-time-wackiest-james-bond-cars.

Hardin, Jeff. "Fearfully and Wonderfully Made? Christians and Embryos in an Era of Biotechnology." In *Technē: Christian Visions of Technology*, edited by Gerald Hiestand and Todd A. Wilson, 172–86. Eugene, OR: Cascade, 2022.

Hartmann, Margaret. "Let's Get to Know Space Force, Trump's Most Misunderstood Creation." *Intelligencer*, Sep 21, 2022. https://nymag.com/intelligencer/article/space-force-guide.html.

Hastings, Conn. "Fish-Shaped Microrobots to Deliver Chemotherapy to Tumors." Med-Tac, Nov 19, 2021. https://tactical-medicine.com/blogs/news/fish-shaped-microrobots-to-deliver-chemotherapy-to-tumors.

Hauskeller, Michael. "Automatic Sweethearts for Transhumanists." In *Robot Sex: Social and Ethical Implications*, edited by John Danaher and Neil McArthur, 203–18. Cambridge, MA: MIT Press.

Headrick, Daniel R. *Technology: A World History*. New York: Oxford University Press, 2009.

Heath, Alex. "Mark Zuckerberg on Why Facebook Is Rebranding to Meta." *The Verge*, Oct 28, 2021. https://www.theverge.com/22749919/mark-zuckerberg-facebook-meta-company-rebrand.

Heeralall, Nirmal, and Raoudha Ben Abdelkrim. "The World's Fastest-Growing Middle Class." https://www.uhy.com/the-worlds-fastest-growing-middle-class/.

Henderson, Mark. "The Dawn of the Fusion Age." YouTube video, Jul 11, 2019. https://www.youtube.com/watch?v=KlxPJ6LnyFc.

Henthorn, Jamie, et al. *The Pokémon Go Phenomenon: Essays on Public Play in Contested Spaces*. Jefferson, NC: McFarland, 2019.

Herbstreuth, Sebastian. *Oil and American Identity: A Culture of Dependency and US Foreign Policy*. New York: I.B. Taurus, 2014.

Herger, Mario. *The Last Driver's License Holder Has Already Been Born: How Rapid Advances in Automotive Technology Will Disrupt Life as We Know It and Why This Is a Good Thing*. New York: McGraw-Hill Education, 2019.

Herrera, Rene J., and Ralph Garcia-Bertrand. *Ancestral DNA, Human Origins, and Migrations*. London: Academic, 2018.

Hershberger, Daniel. *Bitcoin Is Better: Natural Money That Works for the Working Class*. Bitcoin Is Better, 2023.

Hertz, Noreena. *The Lonely Century: How to Restore Human Connection in a World That's Pulling Apart*. New York: Currency, 2021.

Herzog, Albert A., Jr. *The Social Contexts of Disability Ministry: A Primer for Pastors, Seminarians, and Lay Leaders*. Eugene, OR: Cascade, 2017.

Heschel, Abraham Joshua. *The Sabbath: Its Meaning for Modern Man*. New York: Farrar, Straus and Giroux, 2005.

Hill, Andrew E., and John H. Walton. *A Survey of the Old Testament*. 3rd ed. Grand Rapids, MI: Zondervan Academic, 2009.

Hill, Charles W. L., and Gareth R. Jones. *Essentials of Strategic Management*. Mason, OH: Cengage Learning, 2011.

Hill, Michael, and Dan Swinhoe. "The 15 Biggest Data Breaches of the 21st Century." *CSO*, Nov 8, 2022. https://www.csoonline.com/article/2130877/the-biggest-data-breaches-of-the-21st-century.html.

Hinchliffe, Ruby. "Federal Reserve More Worried about Cyber Risk Than Another 2008 Crash." *FinTech Futures*, Apr 14, 2021. https://www.fintechfutures.com/2021/04/federal-reserve-chair-says-cyber-risk-a-greater-threat-than-another-financial-crash/.

Hirst, Jon. "Webinar: AI and Its Impact on Global Mission." Missio Nexus, Jun 1, 2023. https://missionexus.org/webinar-ai-and-its-impact-on-global-mission/.

Hitt, Kevin. "2023 League of Legends Worlds Streaming Creates Record-Breaking Media Value." *Sports Business Journal*, Dec 7, 2023. https://www.sportsbusinessjournal.com/Articles/2023/12/07/esports-shikenso-media-value.

Hjortdal, Magnus. "China's Use of Cyber Warfare: Espionage Meets Strategic Deterrence." *Journal of Strategic Studies* 4.2 (2011) 1–24. https://www.jstor.org/stable/26463924?seq=1.

Holland, Tom. *Dominion: How the Christian Revolution Remade the World*. New York: Basic, 2019.

Holley, Peter. "Domino's Will Start Delivering Pizzas via an Autonomous Robot This Fall." *Washington Post*, Jun 17, 2019. https://www.washingtonpost.com/technology/2019/06/17/dominos-will-start-delivering-pizzas-via-an-autonomous-robot-this-fall.

Holmes, Arthur F. *All Truth Is God's Truth*. Grand Rapids, MI: Eerdmans, 1977.

Holt, Brianna. "Women Are Ditching the Pill in Droves for More Convenient Options." *Quartz*, Oct 24, 2019. https://qz.com/1730175/birth-control-usage-stats-show-the-pill-losing-ground-to-the-iud/.
Homans, Charles. "Energy Independence: A Short History." *Foreign Policy* 191 (Feb 1, 2012) 1–5.
Hornyak, Tim. "The Flying Taxi Market May Be Ready for Takeoff, Changing the Travel Experience Forever." CNBC, Mar 7, 2020. https://www.cnbc.com/2020/03/06/the-flying-taxi-market-is-ready-to-change-worldwide-travel.html.
Horsfjord, Vebjørn L., et al. *Global Christianity: Current Trends and Developments*. Eugene, OR: Wipf & Stock, 2022.
Huggins, Jonathan. "Proceed with Caution: Lessons from Saint Augustine, Jonathan Edwards, and Miroslav Volf." In *Technē: Christian Visions of Technology*, edited by Gerald Hiestand and Todd A. Wilson, 92–108. Eugene, OR: Cascade, 2022.
IED Team. "A Brief History of the 4 Industrial Revolutions That Shaped the World." https://ied.eu/project-updates/the-4-industrial-revolutions.
IIHS. "Fatality Facts 2021: Yearly Snapshot." May 2023. https://www.iihs.org/topics/fatality-statistics/detail/yearly-snapshot.
IMARC. "United States Diabetes Market Report: 2024–2032." https://www.imarcgroup.com/us-diabetes-market.
Immad, Laiba. "25 Countries with Highest Abortion Rates." *Yahoo! Finance*, Mar 12, 2024. https://finance.yahoo.com/news/25-countries-highest-abortion-rates-154002996.html.
Irfan, Umair. "Fusion Energy Is a Reason to Be Excited about the Future." *Vox*, Jan 6, 2022. https://www.vox.com/22801265/fusion-energy-electricity-power-climate-change-research-iter.
Jacobson, Robert C. *Space Is Open for Business: The Industry That Can Transform Humanity*. Self-published, 2020.
Jacona, Alessio. "Porn Industry, the Internet Innovation Engine We (Prefer to) Ignore." Web Observer, May 4, 2013. *The Web Observer* (blog). https://thewebobserver.it/2013/06/04/porn-industry-the-internet-innovation-engine-we-prefer-to-ignore/.
Jenkins, Philip. *The Next Christendom: The Coming of Global Christianity*. 3rd ed. New York: Oxford University Press, 2011.
Johnson, James. *Artificial Intelligence and the Future of Warfare: The USA, China, and Strategic Stability*. Manchester: Manchester University Press, 2021.
Johnson, Thomas A. "Cyber Intelligence, Cyber Conflicts, and Cyber Warfare." In *Cybersecurity: Protecting Critical Infrastructures from Cyber Attack and Cyber Warfare*, edited by Thomas A. Johnson, 155–98. Boca Raton, FL: CRC, 2015.
———. "Cybersecurity Threat Landscape and Trends." In *Cybersecurity: Protecting Critical Infrastructures from Cyber Attack and Cyber Warfare*, edited by Thomas A. Johnson, 287–326. Boca Raton, FL: CRC, 2015.
Jolly, Jennifer L., et al. *Parenting Gifted Children: The Authoritative Guide from the National Association for Gifted Children*. New York: Routledge, 2021.
Joshel, Sandra R. *Slavery in the Roman World*. New York: Cambridge University Press, 2010.
Joshua Project. "Deaf." https://joshuaproject.net/people_groups/19007.
Kaku, Michio. *Quantum Supremacy: How the Quantum Computer Revolution Will Change Everything*. New York: Doubleday, 2023.

Kallenborn, Zachary. "A Partial Ban on Autonomous Weapons Would Make Everyone Safer." *Foreign Policy*, Oct 14, 2020. https://foreignpolicy.com/2020/10/14/ai-drones-swarms-killer-robots-partial-ban-on-autonomous-weapons-would-make-everyone-safer/.
Kane, Herbert J. *A Concise History of the Christian World Mission: A Panoramic View of Missions from Pentecost to the Present*. Rev. ed. Grand Rapids, MI: Baker Academic, 1982.
Katwala, Amit. *Quantum Computing: How It Works and How It Could Change the World*. London: Random, 2021.
Keane, Sean. "Elon Musk Calls for Increased Nuclear Power, Oil and Gas Production." *CNET*, Mar 8, 2022. https://www.cnet.com/science/elon-musk-calls-for-increased-nuclear-power-oil-and-gas-production/.
Keller, Timothy. *Every Good Endeavor: Connecting Your Work to God's Work*. New York: Penguin, 2014.
Kelly, C. Brian. *Best Little Stories from the Life and Times of Winston Churchill*. Nashville: Cumberland, 2008.
Kelly, John. *The Great Mortality: An Intimate History of the Black Death, the Most Devastating Plague of All Time*. New York: Harper Perennial, 2006.
Kelly, Kevin. *The Inevitable: Understanding the 12 Technological Forces That Will Shape Our Future*. New York: Viking, 2016.
Kermorgant, Gaelle, and Odile Siary. "Is the Law Ready for Autonomous Cars?" In *Energy Consumption and Autonomous Driving: Proceedings of the 3rd CESA Automotive Electronics Congress, Paris, 2014*, edited by Jochen Langheim, 89–98. Cham, Switzerland: Springer, 2016.
Kharpal, Arjun. "Baidu Pushes to Put Driverless Taxis on China's Roads, Pledging to Build 1,000 in 3 Years." CNBC, Jun 17, 2021. https://www.cnbc.com/2021/06/17/baidu-pushes-to-put-driverless-taxis-on-china-roads-with-baic-tie-up.html.
Kilner, John F. *Dignity and Destiny: Humanity in the Image of God*. Grand Rapids, MI: Eerdmans, 2015.
Kim, Jay Y. *Analog Church: Why We Need Real People, Places, and Things in the Digital Age*. Downers Grove, IL: InterVarsity, 2020.
King, Celia. "'A Person Standing in the Gap': The Deaf Community as a Mission Field." In *Theology and the Experience of Disability: Interdisciplinary Perspectives from Down Under*, edited by Andrew Picard and Myk Habets, 118–28. London: Routledge, 2016.
Kissinger, Henry A., et al. *The Age of AI: And Our Human Future*. New York: Back Bay, 2022.
Kizer Whitt, Kelly. "Who Owns All the Satellites?" *EarthSky*, Feb 8, 2022. https://earthsky.org/space/who-owns-satellites-company-country/.
Klawans, Justin. "The Rise of the World's First Trillionaire: When Will It Happen, and Who Will It Be?" *The Week*, Feb 15, 2024. https://theweek.com/finance/1019328/the-rise-of-the-worlds-first-trillionaire.
Klebnikov, Sergei. "Tesla Is Now the World's Most Valuable Car Company with a $208 Billion Valuation." *Forbes*, Jul 1, 2020. https://www.forbes.com/sites/sergeiklebnikov/2020/07/01/tesla-is-now-the-worlds-most-valuable-car-company-with-a-valuation-of-208-billion/.
Klepeis, Alicia Z. *The Future of Transportation: From Electric Cars to Jet Packs*. North Mankato, MN: Capstone, 2020.

Kline, Stephen J. "What Is Technology?" *Bulletin of Science, Technology and Society* 5.3 (Jun 1985) 215–18.

Kluger, Jeffrey. "Four Civilian Astronauts. Three Days in Orbit. One Giant Leap. Meet the Inspiration4 Crew." *Time*, Aug 23, 2021. https://time.com/magazine/us/6089812/august-23rd-2021-vol-198-no-7-u-s/.

Kostarelos, Kostas. "Nanorobots for Medicine: How Close Are We?" *Nanomedicine* 5.3 (Apr 2010) 341–42. https://doi.org/10.2217/nnm.10.19.

Kurzweil, Ray. *The Singularity Is Near: When Humans Transcend Biology*. New York: Penguin, 2005.

Labios, Liezel. "Super Productive 3D Bioprinter Could Help Speed Up Drug Development." UC San Diego, Jun 8, 2021. https://jacobsschool.ucsd.edu/news/release/3290?id=3290.

Ladd, George Eldon. *The Presence of the Future: The Eschatology of Biblical Realism*. Grand Rapids, MI: Eerdmans, 1996.

——. *A Theology of the New Testament*. Rev. ed. Grand Rapids, MI: Eerdmans, 1993.

LaGratta, Maria. "CT vs MRI: What's the Difference? And How Do Doctors Choose Which Imaging Method to Use?" Memorial Sloan Kettering Cancer Center, Jul 13, 2022. https://www.mskcc.org/news/ct-vs-mri-what-s-difference-and-how-do-doctors-choose-which-imaging-method-use.

Lambert, Patricia M., and Phillip L. Walker. "Bioarcheological Ethics: Perspectives on the Use and Value of Human Remains in Scientific Research." In *Biological Anthropology of the Human Skeleton*, edited by M. Anne Katzenberg and Anne L. Grauer, 3–42. 3rd ed. Hoboken, NY: Wiley Blackwell, 2019.

Laughlin, Robert B. *Powering the Future: How We Will (Eventually) Solve the Energy Crisis and Fuel the Civilization of Tomorrow*. New York: Basic, 2011.

Lee, Cameron. *Unexpected Blessing: Living the Countercultural Reality of the Beatitudes*. Downers Grove, IL: InterVarsity, 2004.

Lee, Daeyeol. *Birth of Intelligence: From RNA to Artificial Intelligence*. New York: Oxford University Press, 2020.

Lee, Kai-Fu. *AI Superpowers: China, Silicon Valley, and the New World Order*. Boston: Harper, 2018.

Lennox, John C. *2084: Artificial Intelligence and the Future of Humanity*. Grand Rapids, MI: Zondervan Reflective, 2020.

Lenong, Jentley. "State Cybersecurity Governance in the Fourth Industrial Revolution: An International Law Perspective." In *The Disruptive Fourth Industrial Revolution: Technology, Society and Beyond*, edited by Wesley Doorsamy et al., 69–94. Cham, Switzerland: Springer, 2020.

Leonard, John J., et al. "Autonomous Vehicles, Mobility, and Employment Policy: The Road Ahead." https://ouravfuture.org/wp-content/uploads/2020/08/WotF-2020-Research-Brief-Leonard-Mindell-Stayton.pdf.

Levin, Dov H. *Meddling in the Ballot Box: The Causes and Effects of Partisan Electoral Interventions*. New York: Oxford University Press, 2020.

Lewis, C. S. *The Space Trilogy*. San Francisco: HarperOne, 2014.

Li, Jinxing, et al. "Micro/Nanorobots for Biomedicine: Delivery, Surgery, Sensing, and Detoxification." *Science Robotics* 2.4 (Mar 2017). https://doi.org/10.1126/scirobotics.aam6431.

Linde. "Bodyguard 2.0: Pedestrian Warning Band for Maximum Safety." https://www.linde-mh.com/en/About-us/Innovations-from-Linde/Pedestrian-Warning-Band/.
Linkov, Václav, et al. "Human Factors in the Cybersecurity of Autonomous Vehicles: Trends in Current Research." *Frontiers in Psychology* 10.995 (May 3, 2019). https://doi.org/10.3389/fpsyg.2019.00995.
LiVecche, Marc, and Matt Gabush. "The Just War Tradition." https://www.episcopalchurch.org/armed-forces-and-federal-ministries/just-war-education/just-war-tradition/.
Livio, Mario. *Galileo and the Science Deniers*. New York: Simon & Schuster, 2020.
Losey, Stephen. "New in 2024: Air Force Plans Autonomous Flight Tests for Drone Wingmen." *Defense News*, Dec 30, 2023. https://www.defensenews.com/air/2023/12/30/new-in-2024-air-force-plans-autonomous-flight-tests-for-drone-wingmen/.
Low, Linda. *Economics Primer*. Singapore: World Scientific, 2020.
Lurie, Barak. *Rise of the Sex Machines*. Los Angeles: CT3 Media, 2019.
Lutz, Tom, and Heidi Unruh. *Equipping Christians for Kingdom Purpose in Their Work: A Guide for All Who Make Disciples*. Peabody, MA: Hendrickson, 2021.
Maayan, Gilad David. "The IoT Rundown for 2020: Stats, Risks, and Solutions." *Security Today*, Jan 13, 2020. https://securitytoday.com/articles/2020/01/13/the-iot-rundown-for-2020.aspx#:~:text=In%202018%E2%80%94there%20were%207,of%2031%20billion%20IoT%20devices.
Maddison, Angus. *The World Economy*. Paris: OECD, 2006.
Madrigal, Alexis C. "When Did TV Watching Peak?" *Atlantic*, May 30, 2018. https://www.theatlantic.com/technology/archive/2018/05/when-did-tv-watching-peak/561464/.
Madzik, Mateusz T., et al. "Major Breakthrough as Quantum Computing in Silicon Hits 99% Accuracy." *SciTech Daily*, Jan 19, 2022. https://scitechdaily.com/major-breakthrough-as-quantum-computing-in-silicon-hits-99-accuracy/.
Magnuson, William. *Blockchain Democracy: Technology, Law and the Rule of the Crowd*. Cambridge, UK: Cambridge University Press, 2020.
Mahdawi, Arwa. "What Jobs Will Still Be Around in 20 Years? Read This to Prepare Your Future." *Guardian*, Jun 26, 2017. https://www.theguardian.com/us-news/2017/jun/26/jobs-future-automation-robots-skills-creative-health.
Mahmood, Zaigham, ed. *Connected Vehicles in the Internet of Things: Concepts, Technologies and Frameworks for the IoV*. Cham, Switzerland: Springer Nature, 2020.
Malet, André. "The Believer in the Presence of Technique." In *Theology and Technology: Essays in Christian Analysis*, edited by Carl Mitcham et al., 1:61–76. Eugene, OR: Wipf & Stock, 2022.
Maley, Michael. *Video Games and Esports: The Growing World of Gamers*. New York: Lucent, 2020.
Malia Krauss, Stephanie. *Making It: What Today's Kids Need for Tomorrow's World*. Hoboken, NJ: Jossey-Bass, 2021.
Malikyte, Eric. "10 Reasons Colonizing Mars Is a Bad Idea." *Top Tenz*, Sep 14, 2020. https://www.toptenz.net/10-reasons-colonizing-mars-is-a-bad-idea.php.
Malone, Michael Shawn. *Bill and Dave: How Hewlett and Packard Built the World's Greatest Company*. New York: Portfolio, 2007.

BIBLIOGRAPHY

Mamchii, Oleksandra. "Top 10 Countries with Largest Oil Reserves in the World." *Best Diplomats*, Feb 3, 2024. https://bestdiplomats.org/largest-oil-reserves-by-country/.

Mangalwadi, Vishal. *The Book That Made Your World: How the Bible Created the Soul of Western Civilization*. Nashville: Thomas Nelson, 2012.

Manyika, James, et al. "A Future That Works: Automation, Employment, and Productivity." McKinsey, Jan 2017. https://www.mckinsey.com/~/media/McKinsey/Featured%20Insights/Digital%20Disruption/Harnessing%20automation%20for%20a%20future%20that%20works/MGI-A-future-that-works_Full-report.ashx.

Marks, Robert J. *The Case for Killer Robots: Why America's Military Needs to Continue Development of Lethal AI*. Seattle: Discovery Institute, 2020.

Marr, Bernard. "8 Things Every School Must Do to Prepare for the 4th Industrial Revolution." *Forbes*, May 22, 2019. https://www.forbes.com/sites/bernardmarr/2019/05/22/8-things-every-school-must-do-to-prepare-for-the-4th-industrial-revolution.

———. *Tech Trends in Practice: The 25 Technologies That Are Driving the 4th Industrial Revolution*. Chichester, UK: Wiley, 2020.

Marsden, George M. *The Soul of the American University: From Protestant Establishment to Established Nonbelief*. New York: Oxford University Press, 1994.

Marsh, Connor, et al. "The Most Downloaded Mobile Games." *The Gamer*, Jul 15, 2023. https://www.thegamer.com/most-downloaded-mobile-games/.

Martel, Gordon, ed. *Twentieth-Century War and Conflict: A Concise Encyclopedia*. Chichester, UK: Wiley Blackwell, 2015.

Martindale, Jon. "Best Smart Glasses of 2024." *U.S. News and World Report*, last updated Apr 25, 2024. https://www.usnews.com/360-reviews/technology/best-smart-glasses.

Martinez, Sylvia L., and Gary Stager. *Invent to Learn: Making, Tinkering, and Engineering in the Classroom*. 2nd ed. Torrance, CA: Constructing Modern Knowledge, 2019.

———. "The Maker Movement: A Learning Revolution." May 10, 2021. https://www.iste.org/explore/In-the-classroom/The-maker-movement-A-learning-revolution.

Martin, Taylor. "Is the International Space Station Actually a Good Investment?" *MotorBiscuit*, Sep 15, 2021. https://www.motorbiscuit.com/international-space-station-good-investment/.

Marwala, Tshilidzi. *Closing the Gap: The Fourth Industrial Revolution in Africa*. Johannesburg: Pan Macmillan SA, 2020.

Marx, Paris. *Road to Nowhere: What Silicon Valley Gets Wrong about the Future of Transportation*. London: Verso, 2022.

Maths Careers. "The Rice and Chessboard Legend." Apr 26, 2019. https://www.mathscareers.org.uk/the-rice-and-chessboard-legend/.

Matthew, Devitt. "Are Automated Drone Deliveries the Sustainable Future of Logistics?" Oct 1, 2020. https://alphacommerce.xyz/sustainability/logistics/30-minutes-or-less-are-you-ready-for-ecommerce-automated-drone-deliveries/.

Maurice, Lisa. *The Teacher in Ancient Rome: The Magister and His World*. Plymouth, UK: Lexington, 2013.

May, Todd. "Opinion: Would Human Extinction Be a Tragedy?" *New York Times*, Dec 17, 2018. https://www.nytimes.com/2018/12/17/opinion/human-extinction-climate-change.html.

Mazoyer, Marcel, and Laurence Roudart. *A History of World Agriculture: From the Neolithic Age to the Current Crisis*. New York: Monthly Review, 2006.

McArthur, Neil. "The Case for Sexbots." In *Robot Sex: Social and Ethical Implications*, edited by John Danaher and Neil McArthur, 31–45. Cambridge, MA: MIT Press, 2018.

McBride, James, and Anshu Siripurapu. "How Does the U.S. Power Grid Work?" Council on Foreign Relations, last updated Jul 5, 2022. https://www.cfr.org/backgrounder/how-does-us-power-grid-work.

McFadden, Christopher. "Don't Worry, We'll Never Run Out of Oil." *Interesting Engineering*, Nov 9, 2022. https://interestingengineering.com/we-will-never-run-out-of-oil.

McGrath, Michael E. *Autonomous Vehicles: Opportunities, Strategies, and Disruptions*. 2nd ed. Self-published, 2019.

McGregor, Grady. "The World's Largest Surveillance System Is Growing—And So Is the Backlash." *Fortune*, Nov 3, 2020. https://fortune.com/2020/11/03/china-surveillance-system-backlash-worlds-largest/.

McInerney, Thomas, et al. *America's End Game for the 21st Century: A Blueprint for Saving Our Country*. Nashville: Fidelis, 2022.

McKenzie, Hamish. *Insane Mode: How Elon Musk's Tesla Sparked an Electric Revolution to End the Age of Oil*. New York: Dutton, 2018.

McShane, Alex. "Jordan Peterson Releases 'Bitcoin: The Future of Money?'" NASDAQ, Aug 11, 2021. https://www.nasdaq.com/articles/jordan-peterson-releases-bitcoin:-the-future-of-money-2021-08-11.

Meadows, Donella H., et al. *The Limits to Growth: A Report for the Club of Rome's Project on the Predicament of Mankind*. New York: Universe, 1974.

Mehta, Neel, et al. *Bubble or Revolution? The Present and Future of Blockchain and Cryptocurrencies*. 2nd ed. Seattle: Paravane Ventures, 2021.

Merchant, Brian. *The One Device: The Secret History of the iPhone*. New York: Back Bay, 2018.

Metzl, Jamie. *Hacking Darwin: Genetic Engineering and the Future of Humanity*. Naperville, IL: Sourcebooks, 2019.

Meyer, Susan. "The Top Five Causes of Fatal Car Accidents and How to Avoid Them." *The Zebra*, last updated Jan 23, 2024. https://www.thezebra.com/resources/driving/causes-of-fatal-car-accidents/.

Middendorf, J. William, II. "Meet the U.S. Navy's Unmanned Ships of the Future." The Heritage Foundation, Jan 1, 2021. https://www.heritage.org/defense/commentary/meet-the-us-navys-unmanned-ships-the-future.

Miller, Chris. *Chip War: The Fight for the World's Most Critical Technology*. New York: Scribner, 2022.

Miller, Darrow L. *Discipling Nations: The Power of Truth to Transform Cultures*. 3rd ed. Seattle: YWAM, 2018.

Minton Beddoes, Zanny. "Rivalry between America and China Will Shape the Post-Covid World." *Economist*, Nov 8, 2021. https://www.economist.com/the-world-ahead/2021/11/08/rivalry-between-america-and-china-will-shape-the-post-covid-world.

Mitcham, Carl. "Technology as a Theological Problem in the Christian Tradition." In *Theology and Technology: Essays in Christian Analysis*, edited by Carl Mitcham et al., 1:1–17. Eugene, OR: Wipf & Stock, 2022.

Mitchell, C. Ben, and D. Joy Riley. *Christian Bioethics: A Guide for Pastors, Health Care Professionals, and Families.* Nashville: B&H Academic, 2014.

Moon, Steve Sang-Cheol. "Missions from Korea 2017: The Fourth Industrial Revolution and Missions." *International Bulletin of Mission Research* 41.2 (2017) 121–27.

Morgan, Jacob. "The Lab, the Factory and the Future of Work." *Forbes,* Feb 11, 2016. https://www.forbes.com/sites/jacobmorgan/2016/02/11/lab-factory-future-work/.

———. "This Is What the Future of Work Looks Like." YouTube video, Jun 21, 2020. https://www.youtube.com/watch?v=CpQYxNWKWgI.

Morris, Edmund. *Edison.* New York: Random, 2019.

Muck, Terry C., and Frances S. Adeney. *Christianity Encountering World Religions: The Practice of Mission in the Twenty-First Century.* Grand Rapids, MI: Baker, 2009.

Mulvaney, Dustin. *Sustainable Energy Transitions: Socio-Ecological Dimensions of Decarbonization.* Cham, Switzerland: Palgrave Macmillan, 2020.

Murphy, Alexander B., et al. *The European Culture Area: A Systematic Geography.* 7th ed. London: Rowman & Littlefield, 2020.

Murray, Charles. *In Our Hands: A Plan to Replace the Welfare State.* Washington, DC: AEI, 2016.

Musha Doerr, Neriko, and Debra J. Occhi. *The Augmented Reality of Pokémon Go: Chronotopes, Moral Panic, and Other Complexities.* Lanham, MD: Lexington, 2019.

Musonda, Nelson. "Church Online Statistics for 2021." Delmethod, Jan 15, 2021. https://www.delmethod.com/blog/church-online-statistics.

Myers, Bryant L. *Walking with the Poor: Principles and Practices of Transformational Development.* Rev. ed. Maryknoll, NY: Orbis, 2011.

National Archives. "Declaration of Independence: A Transcription." https://www.archives.gov/founding-docs/declaration-transcript.

Nawrat, Allie. "3D Printing in the Medical Field: Four Major Applications Revolutionising the Industry." Medical Device Network, Aug 7, 2018. https://www.medicaldevice-network.com/features/3d-printing-in-the-medical-field-applications.

Nebula Genomics. "What Does Your DNA Say about Your Health and Ancestry?" https://nebula.org/whole-genome-sequencing-dna-test/.

Needle, Flori. "What Jobs Will AI Replace and Which Are Safe in 2023." *Hubspot* (blog), Aug 21, 2023. https://blog.hubspot.com/marketing/jobs-artificial-intelligence-will-replace.

NEI. "Top 15 Nuclear Generating Countries." Last updated Aug 2022. https://www.nei.org/resources/statistics/top-15-nuclear-generating-countries.

The New York Times. "Rates on Overseas Phone Calls Decline." May 19, 1982. https://www.nytimes.com/1982/05/19/garden/rates-on-overseas-phone-calls-decline.html.

Ngo, Madeleine, and Ana Swanson. "The Biggest Kink in America's Supply Chain: Not Enough Truckers." *New York Times,* Nov 9, 2021. https://www.nytimes.com/2021/11/09/us/politics/trucker-shortage-supply-chain.html.

Niebuhr, H. Richard. *Christ and Culture.* New York: HarperCollins, 2001.

Nield, David. "How to Keep All of Your Accounts Safe in a World Where People Want Your Data." *Popular Science,* May 21, 2021. https://www.popsci.com/protect-your-accounts-online/.

NIH. "June 2000 White House Event." June 26, 2000. https://www.genome.gov/10001356/june-2000-white-house-event.

North, Anna. "You Can't Even Pay People to Have More Kids." *Vox*, Nov 27, 2023. https://www.vox.com/23971366/declining-birth-rate-fertility-babies-children.

Nosowitz, Dan. "Why Can't We Get Rid of the 7-Day Week?" *Atlas Obscura*, Sep 17, 2015. http://www.atlasobscura.com/articles/why-cant-we-get-rid-of-the-7day-week.

Numbers, Ronald L. *Galileo Goes to Jail and Other Myths about Science and Religion.* Cambridge, MA: Harvard University Press, 2010.

Oakes, Nick. "Will Humans Ever Go to Mars?" *Astronomy*, Aug 31, 2023. https://www.astronomy.com/space-exploration/will-humans-ever-go-to-mars/.

O'Dowd, Peter, and Allison Hagan. "Take a Ride through Phoenix in a Driverless Car." *Wbur*, Jan 4, 2021. https://www.wbur.org/hereandnow/2021/01/04/waymo-driverless-car.

Olavsrud, Thor. "Rolls-Royce Turns to Digital Twins to Improve Jet Engine Efficiency." *CIO*, Jun 10, 2021. https://www.cio.com/article/188765/rolls-royce-turns-to-digital-twins-to-improve-jet-engine-efficiency.html.

Oleson, John Peter, ed. *The Oxford Handbook of Engineering and Technology in the Classical World.* New York: Oxford University Press, 2009.

Olya, Gabrielle. "16 Companies That Have Pledged to Go Carbon Neutral: Amazon, Starbucks and More Are Fighting against Climate Change." Go Banking Rates, Apr 1, 2021. https://www.gobankingrates.com/money/business/16-companies-that-have-pledged-to-go-carbon-neutral/.

O'Meara, Sarah. "Will China Lead the World in AI by 2030?" *Nature* 572 (Aug 21, 2019) 427–28. https://doi.org/10.1038/d41586-019-02360-7.

Ondruš, Ján, et al. "How Do Autonomous Cars Work?" *Transportation Research Procedia* 44 (2020) 226–33. https://doi.org/10.1016/j.trpro.2020.02.049.

Open to Debate. "Agree to Disagree: Sex Robots?" YouTube video, Feb 18, 2021. https://www.youtube.com/watch?v=YWifv7CgEpo.

Oppenheimer, Andres. *The Robots Are Coming! The Future of Jobs in the Age of Automation.* Translated by Ezra E. Fitz. New York: Vintage, 2019.

Oreskovich, Michael R., et al. "Prevalence of Alcohol Use Disorders among American Surgeons." *Archives of Surgery* 147.2 (Feb 2012) 168–74. https://doi.org/10.1001/archsurg.2011.1481.

Ortlund, Ray. *The Death of Porn: Men of Integrity Building a World of Nobility.* Wheaton, IL: Crossway, 2021.

Osterloff, Emily. "How an Asteroid Ended the Age of the Dinosaurs." Natural History Museum. https://www.nhm.ac.uk/discover/how-an-asteroid-caused-extinction-of-dinosaurs.html#:~:text=The%20impact%20site%2C%20known%20as,largest%20crater%20on%20the%20planet.

O'Sullivan, Donie. "West Virginia to Introduce Mobile Phone Voting for Midterm Elections." CNN, Aug 6, 2018. https://money.cnn.com/2018/08/06/technology/mobile-voting-west-virginia-voatz/index.html.

Palfrey, John, and Urs Gasser. *Born Digital: Understanding the First Generation of Digital Natives.* New York: Basic, 2008.

Palfreyman, David, and Paul Temple. *Universities and Colleges: A Very Short Introduction.* New York: Oxford University Press, 2017.

Palmer, Annie. "Amazon Wins FAA Approval for Prime Air Drone Delivery Fleet." CNBC, Aug 31, 2020. https://www.cnbc.com/2020/08/31/amazon-prime-now-drone-delivery-fleet-gets-faa-approval.html.

Panicola, Michael R., et al. *Health Care Ethics: Theological Foundations, Contemporary Issues, and Controversial Cases*. 2nd ed. Winona, MN: Anselm Academic, 2011.

Pappas, Charles. *One Giant Leap: Iconic and Inspiring Space Race Inventions That Shaped History*. Lanham, MD: Rowman & Littlefield, 2019.

Park Woolf, Beverly. *Building Intelligent Interactive Tutors: Student-Centered Strategies for Revolutionizing E-Learning*. Burlington, MA: Morgan Kaufmann, 2010.

Paukert, Chris. "GM Surprises with Cadillac eVTOL Air Taxi at CES 2021." *CNET*, Jan 12, 2021. https://www.cnet.com/roadshow/news/gm-surprises-with-cadillac-evtol-air-taxi-at-ces-2021/.

Peak Substation Services. "Centralized vs. Decentralized Energy." https://peaksubstation.com/centralized-vs-decentralized-energy/.

Penna, Anthony N. *A History of Energy Flows: From Human Labor to Renewable Power*. London: Routledge, 2019.

Perry, Mark J. "Computer Prices and Speed: 1970 to 2007." AEI, Aug 21, 2007. https://www.aei.org/carpe-diem/computer-prices-and-speed-1970-to-2007/.

Perry, Samuel L. *Addicted to Lust: Pornography in the Lives of Conservative Protestants*. New York: Oxford University Press, 2019.

Peters, Adele. "Here's How Much Space U.S. Cities Waste on Parking." *Fast Company*, Jul 17, 2018. https://www.fastcompany.com/90202222/heres-how-much-space-u-s-cities-waste-on-parking.

Petersen, Steve. "Is It Good for Them Too? Ethical Concerns for the Sexbots." In *Robot Sex: Social and Ethical Implications*, edited by John Danaher and Neil McArthur, 155–68. Cambridge, MA: MIT Press.

Pew. "What Is Medical 3D Printing—And How Is It Regulated?" Oct 5, 2020. https://www.pewtrusts.org/en/research-and-analysis/issue-briefs/2020/10/what-is-medical-3d-printing-and-how-is-it-regulated.

Philipps, Mike. "You're Planning a Heist. What Buildings Have the World's Most Valuable Contents?" *Forbes*, Sep 18, 2017. https://www.forbes.com/sites/bisnow/2017/09/18/youre-planning-a-heist-what-buildings-have-the-worlds-most-valuable-contents/.

PHMSA. "General Pipeline FAQs." Last updated Nov 6, 2018. https://www.phmsa.dot.gov/faqs/general-pipeline-faqs.

Pigman, Geoffrey Allen. *The World Economic Forum: A Multi-Stakeholder Approach to Global Governance*. New York: Routledge, 2007.

Piller, Ingrid. *Linguistic Diversity and Social Justice: An Introduction to Applied Sociolinguistics*. New York: Oxford University Press, 2016.

Platt, David. *Counter Culture: Following Christ in an Anti-Christian Age*. Carol Stream, IL: Tyndale Momentum, 2017.

Porathe, A., et al. "At Least as Safe as Manned Shipping? Autonomous Shipping, Safety, and 'Human Error.'" In *Safety and Reliability: Safe Societies in a Changing World*, edited by Stein Haugen et al., 417–25. Boca Raton, FL: CRC, 2018.

Porter, Jon. "Tesla Raises Price of 'Full Self-Driving' Option to $10,000." *The Verge*, Oct 30, 2020. https://www.theverge.com/2020/10/30/21541571/tesla-full-self-driving-price-increase-10000-dollars-autopilot-beta.

Powell McNutt, Jennifer. "Partnering with Pastors: How Early Modern Printers Advanced the Reformation." In *Technē: Christian Visions of Technology*, edited by Gerald Hiestand and Todd A. Wilson, 221–36. Eugene, OR: Cascade, 2022.

Prensky, Marc R. *Teaching Digital Natives: Partnering for Real Learning*. Thousand Oaks, CA: Corwin, 2010.

Prince, Derek. *Fasting: The Key to Releasing God's Power in Your Life*. New Kensington, PA: Whitaker, 1993.

Prior, Karen Swallow. "The Technology of Reading." In *Technē: Christian Visions of Technology*, edited by Gerald Hiestand and Todd A. Wilson, 187–201. Eugene, OR: Cascade, 2022.

Prior, Matthew T. *Confronting Technology: The Theology of Jacques Ellul*. Eugene, OR: Pickwick, 2020.

Pruitt, Sarah. "6 Major Breakthroughs in Hunter-Gatherer Tools." *History*, Aug 5, 2019. https://www.history.com/news/hunter-gatherer-tools-breakthroughs.

Puiu, Tibi. "How Big Is a Petabyte, Exabyte or Yottabyte? Let's Look at the Largest Units of Data Storage." *ZME Science*, Dec 21, 2022. https://www.zmescience.com/science/how-big-data-can-get/.

Pyle, Rod. *Space 2.0: How Private Spaceflight, a Resurgent NASA, and International Partners Are Creating a New Space Age*. Dallas: BenBella, 2019.

Raines, J. Patrick, and Charles G. Leathers. *The Economic Institutions of Higher Education: Economic Theories of University Behaviour*. Cheltenham, UK: Edward Elgar, 2003.

Rankin, Alisha. *The Poison Trials: Wonder Drugs, Experiment, and the Battle for Authority in Renaissance Science*. Chicago: University of Chicago Press, 2021.

Raphael, JR. "The Internet's 100 Oldest Dot-Com Domains." *PC World*, Dec 21, 2008. https://www.pcworld.com/article/532545/oldest_domains.html.

Rapier, Robert. "Environmental Implications of Lead-Acid and Lithium-Ion Batteries." *Forbes*, Jan 19, 2020. https://www.forbes.com/sites/rrapier/2020/01/19/environmental-implications-of-lead-acid-and-lithium-ion-batteries/?sh=59590b757bf5.

———. "World Energy Outlook 2023: Fossil Fuels Peak and Renewable Surges." *Forbes*, Oct 26, 2023. https://www.forbes.com/sites/rrapier/2023/10/26/world-energy-outlook-2023-fossil-fuels-peak-and-renewable-surges/?sh=4a9a3bd72e8b.

Rashdall, Hastings. *The Universities of Europe in the Middle Ages*. Vol. 1, *Salerno, Bologna, Paris*. New York: Cambridge University Press, 2010.

Reddy, Namireddy Praveen, et al. "Zero-Emission Autonomous Ferries for Urban Water Transport: Cheaper, Cleaner Alternative to Bridges and Manned Vessels." *IEEE Electrification Magazine* 7.4 (Dec 2019) 32–45. https://doi.org/10.1109/MELE.2019.2943954.

Reed, Aaron A., et al. *Adventure Games: Playing the Outsider*. New York: Bloomsbury Academic 2020.

Reich, Justin. *Failure to Disrupt: Why Technology Alone Can't Transform Education*. Cambridge, MA: Harvard University Press, 2020.

Reinke, Tony. *12 Ways Your Phone Is Changing You*. Wheaton, IL: Crossway, 2017.

———. *Competing Spectacles: Treasuring Christ in the Media Age*. Wheaton, IL: Crossway, 2019.

———. *God, Technology, and the Christian Life*. Wheaton, IL: Crossway, 2022.

Renteria, Nelson, et al. "El Salvador to Transfer 'Big Chunk' of Bitcoin to Physical Vault." Reuters, Mar 14, 2024. https://www.reuters.com/technology/el-salvador-transfer-big-chunk-bitcoin-physical-vault-2024-03-15/.

Rhodes, Richard. *Energy: A Human History*. New York: Simon & Schuster, 2018.

Rice, Doyle. "How Long Does It Take to Get to the End of the Universe?" *USA Today*, May 2, 2014. https://www.usatoday.com/story/news/nation-now/2014/05/02/space-day-distances/8618041/.

———. "This Isn't Your Typical Space Rock: There's a Metal Asteroid out There Worth $10,000 Quadrillion." *USA Today*, Oct 29, 2020. https://www.usatoday.com/story/news/nation/2020/10/29/metal-asteroid-psyche-nasa-hubble-images/6069223002/.

Rice Hasson, Mary, and Theresa Farnan. *Get Out Now: Why You Should Pull Your Child from Public School before It's Too Late*. Washington, DC: Regnery Gateway, 2018.

Richards, Neil. *Why Privacy Matters*. New York: Oxford University Press, 2022.

Rinehart, Will, and Allison Edwards. "Understanding Job Loss Predictions from Artificial Intelligence." American Action Forum, Jul 11, 2019. https://www.americanactionforum.org/insight/understanding-job-loss-predictions-from-artificial-intelligence/.

Roberts, Ken. "Percent of U.S. Oil Imports from Russia Highest in Decades—At 3.5%." *Forbes*, Mar 5, 2022. https://www.forbes.com/sites/kenroberts/2022/03/05/percent-of-us-oil-imports-from-russia-highest-in-decades---at-35/.

Robinson, Ken. "Changing Education Paradigms." TED, Oct 2010. https://www.ted.com/talks/sir_ken_robinson_changing_education_paradigms.

Robinson, Ken, and Lou Aronica. *Creative Schools: The Grassroots Revolution That's Transforming Education*. New York: Penguin, 2015.

Rodgers, Daniel T. *As a City on a Hill: The Story of America's Most Famous Lay Sermon*. Princeton, NJ: Princeton University Press, 2020.

Rollins, Amanda. "What's a MOOC? History, Principles, and Characteristics." eLearning Industry, Sep 3, 2018. https://elearningindustry.com/whats-a-mooc-history-principles-characteristics.

Romanowski, Michael H., and Teri McCarthy. *Teaching in a Distant Classroom: Crossing Borders for Global Transformation*. Downers Grove, IL: InterVarsity, 2009.

Rose, Joel. "How to Break Free of Our 19th-Century Factory-Model Education System." *Atlantic*, May 9, 2012. https://www.theatlantic.com/business/archive/2012/05/how-to-break-free-of-our-19th-century-factory-model-education-system/256881/.

Rosen, William. *The Most Powerful Idea in the World: A Story of Steam, Industry, and Invention*. Chicago: University of Chicago Press, 2012.

Roston, Eric. "Investors Get Serious about Nuclear Fusion, Energy's Eternal Grail." *Bloomberg*, Aug 17, 2021. https://www.bloomberg.com/news/articles/2021-08-17/investors-get-serious-about-nuclear-fusion-energy-s-eternal-grail.

Roth, Carol. *You Will Own Nothing: Your War with a New Financial World Order and How to Fight Back*. New York: Broadside, 2023.

Ryken, Leland, and Glenda Mathes. *Recovering the Lost Art of Reading: A Quest for the True, the Good, and the Beautiful*. Wheaton, IL: Crossway, 2021.

SAE International. "SAE Levels of Driving Automation™ Refined for Clarity and International Audience." May 3, 2021. https://www.sae.org/blog/sae-j3016-update.

Sagen, Erin. "Car Accidents Cause Death, Injury and Trauma. Why Do We Shrug Them Off?" NBC News, Oct 24, 2021. https://www.nbcnews.com/think/opinion/car-accidents-cause-death-injury-trauma-why-do-we-shrug-ncna1282193.
Sandel, Michael J. *The Case against Perfection: Ethics in the Age of Genetic Engineering.* Cambridge, MA: Harvard University Press, 2009.
Sanz, Crickette M., et al. *Tool Use in Animals: Cognition and Ecology.* New York: Cambridge University Press, 2013.
Satter, Raphael. "U.S. Court: Mass Surveillance Program Exposed by Snowden Was Illegal." Reuters, Sep 2, 2020. https://www.reuters.com/article/us-usa-nsa-spying-idUSKBN25T3CK.
Sawers, Paul. "Rolls-Royce Demonstrates Fully Autonomous Passenger Ferry in Finland." *Venture Beat,* Dec 3, 2018. https://venturebeat.com/ai/rolls-royce-demonstrates-fully-autonomous-passenger-ferry-in-finland/.
Sawh, Michael. "Best Smart Rings 2024: Top Fitness Tracking and Payment Rings." Wareable, May 1, 2024. https://www.wareable.com/fashion/best-smart-rings-1340.
Saxon, Dan. *Fighting Machines: Autonomous Weapons and Human Dignity.* Philadelphia: University of Pennsylvania Press, 2022.
Scarlata, Mark. *Sabbath Rest: The Beauty of God's Rhythm for a Digital Age.* London: SCM, 2019.
Schaer, Cathrin, and Kersten Knipp. "Is Saudi Arabia Wining the Fight to Rehabilitate Its Image?" DW, Dec 7, 2021. https://www.dw.com/en/saudi-arabia-winning-fight-to-rehabilitate-image/a-60044292.
Scharre, Paul. *Army of None: Autonomous Weapons and the Future of War.* New York: Norton, 2019.
Schatt, Stan. *Still Room for Humans: Career Planning in an AI World.* New York: Business Expert, 2023.
Schatzberg, Eric. *Technology: Critical History of a Concept.* Chicago: University of Chicago Press, 2018.
Schmidt, Alvin J. *How Christianity Changed the World.* Grand Rapids, MI: Zondervan, 2004.
Schuman, Samuel. *Seeing the Light: Religious Colleges in Twenty-First-Century America.* Baltimore, MD: Johns Hopkins University Press, 2010.
Schwab, Klaus. "The Fourth Industrial Revolution." *Encyclopaedia Britannica.* https://www.britannica.com/topic/The-Fourth-Industrial-Revolution-2119734.
———. *The Fourth Industrial Revolution.* New York: Currency, 2017.
Schwab, Klaus, and Nicholas Davis. *Shaping the Fourth Industrial Revolution.* New York: Currency, 2018.
Schwartz, Jeff. *Work Disrupted: Opportunity, Resilience, and Growth in the Accelerated Future of Work.* Hoboken, NJ: John Wiley & Sons, 2021.
Schwartz, Samuel I. *No One at the Wheel: Driverless Cars and the Road of the Future.* New York: PublicAffairs, 2018.
Schwichtenberg, Lars. "Solar aus dem Weltraum: Europäisches Land will Sonne aus dem All zapfen." Efahrer, Mar 22, 2022. https://efahrer.chip.de/news/solar-aus-dem-weltraum-europaeisches-land-will-sonne-aus-dem-all-zapfen_107537.
Scranton Law Firm. "Death from War vs Death from Motor Vehicle Collisions: Fatal Car Accident Statistics vs War Casualties." https://scrantonlawfirm.com/death-war-vs-death-motor-vehicle-collisions/.

Seba, Tony, and Adam Dorr. "100% Solar, Wind and Batteries Is Just the Start—the 'Super' Power They Produce Will Change the World." *Utility Dive*, Nov 5, 2020. https://www.utilitydive.com/news/100-solar-wind-and-batteries-is-just-the-start-the-super-power-they-p/588412/.

Sedgwick, Mark. "Islam and Popular Culture." In *Islam in the Modern World*, edited by Jeffrey T. Kenney and Ebrahim Moosa, 279–98. New York: Routledge, 2013.

Segal, Seth. "Harvard Is Wealthier Than More Than Half of the World's Countries." *Campus Reform*, Aug 28, 2019. https://www.campusreform.org/?ID=13635.

Seldon, Anthony. *The Fourth Education Revolution: Will Artificial Intelligence Liberate or Infantilise Humanity*. London: University of Buckingham Press, 2018.

Selwyn, Neil. *Should Robots Replace Teachers? AI and the Future of Education*. Cambridge, UK: Polity, 2019.

Semuels, Alana. "The Truck Driver Shortage Doesn't Exist. Saying There Is One Makes Conditions Worse for Drivers." *Time*, Nov 12, 2021. https://time.com/6116853/truck-driver-shortage-supply-chain.

Shaban, Dean. "ADHD in Children: Symptoms, Causes, Treatment." WebMD, Nov 15, 2023. https://www.webmd.com/add-adhd/news/20181126/adhd-rising-in-the-us-but-why.

Shackelford, Scott J. *The Internet of Things: What Everyone Needs to Know*. New York: Oxford University Press, 2020.

Shackelford, Scott J., and Steven Myers. "Block-by-Block: Leveraging the Power of Blockchain Technology to Build Trust and Promote Cyber Peace." Kelly School of Business Research Paper, Nov 23, 2016. https://ssrn.com/abstract=2874090.

Shah, Dhawal. "Capturing the Hype: Year of the MOOC Timeline Explained—Class Central." *The Report*, Feb 4, 2020. https://www.classcentral.com/report/mooc-hype-year-1/.

Shannon, Leslie. *Interconnected Realities: How the Metaverse Will Transform Our Relationship with Technology Forever*. Hoboken, NJ: Wiley, 2023.

Shatzer, Jacob. *Transhumanism and the Image of God: Today's Technology and the Future of Christian Discipleship*. Downers Grove, IL: IVP Academic, 2019.

Shaw, Adrienne, and Shira Chess. "Reflections on the Casual Games Market in a Post-GamerGate World." In *Social, Casual and Mobile Games: The Changing Gaming Landscape*, edited by Tama Leaver and Michele Willson, 277–89. New York: Bloomsbury Academic, 2016.

Shead, Sam. "Climate Change Is Making People Think Twice about Having Children." CNBC, Aug 12, 2021. https://www.cnbc.com/2021/08/12/climate-change-is-making-people-think-twice-about-having-children.html.

Sherman, Maria. "It's the Ultimate Disaster Scenario, but How Likely Is It? A Planetary Scientist Breaks Down *Don't Look Up*." *Tudum by Netflix*, Dec 24, 2021. https://www.netflix.com/tudum/articles/dont-look-up-could-a-comet-destroy-the-earth.

Shetty, Sameepa. "Uber's Self-Driving Cars Are a Key to Its Path to Profitability." CNBC, Jan 28, 2020. https://www.cnbc.com/2020/01/28/ubers-self-driving-cars-are-a-key-to-its-path-to-profitability.html.

Shimer, David. *Rigged: America, Russia, and One Hundred Years of Covert Electoral Interference*. New York: Knopf, 2020.

Shumaker, Robert W., et al. *Animal Tool Behavior: The Use and Manufacture of Tools by Animals*. Baltimore, MD: Johns Hopkins University Press, 2011.

Shwayder, Maya. "Debunking a Myth: In Medieval Christianity, Dissection Was Often Practiced." *Harvard Gazette*, Apr 7, 2011. https://news.harvard.edu/gazette/story/2011/04/debunking-a-myth.

Sidel, Robin, et al. "Almost Half a Billion Worth of Bitcoin Vanish: Mt. Gox Says It Lost 750,000 of Customers' Bitcoin to Fraud." *Wall Street Journal*, Feb 28, 2014. https://www.wsj.com/articles/SB10001424052702303801304579410010379087576.

SIL International. "SIL AI and NLP Projects." https://ai.sil.org/projects.

Singleton, Patrick A. "Discussing the 'Positive Utilities' of Autonomous Vehicles: Will Travellers Really Use Their Time Productively?" *Transport Reviews* 39.1 (Jan 2019) 50–65.

Sirani, Jordan. "The 10 Best-Selling Video Games of All Time." IGN, last updated May 16, 2024. https://www.ign.com/articles/best-selling-video-games-of-all-time-grand-theft-auto-minecraft-tetris.

Sivolella, Davide. *Space Mining and Manufacturing: Off-World Resources and Revolutionary Engineering Techniques*. Cham, Switzerland: Springer, 2019.

Slade, Giles. *Big Disconnect: The Story of Technology and Loneliness*. New York: Prometheus, 2012.

Smil, Vaclav. *Energy and Civilization: A History*. Cambridge, MA: MIT Press, 2018.

Smith, David I., et al. *Digital Life Together: The Challenge of Technology for Christian Schools*. Grand Rapids, MI: Eerdmans, 2020.

Smith, Jeff. *Becoming Amish: A Family's Search for Faith, Community, and Purpose*. Cedar, MI: Dance Hall, 2016.

Sohn, Pam. "Opinion: Our Nuclear Facilities Pose Their Own Risks; Being a Target of War Is Just One More." *Chattanooga Times Free Press*, Mar 6, 2022. https://www.timesfreepress.com/news/opinion/times/story/2022/mar/06/opinion-our-nuclear-facilities-pose-their-own/564512/.

Soto, Fernando, et al. "Medical Micro/Nanorobots in Precision Medicine." *Advanced Science* 7.21 (2020). https://doi.org/10.1002/advs.202002203.

Speake, Wendy. *The 40-Day Social Media Fast: Exchange Your Online Distractions for Real-Life Devotion*. Grand Rapids, MI: Baker, 2010.

Spector, Ronald H. "Vietnam War: 1954–1975." *Encyclopaedia Britannica*, last updated May 22, 2024. https://www.britannica.com/event/Vietnam-War.

Spoonauer, Mark. "AR Goggles Will Replace Phones, Says Facebook CEO Zuckerberg." *Christian Science Monitor*, Jul 1, 2015. https://www.csmonitor.com/Technology/2015/0701/AR-goggles-will-replace-phones-says-Facebook-CEO-Zuckerberg.

Standage, Tom. *A Brief History of Motion: From the Wheel, to the Car, to What Comes Next*. New York: Bloomsbury, 2021.

Stantcheva, Stefanie. "Inequalities in the Times of a Pandemic." 2022. https://scholar.harvard.edu/files/stantcheva/files/inequalities_pandemic.pdf.

Stark, Rodney. *The Victory of Reason: How Christianity Led to Freedom, Capitalism, and Western Success*. New York: Random, 2006.

Statista. "Countries and Territories with the Largest Number of Operational Coal Power Plants Worldwide as of July 2023." Dec 6, 2023. https://www.statista.com/statistics/859266/number-of-coal-power-plants-by-country/.

———. "Number of Public and Private Airports in the United States from 1990 to 2022." Dec 19, 2023. https://www.statista.com/statistics/183496/number-of-airports-in-the-united-states-since-1990/.

Stearns, Peter N. *The Industrial Revolution in World History*. New York: Routledge, 2018.
Steinberg, Joseph, et al. *Cybersecurity All-in-One for Dummies*. Hoboken, NJ: Wiley, 2023.
Steinberg, Stacey. *Growing Up Shared: How Parents Can Share Smarter on Social Media—And What You Can Do to Keep Your Family Safe in a No-Privacy World*. Naperville, IL: Sourcebooks, 2020.
Stein, Scott. "Best VR Headset of 2024." *CNET*, Feb 12, 2024. https://www.cnet.com/tech/gaming/best-vr-headsets/.
Stevens, Tina, and Stuart Newman. *Biotech Juggernaut: Hope, Hype, and Hidden Agendas of Entrepreneurial BioScience*. New York: Routledge, 2019.
Stone, Dan. "Churches and Christian Schools: They Can and Should Work Together." *The Dayspring Blog*, Jun 29, 2018. https://www.dayspringchristian.com/blog/churches-christian-schools-should-work-together.
Stone, Ken. "Jeff Bezos in San Diego: To Save Planet, 'Move All Heavy Industry into Space.'" *Times of San Diego*, Nov 23, 2019. https://timesofsandiego.com/tech/2019/11/23/jeff-bezos-in-san-diego-to-save-planet-move-all-heavy-industry-into-space/.
Stouffer, Clare. "Password Security: How to Create Strong Passwords in 5 Steps." LifeLock by Norton, Jul 8, 2022. https://lifelock.norton.com/learn/internet-security-password-security.
Suh, Edward Y. *The Empowering God: Redeeming the Prosperity Movement and Overcoming Victim Trauma in the Poor*. Eugene, OR: Pickwick, 2021.
Susskind, Daniel. *A World without Work: Technology, Automation, and How We Should Respond*. New York: Metropolitan, 2020.
Sutor, Robert S. *Dancing with Qubits: From Qubits to Algorithms, Embark on the Quantum Computing Journey Shaping Our Future*. 2nd ed. Birmingham, UK: Packt, 2024.
Sutton, L. "An Appropriation of Psalm 82 against the Background of the Fourth Industrial Revolution: The Christian Church as a Change Agent in the Fourth Industrial Revolution." *HTS Teologiese Studies/Theological Studies* 76 (2020). https://doi.org/10.4102/hts.v76i2.6126.
Swann, John Thomas. *The Imago Dei: A Priestly Calling for Humankind*. Eugene, OR: Wipf & Stock, 2017.
Swoboda, A. J. *Subversive Sabbath: The Surprising Power of Rest in a Nonstop World*. Grand Rapids, MI: Baker, 2018.
Tabb, Michael, et al. "How Does a Quantum Computer Work?" *Scientific American*, Jul 7, 2021. https://www.scientificamerican.com/video/how-does-a-quantum-computer-work/.
Tardi, Carla. "What Is Moore's Law and Is It Still True?" *Investopedia*, last updated Apr 2, 2024. https://www.investopedia.com/terms/m/mooreslaw.asp.
Tarnoff, Ben. "How the Internet Was Invented." *Guardian*, Jul 15, 2016. https://www.theguardian.com/technology/2016/jul/15/how-the-internet-was-invented-1976-arpa-kahn-cerf.
Tartar, Andre. "The Hiring Gap." *Intelligencer*, Apr 15, 2011. https://nymag.com/news/intelligencer/topic/hiring-gap-2011-4/.

Taylor, Chloe. "Robots Could Take Over 20 Million Jobs by 2030, Study Claims." CNBC, Jun 26, 2019. https://www.cnbc.com/2019/06/26/robots-could-take-over-20-million-jobs-by-2030-study-claims.html.

Taylor Tillman, Nola, and Daisy Dobrijevic. "How Long Does It Take to Get to Mars?" *Space*, last updated Aug 8, 2023. https://www.space.com/24701-how-long-does-it-take-to-get-to-mars.html.

Tegmark, Max. *Life 3.0: Being Human in the Age of Artificial Intelligence*. New York: Knopf, 2017.

Tesla. "Advanced Sensor Coverage." Accessed March 26, 2024. https://www.tesla.com/autopilot.

Thacker, Jason. *The Age of AI: Artificial Intelligence and the Future of Humanity*. Grand Rapids, MI: Zondervan, 2020.

TheCoconetTV. "Pacific Climate Change Leader Brianna Fruean's Full Speech at COP26." YouTube video, Nov 1, 2021. https://www.youtube.com/watch?v=3HZ5xS5J9Go&t=5s.

Thelen, Mathias D. *Biblical Foundations for the Role of Healing in Evangelization*. Eugene, OR: Wipf & Stock, 2017.

Thomas, Mike. "30 Internet-of-Things Examples You Should Know." BuiltIn, last updated Mar 19, 2024. https://builtin.com/internet-things/iot-examples.

Threewitt, Cherise. "10 Cars That Are Almost Self-Driving." *U.S. News and World Report*, last updated May 15, 2024. https://cars.usnews.com/cars-trucks/advice/cars-that-are-almost-self-driving.

Thrun, Sebastian. "Flying Cars, Autonomous Vehicles, and Education: Lex Fridman Podcast #59." YouTube video, Dec 21, 2019. https://www.youtube.com/watch?v=ZPPAOakITeQ.

Tight, Malcolm. "Mass Higher Education and Massification." *Higher Education Policy* 32.1 (Mar 2019) 93–108.

Tizon, Al. "Reconciling All Things: Missional Competencies in a Broken World." In *Ambassadors of Reconciliation: God's Mission through Missions for All*, edited by Geoff Hartt et al., 3–12. Littleton, CO: William Carey, 2023.

Topf, Daniel. "America's New Independence Day: Envisioning an Era of Self-Sufficiency in a Deglobalizing World." *Journal of Interdisciplinary Studies* 35.1/2 (2023) 123–44.

———. "The Global Crisis of Unemployment in an Age of Automation and Artificial Intelligence: Missiological Implications of the Fourth Industrial Revolution." *Occasional Bulletin of EMS* 33.2 (Spring 2020) 9–15, 36–37.

———. *Pentecostal Higher Education: History, Current Practices, and Future Prospects*. Cham, Switzerland: Springer Nature, 2021.

———. "Technology as a Modern-Day Tower of Babel: The Garden of Eden as an Alternative Vision for Missionally Engaging a Media-Saturated Culture." *Global Missiology* 18.2 (Apr 22, 2021). http://ojs.globalmissiology.org/index.php/english/article/view/2425.

———. "'Useless Class' or Uniquely Human? The Challenge of Artificial Intelligence." *Journal of Interdisciplinary Studies* 32.1–2 (2020) 17–38.

Topol, Eric. *The Creative Destruction of Medicine: How the Digital Revolution Will Create Better Health Care*. New York: Basic, 2013.

———. *Deep Medicine: How Artificial Intelligence Can Make Healthcare Human Again*. New York: Basic, 2019.

———. *The Patient Will See You Now: The Future of Medicine Is in Your Hands.* New York: Basic, 2016.

Torchinsky, Jason. *Robot, Take the Wheel: The Road to Autonomous Cars and the Lost Art of Driving.* New York: Apollo, 2019.

Townsend, Anthony M. *Ghost Road: Beyond the Driverless Car.* New York: Norton, 2020.

Trudolyubov, Maxim. *The Tragedy of Property: Private Life, Ownership and the Russian State.* Translated by Arch Tait. Cambridge, UK: Polity, 2018.

Trumbore, Anne. "ChatGPT Could Become a Personal Tutor to Millions of Students If It Learns Lessons from the Robot Teachers That Came Before." *Fortune*, Feb 22, 2023. https://fortune.com/2023/02/22/chatgpt-ai-openai-educatoin-tutor-teaching-school/.

Turkle, Sherry. *Alone Together: Why We Expect More from Technology and Less from Each Other.* 3rd ed. New York: Basic, 2017.

Turner, Ben. "Nuclear Fusion Reactor in South Korea Runs at 100 million Degrees C for a Record-breaking 48 Seconds." *Space*, Apr 14, 2024. https://www.space.com/nuclear-fusion-reactor-south-korea-runs-48-seconds#xenforo-comments-65997.

Turton, William, and Kartikay Mehrotra. "Hackers Breached Colonial Pipeline Using Compromised Password." *Bloomberg*, Jun 4, 2021. https://www.bloomberg.com/news/articles/2021-06-04/hackers-breached-colonial-pipeline-using-compromised-password.

Ungar-Sargon, Batya. *Bad News: How Woke Media Is Undermining Democracy.* New York: Encounter, 2021.

Unwin, Tim. "Five Problems with the Fourth Industrial Revolution." *ICT Works*, Mar 23, 2019. https://www.ictworks.org/problems-fourth-industrial-revolution.

Urbain, Tom. "How Long Does It Take to Get to the Moon? Distance and Travel Time." *Starlust*, last updated Nov 23, 2022. https://starlust.org/how-long-does-it-take-to-travel-to-the-moon/.

US Army. "Army Researchers Augment Combat Vehicles with AI." Jun 25, 2020. https://www.army.mil/article/236733/army_researchers_augment_combat_vehicles_with_ai.

———. "Welcome to Fort Knox." https://home.army.mil/knox/index.php/about/visitor-information.

USDA. "Farming and Farm Income." Last updated Feb 29, 2024. https://www.ers.usda.gov/data-products/ag-and-food-statistics-charting-the-essentials/farming-and-farm-income/.

Van Engen, Abram C. *City on a Hill: A History of American Exceptionalism.* New Haven, CT: Yale University Press, 2020.

Van Engen, Charles E., and Jude Tiersma. *God So Loves the City: Seeking a Theology for Urban Mission.* Eugene, OR: Wipf & Stock, 2009.

Van Engen, John H., ed., *Educating People of Faith: Exploring the History of Jewish and Christian Communities.* Grand Rapids, MI: Eerdmans, 2004.

Vazharov, Stefan. "The 7 Best Video Game Consoles Based on Hands-on Testing." *Best Products*, last updated Jan 18, 2023. https://www.bestproducts.com/tech/electronics/g235/best-video-game-consoles-systems/.

Véliz, Carissa. *Privacy Is Power: Why and How You Should Take Back Control of Your Data.* Brooklyn, NY: Melville, 2021.

The Verge. "SpaceX Lands Rocket at Sea, Makes History." YouTube video, Apr 8, 2016. https://www.youtube.com/watch?v=lEr9cPpuAx8.

Vernon, Austin, and Eli Dourado. "Energy Superabundance: How Cheap, Abundant Energy Will Shape Our Future." Center for Growth and Opportunity, Jun 30, 2022. https://www.thecgo.org/research/energy-superabundance/.

Vigderman, Aliza, and Gabe Turner. "The Best VPN Services of 2024." *Security.org*, last updated May 17, 2024. https://www.security.org/vpn/best/.

Vincent, James. "Putin Says the Nation That Leads in AI 'Will Be the Ruler of the World.'" *The Verge*, Sep 4, 2017. https://www.theverge.com/2017/9/4/16251226/russia-ai-putin-rule-the-world.

Violino, Bob. "What 5G Promises for IoT." *NetworkWorld*, Oct 12, 2020. https://www.networkworld.com/article/3584385/what-5g-brings-to-iot-today-and-tomorrow.html.

Volf, Miroslav. *Work in the Spirit: Toward a Theology of Work*. Eugene, OR: Wipf & Stock, 2001.

Walden, Nick. "Delivering Fusion Energy." TEDx Talks, Jan 7, 2021. YouTube video. https://www.youtube.com/watch?v=foKofSsjOak.

Walker, Zachary, et al., eds. *Flipped Classrooms with Diverse Learners: International Perspectives*. Singapore: Springer, 2020.

Wallach, Omri. "Race to Net Zero: Carbon Neutral Goals by Country." *Visual Capitalist*, Jun 8, 2021. https://www.visualcapitalist.com/race-to-net-zero-carbon-neutral-goals-by-country/.

Wall, Mike. "SpaceX Launches 23 Starlink Satellites from Florida." *Space*, last updated Apr 17, 2024. https://www.space.com/spacex-starlink-launch-group-6-51.

Weber, Andrew, and Mose Buchele. "Texas Has an Official Death Count from the 2021 Blackout. The True Toll May Never Be Known." *Texas Standard*, Aug 5, 2022. https://www.texasstandard.org/stories/texas-freeze-winter-storm-2021-death-count/.

Weber, Max. *The Protestant Ethic and the Spirit of Capitalism*. Translated by Talcott Parsons. Mineola, NY: Dover, 2003.

Webster, Larry, et al., eds. *Never Stop Driving: A Better Life behind the Wheel*. Beverly, MA: Motorbooks, 2019.

Weidner, Justin Burton. "Why Google Glass Failed." *Investopedia*, Jul 20, 2023. https://www.investopedia.com/articles/investing/052115/how-why-google-glass-failed.asp.

Weinersmith, Kelly, and Zach Weinersmith. *A City on Mars: Can We Settle Space, Should We Settle Space, and Have We Really Thought This Through?* New York: Penguin, 2023.

Weissmann, Mikael, et al., eds. *Hybrid Warfare: Security and Asymmetric Conflict in International Relations*. London: I.B. Tauris, 2021.

West, Darrell M. *The Future of Work: Robots, AI, and Automation*. Washington, DC: Brookings Institution, 2019.

Wetmore, Jameson M. "Amish Technology: Reinforcing Values and Building Community." In *Technology and Society: Building Our Sociotechnical Future*, edited by Deborah G. Johnson and Jameson M. Wetmore, 247–66. 2nd ed. Cambridge, MA: MIT Press, 2021.

Whittington, Keith E. *Speak Freely: Why Universities Must Defend Free Speech*. Princeton, NJ: Princeton University Press, 2018.

Wilkins, Alex. "Record-Breaking Quantum Computer Has More Than 1000 Qubits." *NewScientist*, Oct 24, 2023. https://www.newscientist.com/article/2399246-record-breaking-quantum-computer-has-more-than-1000-qubits/.

Wilkins, Neil. *Internet of Things: What You Need to Know about IoT, Big Data, Predictive Analytics, Artificial Intelligence, Machine Learning, Cybersecurity, Business Intelligence, Augmented Reality and Our Future.* Self-published, 2019.

Williams, Matt. "How Far Is the Asteroid Belt from Earth?" *Universe Today*, Aug 10, 2016. https://www.universetoday.com/130136/far-asteroid-belt-earth/.

Williams, Tony. "Essay 92—October 4, 1957: USSR Launches Sputnik, Shocks U.S. Into Space Age." https://html5-player.libsyn.com/embed/episode/id/14961332/height/90/theme/custom/thumbnail/yes/direction/backward/render-playlist/no/custom-color/87A93A/.

Willings, Adrian. "32 Interesting and Incredibly Futuristic Weapons and Modern Fighting Vehicles." *Pocket-lint*, Mar 20, 2023. https://www.pocket-lint.com/gadgets/news/142272-28-incredible-futuristic-weapons-showing-modern-military-might/.

Wilson, Douglas. *Ploductivity: A Practical Theology of Work and Wealth*. Moscow, ID: Cannon, 2020.

Winston, Clifford, and Quentin Karpilow. *Autonomous Vehicles: The Road to Economic Growth?* Washington, DC: Brookings Institution, 2020.

WION Web Team. "NASA Is Recruiting to Send Humans to Mars as Soon as 2037." WION, Aug 7, 2021. https://www.wionews.com/science/nasa-is-recruiting-to-send-humans-to-mars-as-soon-as-2037-403689.

Witkowski, Wallace. "Videogames Are a Bigger Industry Than Movies and North American Sports Combined, Thanks to the Pandemic." *MarketWatch*, last updated Jan 2, 2021. https://www.marketwatch.com/story/videogames-are-a-bigger-industry-than-sports-and-movies-combined-thanks-to-the-pandemic-11608654990.

Witherington, Ben, III. *The Rest of Life: Rest, Play, Eating, Studying, Sex from a Kingdom Perspective*. Grand Rapids, MI: Eerdmans, 2012.

———. *Work: A Kingdom Perspective on Labor*. Grand Rapids, MI: Eerdmans, 2011.

Wolf, Harrison. "Who Are the Big 3 in U.S. Drone Delivery?" *Forbes*, Jan 26, 2024. https://www.forbes.com/sites/harrisonwolf/2024/01/26/who-are-the-big-3-in-us-drone-delivery/?sh=6131fd6b54e2.

Woodberry, Robert D. "The Missionary Roots of Liberal Democracy." *American Political Science Review* 106.2 (May 2012) 244–74.

Wood, Sarah. "15 National Universities with the Biggest Endowments." *US News*, Oct 2, 2023. https://www.usnews.com/education/best-colleges/the-short-list-college/articles/10-universities-with-the-biggest-endowments.

Workman, Daniel. "Crude Oil Exports by Country." *World's Top Exports*. https://www.worldstopexports.com/worlds-top-oil-exports-country/.

World Council of Churches. "Together towards Life: Mission and Evangelism in Changing Landscapes." https://www.oikoumene.org/sites/default/files/Document/Together_towards_Life.pdf.

World Economic Forum. "What Is the Fourth Industrial Revolution?" YouTube video, Jul 18, 2016. https://www.youtube.com/watch?v=kpW9JcWxKqo.

World Food Programme. "WFP at a Glance: A Guide to the Facts, Figures and Frontline Work of the World Food Programme." Last updated Jan 29, 2024. https://www.

wfp.org/stories/wfp-glance#:~:text=Quick%20facts,5.2%20billion%20short%20 of%20requirements.

World Health Organization. "Deafness and Hearing Loss." Last updated Feb 2, 2024. https://www.who.int/news-room/fact-sheets/detail/deafness-and-hearing-loss.

———. "Road Traffic Injuries." Last updated Dec 13, 2023. https://www.who.int/news-room/fact-sheets/detail/road-traffic-injuries.

Worldometers. "World Population." https://www.worldometers.info/world-population/.

World Population Review. "Countries with Space Programs 2024." https://worldpopulationreview.com/country-rankings/countries-with-space-programs.

Worrachate, Anchalee. "Bitcoin Could Pass $100,000 If It Replaces Gold as a Store of Value, Says Goldman Sachs." *Fortune*, Jan 4, 2022. https://fortune.com/crypto/2022/01/04/bitcoin-price-100k-gold-store-of-value-goldman-sachs/.

Wrangham, Richard. *Catching Fire: How Cooking Made Us Human*. New York: Basic, 2010.

Wray, Sarah. "Flying Taxi Trials in Cities Set to Expand." Cities Today, Aug 27, 2020. https://cities-today.com/cities-progress-flying-taxi-plans/.

Wünschiers, Röbbe. *Genetic Engineering: Reading, Writing and Editing Genes*. Wiesbaden, Germany: Springer, 2021.

Wu Song, Felicia. "Digital Life and Social Media as Secular Liturgy: A Matter of Christian Formation." In *Technē: Christian Visions of Technology*, edited by Gerald Hiestand and Todd A. Wilson, 202–20. Eugene, OR: Cascade, 2022.

Yang, Andrew. *The War on Normal People: The Truth about America's Disappearing Jobs and Why Universal Basic Income Is Our Future*. New York: Hachette, 2019.

Zegart, Amy B. *Spies, Lies, and Algorithms: The History and Future of American Intelligence*. Princeton, NJ: Princeton University Press, 2022.

Zubrin, Robert. *The Case for Space: How the Revolution in Spaceflight Opens Up a Future of Limitless Possibility*. Amherst, NY: Prometheus, 2019.

General Index

3D printing 2, 42n33, 60, 91–94, 137

abortion, pro-life cause 97, 100–102, 104–5
"already" but "not yet," age of tension 13, 49, 103, 172
Amish 179, 181
artificial intelligence (AI) 2–3, 4n14, 9, 14–15, 19, 22, 27, 34, 36–38, 41–42, 46, 52, 54, 57, 61–62, 65, 70–71, 77, 95, 103, 105, 112–16, 120, 123, 128, 147, 165n16, 167, 174, 176, 180
    artificial general intelligence (AGI) 3, 4
asteroids, meteorites 147, 163–71, 174
automation (incl. job loss due to) 8–9, 18n9, 21, 22n29, 30, 23, 30, 35–36, 38, 43n34, 46–47, 50, 53, 62n36, 78n26, 91, 131, 134
autonomous vehicles (AV), self-driving cars 2, 14, 16–33, 35, 39, 112–16, 128, 176
autonomous weapons (incl. "killer robots") 107, 115–17, 122–23

billionaires 42, 48, 162
    Allen, Paul 162n5
    Bezos, Jeff 152, 162, 169n35
    Branson, Richard 48, 162
    Moore, Gordon 125
    Musk, Elon 33, 49, 153n37, 158, 162, 166n22, 173n45
    Zuckerberg, Mark 49, 58, 76

blockchain 2, 57, 109, 122, 125, 131–35, 137, 142, 147n13, 176
    Bitcoin 42n33, 109, 131–33, 142, 147
blue-collar, white-collar 7, 36, 43

ChatGPT 62n35, 71
China 5, 6n25, 10, 17–18, 91, 109, 111–12, 114, 116, 120, 127n9, 11, 137, 146, 162
climate change, climate justice 127, 147–48, 152, 154–56, 160, 170
conveyor-belt, production line 56, 89, 128
COVID-19 47, 54, 67, 84
creation mandate, dominion 49, 78, 138, 170–71
CRISPR 96, 99, 104
Crouch, Andy 4n13, 87
cyberattacks, cybercrime 29, 106–7, 109–11, 117, 119
cybersecurity 29, 43, 46, 68, 104, 108n11, 109, 111n22, 115, 118–19, 122, 128n14

DARPA 16, 113, 116
data 9, 15, 19–20, 22, 36–37, 40, 43, 46, 58–59, 65, 68, 89–90, 92, 95, 98–99, 104, 107, 109, 111–12, 117–22, 127, 129–30, 134, 147, 152, 156, 162
decentralization, democratization 90, 131, 135, 137, 142, 152–53
digital detox 70, 179
disability, special needs 25, 31, 48, 51, 58, 63–65, 77

DNA 12, 94, 95n37, 96, 101, 144n2
Dyer, John 5n17, 13n50, 15, 29, 77n23

Ellul, Jacques 177, 180–81
ethics, ethical/moral questions 2, 12n48, 25n40, 53, 78, 81, 87, 96, 98n48, 102–3, 105, 115–17, 174, 176

Ferngren, Gary B. 11n46, 98n45, 105
fossil fuels (incl. coal, oil, and gas) 9, 22n31, 30, 33, 35, 43, 48, 118, 145–46, 148–49, 152, 156–58, 160, 176
Fourth Industrial Revolution 1, 2, 3n9, 4, 9, 10, 12, 14–15, 21, 25, 29, 32, 34, 36, 38, 42–44, 46, 50, 52, 54, 56–57, 59, 61, 63, 68, 81, 89, 93, 96, 98, 100, 102–3, 107, 112, 114–15, 125, 127n11, 128, 135, 137, 140, 145, 147, 150, 154, 158, 161, 167, 171, 174, 176, 179, 180
fusion energy 150–52, 159, 166, 168, 176

Galilei, Galileo 11
Garden of Eden, paradise 49, 78–79, 83, 138, 140, 155, 169
genetic engineering, genomics 2, 42, 95n37, 96, 104–5, 176
Great Commission, unreached people groups 64, 83
Greengard, Samuel 128n17, 129n18, 19, 130, 142
Guiness, Os 50, 51n62, 63, 53

Harari, Yuval Noah 3, 6n26, 15, 37, 46n46
Hertz, Noreena 140, 143

imago Dei, image of God 43, 50n61, 51, 81, 96, 99, 138
Industrial Revolution (the first) 5–11, 61, 137, 145
internet of things (IoT) 2, 9–10, 21, 125, 128–31, 137, 142, 176
  industrial internet of things (IIoT) 128n16
  internet of everything (IoE) 128n16
  internet of vehicles (IoV) 21n21

just war theory 117

Kelly, Kevin 30n60, 43n34, 50n59, 76n15, 181
kingdom of God 13, 49n57, 51, 53, 67, 80–81, 87, 136, 139, 141–42, 155
Kurzweil, Ray 3, 4n13, 15

laser-powered weapons 107, 114, 117, 147
Lennox, John C. 3, 15, 120
LiDAR 20, 128
Luther, Martin 44–45

massification (incl. mass medicalization, mass screening) 61n33, 89–90, 137
massive open online course (MOOC) 62–63
materials science, new materials 2, 60, 128, 150n26, 167, 174
McGrath, Michael E. 17n4, 20n16, 25n40, 27, 29n59, 31n65, 33
metaverse 76, 84–87
missio Dei 2, 44
missional challenges/opportunities 3, 45, 64–65, 85, 97, 140, 141n62, 179–80
Murray, Charles 49, 53

nanotechnology 2, 46, 89, 92, 99, 104, 176
NASA 149, 162, 164, 173n47, 174
Neolithic Revolution 5–7
New Jerusalem 140, 155

personalized/customized products and services 40, 54, 61, 62n36, 64–65, 71, 89–90, 93, 95, 121, 128, 137, 180
planets (incl. Mars, Jupiter, Saturn) 14, 147, 161, 163–76
Protestant work ethic 11, 78
public theology, common good 30, 44, 118, 137

quantum computers 2, 125–28, 143, 176

Reinke, Tony 3, 5n17, 15, 29, 83n40, 179n12
renewable energy 22n29, 144, 148, 153, 158–59
robots (incl. microrobots and armed robots) 2, 9, 18, 34–35, 38, 40, 42n33, 46, 50n59, 54–55, 59n20, 21, 60–61, 62n36, 70–71, 89, 91–92, 93n24, 99, 104, 107, 113, 115–16, 123, 131, 139, 150n26, 167, 174

Sabbath 69, 78–80, 177, 178n6, 181
Scharre, Paul 114n37, 116n46, 47, 49, 50, 117n51, 52, 118n59
Schwab, Klaus 1, 2n5, 4n15, 15, 161n2
second coming, Christ's return in glory 13, 49, 103, 155, 172
Selwyn, Neil 59n20, 21, 60, 61n29, 30, 71
sex robots 77–78, 81–82, 86–87
smartphones (incl. the iPhone) 3, 9, 54, 58, 68, 74–76, 92, 101, 125, 139, 147
smart products (incl. smart cities) 9, 58, 60, 75, 98n50, 128, 130–34, 139, 162
social media 3, 4n14, 108, 120, 122, 139, 147, 177, 178n7, 180n19
solar energy, photovoltaic panels 30, 148, 153, 159–60, 169
steam engine 7–10, 36
surveillance, privacy 107, 111–12, 115, 119–22, 131, 133, 137
Susskind, Daniel 6n27, 41–42, 47n48, 49, 50, 53

tech companies 8, 16, 22, 24, 35, 48, 60, 83, 105, 119–22, 129, 151–52, 162, 165
  Amazon 23, 41n30, 58, 60, 63, 75, 121
  Apple 9, 48, 58, 60, 63, 74, 76, 83, 121
  Baidu 17, 121
  Didi Chuxing 17
  Google (incl. Waymo, YouTube) 17–18, 19n13, 22, 58, 60, 74, 76n15, 77, 119, 121, 126–27, 152

Hewlett Packard (HP) 8
IBM 19n13, 37, 124, 126n9, 127, 134
Intel 9, 20, 125
Meta (incl. Facebook, Instagram, WhatsApp) 48, 74, 76, 108, 119, 121
Microsoft 48, 73, 134, 162n5
Netflix 77, 121, 170n36
SpaceX 161–63
Starlink 162
Tesla 17–18, 19n14, 20n15, 30, 33, 153n37
Uber, Lyft 17, 22, 24, 32, 41
technological unemployment 42, 52–53
technophobia, technophilia 63, 64n43, 68, 179
Thacker, Jason 4n14, 116n48
tools 4–5, 8–9, 13–14, 36, 54, 60, 64, 81, 85, 91, 96, 116n48, 138–39, 142, 179–81
Topol, Eric 89–90, 91n14, 93n27, 95n36, 37, 99, 104n69, 105

universal basic income (UBI) 34, 48–49, 52–53
universities, higher education 5, 45–46, 52, 57, 61n33, 62–63, 67–70, 77, 119
  Baylor University 123
  Boston University 39
  Caltech 165
  Carnegie Mellon University 118
  Columbia University 149
  Indiana University 132
  MIT 14n55, 46, 63, 125n2, 151
  Oxford University 35
  Princeton University 171
  Stanford University 16, 62, 122
  University of al-Qarawiyyin 5n20
  University of Manitoba 62
  University of Santo Domingo 45
  University of Santo Tomas 45
  University of Science and Technology in Hefei 127n9
  University of Texas in San Antonio 92

virtual reality (VR), augmented reality (AR) 2, 43, 57–58, 60, 65, 70–71, 74–78, 82, 84–86, 114, 176, 180

Wilson, Douglas 83, 138–39, 142
Witherington, Ben, III 50n60, 52–53, 87, 139
World Economic Forum (WEF) 1–2

World Health Organization (WHO) 28, 64n45

Yang, Andrew 34–35, 38n18, 48, 53

Zubrin, Robert 164n15, 165n20, 166n21, 23, 25, 167n28, 29, 168, 175

Scripture Index

Genesis

1–2	26, 78
1:1	171
1:26–28	51, 138
2	138
2:2–3	69
2:12	140
2:15	49
3	26, 103
3:17–19	49
4:2, 20–22	5n17
5:1	51
6:1	172
6:14–16	5n17
8:2	172
9:6	51
10:10–12	5n17
11:3–4	5n17
11:9	171n41

Exodus

7:16	79
8:1, 20	79
9:1, 13	79
10:3	79
20:2	79
20:8–11	69, 79
20:15	135
21:33—22:15	136
23:10–12	79

Leviticus

6:1–5	136
11:45	79
25:2–6	79
25:8–34	136
26:27–35, 43	79

Numbers

5:6–7	136
15:41	79
27:1–11	136
34–36	136

Deuteronomy

4:9	67
4:19	172
5:12–15	79
5:15	69
5:19	135
5:21	136
6:6–9	67
6:20–23	79
8:10–20	142
19:14	136
21:15–17	136
27:17	136
28:13	179

Joshua

13–19	136
24:5–17	79

Judges
6:8–9	79

1 Samuel
10:18	79

1 Kings
4:25	136
8:30	172
8:51–53	79
21	136

1 Chronicles
16:30	170

2 Chronicles
18:18	172
36:21	79

Nehemiah
10:31	79
13:15–21	69

Job
34:13	171n41

Psalms
2	141
8:6–8	172
11:4	172
19:1	168
33:13–14	172
36:9	26
51:5–6	100
72	141
78:42–52	79
97:4	171n41
104:5	170
115:3	172
115:16	172
119:89–90	170
146:6	171

Proverbs
1:8	67
22:6	67

Ecclesiastes
1:4	170

Isaiah
5:8	136
9:6–7	141
11	141
57:15	172
58:13–14	69
66:1	172

Jeremiah
17:21–27	69
32:20–21	79

Ezekiel
20:5–10	79
45:8	136
47–48	136

Daniel
2:44	51, 141
7:13–14, 27	141
7:18, 22, 27	51
9:15	79

Hosea
13:4	79

Micah
2:1–2	136
4:4	136, 154

Zechariah
3:10	136

Scripture Index

Matthew

4:23	141
4:23–24	97
5:9	51
5:13–16	63
5:14	67n54
5:28	81
6:19–34	32
8:11	141
8:16	97
9:35	97, 141
10:1–8	97
10:7–8	141, 155
11:25	171
12:15	97
12:28	141
13:1–23	138
13:31–33	141, 155
14:14	97
15:30	97
16:26	32
18:1–4	81
19:14	81
19:16–30	32
19:18	135
21:14	97
22:34–40	82
24:14	155
24:35	171
25	156
25:31–46	155
25:34	141
26:29	141
28:18–20	83, 155

Mark

1:29–34	97
4:1–20	138
4:9–25	64
10:14–15	81
10:17–31	32
10:19	135
12:28–34	82
16:15–18	83

Luke

3:11	136
4:16	69
6:19	97
6:20–26	32
6:35–36	51
8:4–15	138
8:18	64
8:49–56	97
10:25–37	82, 97
11:28	64
12:13–34	32
12:22–34	136
14:33	32
16:19–31	32
17:21	141
18:16–17	81
18:18–30	32
18:20	135
18:29–30	141
19:11–27	141
20:34–36	51
22:29–30	141
24:46–49	83

John

1:12–13	51
3:13	172
3:16	171n41
4:46–53	97
5:5–9	97
5:26a	26
6:63	26
8:47	64
10:10	26
11:52	51
13:1	12
13:34	140
14:2	172
14:6c	26
15:1–8	138
15:19	12
16:33	12
17:6–18	12
20:21–23	83

Acts

1:8	83
5:3	136
5:4	137
9:33–34	97
15:7	64
17:24	171
17:25b	26

Romans

8:14–29	51
9:6–8	51
10:13–15, 17	64
10:18	171n41
13:4	118
13:9	135

1 Corinthians

7:31	12n49
15:20–58	103

2 Corinthians

6:18	51
12:2	172

Galatians

3:2, 5	64
3:26–29	51
4:1–7	51
6:2	140

Ephesians

1:5	51
6:4	67

Phillipians

2:15	51

Colossians

3:21	67

1 Thessalonians

2:13	64
4:13–18	103
5:11	140

1 Timothy

6:6–10	136
6:13b	26

2 Timothy

3:14–15	67

Hebrews

9:24	172
12:28	51

James

3:9	51

1 Peter

4:9	140

1 John

2:15–17	12
3:1–2, 9–10	51
5:1–2	51

Revelation

1:3	64
3:15–16	179
5:13–14	172
13:16–18	104
21:1	171
21:1–4	103
21:1—22:5	140
21:7	51

www.ingramcontent.com/pod-product-compliance
Lightning Source LLC
Chambersburg PA
CBHW062019220426
43662CB00010B/1388